CHINA FINANCE 2016
中国财政 2016
Budget Taxation Treasury

图书在版编目（CIP）数据

中国财政2016：预算　税收　国库 = China Finance 2016：Budget Taxation Treasury：英文 / 国际财经中心编. -- 北京：中国财政经济出版社，2017.7

书名原文：China Finance 2016：Budget Taxation Treasury

ISBN 978 – 7 – 5095 – 7490 – 4

Ⅰ.①中… Ⅱ.①国… Ⅲ.①财政 – 概况 – 中国 – 2016 – 英文 Ⅳ.①F812

中国版本图书馆 CIP 数据核字（2017）第 115472 号

Copyright © 2016 by China Financial & Economic Publishing House.
All rights reserved. No part of this publication may be reproduced, distributed, or transmitted in any form, including photocopying, electronic or mechanical methods, without the prior written permission of the publisher.

责任编辑：罗亚洪　　　　　　　　责任校对：孙　腾
封面设计：傅　伟　　　　　　　　版式设计：齐　林

中国财政经济出版社 出版

URL：http://www.cfeph.cn

E – mail：cfeph@cfeph.cn

（版权所有　翻印必究）

社址：北京市海淀区阜成路甲 28 号　邮政编码：100142

发行处电话：010 – 88190406　北京财经书店电话：010 – 64033436

天津市银博印刷集团有限公司印刷　各地新华书店经销

889×1 194 毫米　16 开　15.5 印张　360 000 字

2017 年 9 月第 1 版　2017 年 9 月天津第 1 次印刷

定价：128.00 元

ISBN 978 – 7 – 5095 – 7490 – 4

（图书出现印装问题，本社负责调换）

本社质量投诉电话：010 – 88190744

打击盗版举报热线：010 – 88190492、QQ：634579818

Acronyms

ADB	Asian Development Bank
AIIB	Asian Infrastructure Investment Bank
AMRO	ASEAN+3 Macroeconomic Research Office
AoA	Articles of Agreement
APEC	Asia-Pacific Economic Cooperation
ASEAN	Association of Southeast Asian Nations
ASEAN+3	Association of Southeast Asian Nations, China, Korea and Japan
BAI	Business Activity Index
BEPS	Tax Base Erosion and Profit Transfer
BRICS	Brazil, Russia, India, China, and South Africa
CAREC	Central Asia Regional Economic Cooperation
CBRC	China Banking Regulatory Commission
CIRC	China Insurance Regulatory Commission
CPC	The Communist Party of China
CPI	Consumer Price Index
CPPCC	The Chinese People's Political Consultative Conference
CSRC	China Securities Regulatory Commission
FDI	Foreign Direct Investment
FTA	Free Trade Agreement
G20	Group of Twenty countries: Argentina, Australia, Brazil, Canada, China, the European Union, France, Germany, India, Indonesia, Italy, Japan, Mexico, Russia, Saudi Arabia, South Africa, South Korea, Turkey, the United Kingdom and the United States
GAC	General Administration of Customs, China
GDP	Gross Domestic Product
IFAD	International Fund for Agriculture Development
IMF	International Monetary Found
MDBs	Multilateral Development Banks
MIIT	Ministry of Industry and Information Technology, China
MOA	Ministry of Agriculture, China
MOE	Ministry of Education, China
MOF	Ministry of Finance, China

MOFCOM	Ministry of Commerce, China
MOHURD	Ministry of Housing and Urban-Rural Development, China
MOU	Memorandum of Understanding
NBS	National Bureau of Statistics, China
NDB	New Development Bank
NDRC	National Development and Reform Commission, China
NPC	National People's Congress, China
OECD	Organisation of Economic Co-operation and Development
PBOC	People's Bank of China
PMI	Purchasing Managers' Index
PPI	Producer Price Index
PPP	Public-Private-Partnership
S&ED	China-U.S. Strategic and Economic Dialogue
SASAC	State Assets Supervision and Administration Commission, China
SAT	State Administration of Taxation, China
SCO	Shanghai Cooperation Organization
SMEs	Small And Medium-Sized Enterprises
SOEs	State-Owned Enterprises
UNIDO	United Nations Industrial Development Organization
VAT	Value-Added Tax
WTO	World Trade Organization

Preface

It has been nearly nine years since the outbreak of the international financial crisis, but its repercussions are still being felt. The growth of global economy is still weak, while the uncertainties are on the rise, including unclear policy direction and spillover effects of major economies, geopolitical risks and other factors. China's economy has maintained steady growth during the critical stage of transformation, and great achievements have been made in deepening the comprehensive reform and building a moderately prosperous society in an all-round way. In 2016, China's GDP grew by 6.7%, contributing to over 30% of the global economic growth. The supply side structural reform has generated prominent results, as demonstrated in greater contribution by consumption in driving the economy, and higher quality and efficiency of economic development.

In the past year, the Chinese fiscal authorities conscientiously performed their duties, and public finance has played its role as the foundation and an important pillar in the state governance. We have effectively implemented the proactive fiscal policy, and rolled out the VAT pilot reform, which reduced more than 500 billion yuan of tax for businesses. We have promoted the reform of cutting excess capacity, de-leveraging, de-stock, reducing costs and shoring up weak areas of the national economy. A special fund was established to support the reallocation of laid-off workers during the process of cutting over capacity in the steel and coal industries. Reforms in the fiscal system were intensified, and progress was made in the reforms of budget management, tax and financial systems. We also further promoted international financial cooperation by successfully holding a series of meetings in the finance track of the G20 Hangzhou Summit, with tangible outcomes in advancing structural reforms and strengthening infrastructure development. We have carried out pragmatic multi-bilateral financial cooperation. The Asian Infrastructure Investment Bank and the BRICS New Development Bank were officially launched and have achieved their annual operational objectives.

"China Finance 2016" compiled important fiscal and tax reform policies, macroeconomic data, as well as the reform practices in local fiscal authorities, issued in 2016 by the Ministry of Finance and other relevant government departments. It also covered academic discussions by fiscal officials and financial experts. The book is helpful for the international community to better understand China's reform and opening up process, its direction of macroeconomic policies, and tax reform progress.

China's development means opportunity for the world. China is a beneficiary of the economic globalization, and also a contributor. Currently, the global economy is lackluster and the anti-globalization and trade protectionist sentiment is on the rise. The Chinese fiscal authorities will focus on coordinated progress of ecological, economic, political, cultural and social development, following the Four-Pronged Comprehensive Strategy. We will make steady progress while maintaining stability, firmly establish and implement the new development concept, and guide and adapt to the economic new normal. We will focus on improving the quality and efficiency of development, push forward the supply side structural reform, expand the aggregate demand as appropriate, so as to foster the sustained and sound economic and social development of China. We will work with international counterparts to strengthen macroeconomic policy coordination under G20, advocate innovation-driven and dynamic growth, and promote global trade and investment, so as to achieve sound coordinated development of the world economy.

Vice Minister
Ministry of Finance, China
May, 2017

Contents

- **Policy Update** — 1
- **Facts & Figures** — 95
- **MOF Events** — 133
- **Local Finance** — 155
- **Remarks & Opinions** — 199

POLICY UPDATE

CHINA FINANCE 2016

POLICY UPDATE

MOF issued a circular on stamp duty policy for financial leasing contracts

On December 31, 2015, the Ministry of Finance (MOF) issued a circular on stamp duty policy for financial leasing contracts. First, financial leasing contracts (including sale-leaseback financing contracts) are subject to 0.005% stamp duty on the total rent, under the tax item of loan contract. Second, in the sale-leaseback financing business, the contracts for sale or repurchase of leased assets are exempt from stamp duty.■

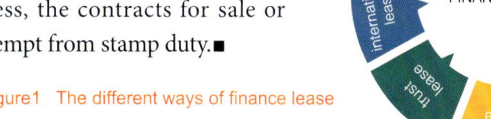

Figure1　The different ways of finance lease

Source: Ministry of Finance of China

MOF issued *Interim Measures on the Management of the Special Funds Allocated by the Central Government to Support Public Cultural Service System at Local Level*

On December 31, 2015, MOF issued *Interim Measures on the Management of the Special Funds Allocated by the Central Government to Support Public Cultural Service System at Local Level*, which provides the following. First, the special funds are arranged to support basic public cultural service by local governments, and improve grass-root public cultural and sports facilities. Second, the special funds are composed of subsidies and incentive awards, the specific amount of which is to be determined by MOF based on the size of annual earmarked funds. Third, the funds are allocated based on production factors, including basic factors, business factors and financial factors. Fourth, when the funds are transferred to the provincial finance departments, they have to be allocated to provincial agencies and finance authorities at municipal and county levels according to budget procedures within 30 days. Fifth, finance authorities at various levels should establish and improve the supervision and performance evaluation mechanism of the special funds in conjunction with other relevant departments.■

MOF issued a circular on improving port construction fee collection

On January 4, 2016, MOF issued a circular on improving port construction fee collection, which provides the following. First, when the waterway inbound cargo undergoes lightering operation or direct transshipment after unloading from the storage yard, the port construction fee is collected only once in the whole process of water transport. Second, when domestic exported goods are loaded in non-open domestic ports in the upper reaches of Nanjing Yangtze River Bridge or other inland rivers, and are unloaded or transferred in open coastal ports or open ports in the lower reaches of the Nanjing Yangtze River Bridge, the port construction fee is collected at the unloading or transshipment port and reduced by half based on the current collection standard. Third, when the cargo is loaded and unloaded at both open ports, the port construction fee is to be collected at the unloading port, and is subject to the higher toll standard of the loading or unloading port.■

MOF issued the *No.8 Interpretation for the Enterprise Accounting Standard*

On January 4, MOF issued the *No.8 Interpretation for the Enterprise Accounting Standard*, which provides the following. First, when financial assets or financial liabilities are held as wealth management products, they should be properly classified in accordance with the *Guidelines of Financial Instruments Recognition Measurement*. Second, when financial assets or financial liabilities are measured at fair value, their fair value should be determined in accordance with the relevant provisions of the *Fair Value Measurement Criteria*. Third, when financial assets are held as wealth management products, except for those measured at fair value and recorded in current profits and losses, they should be subject to impairment evaluation according to the *Guidelines of Financial Instruments Recognition Measurement*, and the amount of impairment loss should be determined and duly recorded in accounting. ■

The State Council issued guidance on promoting coordinated development of the primary, secondary and tertiary industries in rural areas

On January 5, the State Council issued guidance on promoting coordinated development of the primary, secondary and tertiary industries in rural areas. First, various industrial co-development models are encouraged in rural areas. Efforts are to be made to foster the new type of urbanization, speed up agricultural structural adjustment, extend agricultural industrial chain, expand multiple functions of agriculture, and develop new agricultural businesses. Second, multiple market players are encouraged to enter rural industries. Measures are to be taken to strengthen farmers' cooperatives and family farms, support leading enterprises to deliver showcase effects, amplify the advantages of integrated services by supply and marketing cooperatives, and encourage private investment. Third, interest and benefit coalition are to be established. Incentives are to be designed to support innovative contract farming, encourage the development of cooperative shares, strengthen industrial and commercial corporate social responsibility, and improve risk prevention mechanism. Fourth, multi-channel services are to be improved to support integration of rural industries. Government agencies are to build public service platforms, provide innovative rural financial services, strengthen personnel and technological support to improve agricultural and rural infrastructure, and support integration and development of rural industries in poor areas. Fifth, the mechanism for promoting integrated growth of rural industries is to be improved. Measures are to be taken to enhance fiscal support, roll out pilot demonstration, and strengthen inter-agency collaboration. ■

MOF issued guidance on comprehensively enhancing internal control of administrative institutions

On January 7, MOF issued guidance on comprehensively enhancing internal control of administrative institutions. First, the institutions are to set up internal control system based on their actual situations, specify the overall operation processes and procedures, analyze potential risks, improve risk assessment mechanisms, and design risk coping strategies. Second, the institutions

POLICY UPDATE

should delegate administrative power in line with specified responsibilities, posts and hierarchies, and design a regular rotation mechanism, which is to form effective check and balance on the exercise of power, and ensure rigorous internal control. Third, based on the establishment and implementation of internal control, the institutions should actively carry out self-evaluation according to the requirements of the *Internal Control Guidelines*. Fourth, measures are to be taken to strengthen inspection and enhance accountability. ∎

The central public finance stepped up support for the agricultural insurance for rice, wheat and corn in the major counties that grow such crops

According to the news released by MOF on January 8, MOF has recently issued a circular to step up support for the agricultural insurance for rice, wheat and corn in the major counties that grow such crops. (1) Prior to the introduction of the policy, if the provincial subsidies as a percentage of premium exceed 25% (the standard threshold proportion), the central public finance will fund 50% of the subsidies that exceed the threshold. (2) If the provincial subsidies as a percentage of premium rise further and help reduce the fiscal burden of counties, the central public finance will also fund 50% of the costs that result in the lower subsidy expenses for counties. ∎

MOF, GAC and SAT jointly published the *Interim Measures for the Exemption of Import Tax for Charitable Donations*

On January 8, MOF, the General Administration of Customs (GAC) and the State Administration of Taxation (SAT) jointly published the *Interim Measures for the Exemption of Import Tax for Charitable Donations*. (1) The donations made by overseas donors for charitable purposes are exempted from import duties and import VAT. (2) The recipients of donations shall apply to the customs authorities for tax exemption on the eligible donations, and the customs authorities shall review and approve the application according to rules and regulations. (3) If the donations are subject to special quota, registration and licensing requirements as prescribed by the state, the recipients shall apply to relevant authorities for the quota, registration and import license before the customs authorities permit the clearance. (4) Unless with the approval of the customs authorities, the tax-free import of donations shall not be transferred, mortgaged, pledged or used for other purposes. ∎

MOF published the *Measures for the Administration of the Special Funds for Enhancing the Quality of Modern Vocational Education*

On January 11, MOF published the *Measures for the Administration of the Special Funds for Enhancing the Quality of Modern Vocational Education*. (1) The targeted areas for the use of the special funds are determined by MOF and the Ministry of Education (MOE) according to the plan of the CPC Central Committee and the State Council as well as the priorities for vocational education development. (2) The special funds are mainly disbursed by the factor method. (3) The special funds are jointly administered by MOF and MOE. (4) Each year, MOF and MOE will inform the lower-level governments the budgeted sum of the special funds within 90 days after the approval of the central budget by the National People's Congress (NPC). (5) More efforts shall be put on the holistic administration of funds at provincial levels when provincial finance and education authorities allocate the special funds. (6) A robust internal management system and sound rules for fund management shall be put into place and budget execution shall be accelerated in accordance with relevant requirements of budget and treasury management. (7) Provincial finance and education authorities shall administer the funds in a holistic way and make rational allocation. (8) MOF and MOE will conduct inspection and performance evaluation when appropriate based on the use of the special funds in different localities.∎

MOF published the guidelines on subjecting local government debt to the prescribed limit

On January 11, MOF published the guidelines on subjecting local government debt to the prescribed limit. (1) Keeping the local government debt within the prescribed limit. It is important to determine a limit on total local government debt and set the sub-limits by regions. Local governments are required to borrow strictly within the limit and incorporate their debt into budget management. (2) Improving the risk prevention and control system. The risks of local government debt shall be comprehensively assessed and alerted, the risk diffusion and contingency response system be established and the debt supervision and accountability system be improved. (3) Properly handling the stock of debt. The local governments shall earnestly fulfill their debt repayment obligations and properly handle the contingent liabilities according to the laws.∎

MOF published the *Guidelines on Further Regulating and Strengthening the State Asset Management in Public Institutions*

On January 14, MOF published the *Guidelines on Further Regulating and Strengthening the State Asset Management in Public Institutions*. (1) Further defining the mandates of finance authorities, competent authorities and public institutions and strengthening finance authorities' comprehensive management function and competent authorities' specific supervision function. (2) Emphasizing the role of public institutions as entities accountable for possessing and using state assets, calling for more efficient use and more regulated disposal of state assets, and specifying the requirements for better managing asset allocation, use and disposal. (3) Raising requirements concerning the management of public infrastructure, government reserve assets and natural resource assets as well as the enterprises affiliated to public institutions.∎

The State Council issued the *Plan for Promoting Inclusive Financial Development (2016-2020)*

On January 18, the State Council issued the *Plan for Promoting Inclusive Financial Development*

POLICY UPDATE

(2016-2020), which outlined the following. First, the financial system should be composed of diversified and broad-coverage institutions. Various types of banking institutions are encouraged to play an active role. The development of new institutions should be properly regulated. Insurance companies should tap into their advantages as safeguarding institutions. Second, innovative financial products and services are encouraged. Incentives should be given to financial institutions in their innovation and technology upgrading, and using the Internet to enhance the development of inclusive finance. Third, financial infrastructure development is to be accelerated. Priority should be given to the development of rural payment system, inclusive financial credit information system, and inclusive financial data-banks. Fourth, policies are to play an important role in guidance and incentives. Efforts should be made to improve the monetary and credit policies, and apply differentiated incentives in financial supervision. Fiscal policy is to play its role with stronger local support. ∎

The State Council issued guidance on promoting innovative development of processing trade

On January 19, the State Council issued guidance on promoting innovative development of processing trade, which provides the following. First, enhance the division of labor and cooperation among industrial chains, in a bid to promote industrial integration and innovation. Second, maintain strength in traditional industries, and push forward the development of advanced manufacturing and emerging industries. The development of producer services should be emphasized, with coastal areas continuing to play a leading role. Third, promote the development of processing trade industry cluster and the establishment of processing trade industry transfer cooperation mechanisms. Key inland areas should be prepared to take over industrial transfers from coastal areas, and differentiated supporting policies should be designed. Fourth, cultivate overseas cooperation in processing trade, and improve international cooperation mechanisms. Industrial cooperation with countries along the Belt and Road should be deepened, and so should be the cooperation with African states. Fifth, deepen the reform in administrative examination and approval system by adopting new and better regulatory approaches, accelerate the domestic sales facilitation, and speed up the optimization of special customs areas. ∎

MOF issued a circular on the use of official card for the financial settlement of research programs delegated by the central finance authority

On January 20, MOF issued a circular on the use of official card for the financial settlement of research programs delegated by the central finance authority, which provides the following. First, the official card should be used to settle the expenses of research programs which belong to the *Mandatory Official Card Settlement Catalog for Central Budgetary Agencies*, and related small amount of material costs and testing laboratory fees. Second, relevant agencies should standardize the payment procedure of official card, and strictly follow the required procedures. Third, relevant agencies should delegate agent banks to exam the reimbursement of official card. Fourth, except for official expenses, the agencies should not be liable for personal spending incurred on the official card and related obligations entailed on the personal spending. Fifth, during the financial acceptance inspection for the research projects, the use of official card for financial settlement is one of the acceptance requirements.■

MOF issued a circular on the incentives for the development of new energy vehicle charging facilities and broader use of new energy vehicles during the 13th Five-Year Plan period

On January 20, MOF issued a circular on the incentives for the development of new energy vehicle charging facilities and broader use of new energy vehicles during the 13th Five-Year Plan period. First, provinces (autonomous regions and municipalities) with broad market, rational policies and fair market access for new energy vehicles are eligible for the charging facility operation subsidies provided by the central finance authority. Second, the subsidies are lump-sum funds allocated from the central finance to local authorities in provinces (autonomous regions and municipalities), which are to make coordinated arrangement of the development of charging facilities and relevant operation. Third, the amount of subsidies is mainly determined by the number of new energy vehicles put into use in the provinces (autonomous regions and municipalities). Fourth, the subsidies are earmarked for the construction, operation and upgrading of charging facilities and related field monitoring system, and should not be used for supplementing local finance or supporting the purchase and operation of new energy vehicles.■

MOF issued the *Piloting Management Measures for the Agency Official Card*

On January 21, MOF issued the *Piloting Management Measures for the Agency Official Card*, which provides the following. First, the budget agency is to choose a bank within the scope of designated banks to be the issuing bank for the agency official card. Second, the official cardholders should be formal and permanent staff in the budget agency. Third, the credit ceiling of the official card is to be applied by the budget agency and examined by the issuing bank. Fourth, the budget agency is liable for the repayment in the official card. Fifth, the official card should only be used for official purposes. Personal expenses, installment, cashing or cash dividend return should not be incurred on the agency financial card. Sixth, both the agency and personal official card can be used to settle the business item within the mandatory settlement catalog. Seventh, the reimbursement of the agency official card is to go through the supporting system of the delegated bank, and is subject to dynamic monitoring of budget management.■

MOF published a circular on adjusting the relevant matters on verifying and approving the eligibility of public-interest-purpose donations for pre-tax deduction

On January 22, MOF published the circular on adjusting the relevant matters on verifying and

POLICY UPDATE

approving the eligibility of public-interest-purpose donations for pre-tax deduction. (1) The requirement for social organizations to submit application and relevant paperwork for pre-tax deduction of such donations will be scrapped. (2) MOF, SAT and the Ministry of Civil Affairs (MOCA) will jointly publish announcements to confirm the eligibility of qualified public-interest social organizations for pre-tax deduction. (3) The inspection and oversight will be intensified over the public-interest social organizations, so will be the penalty if they are found violating relevant rules and regulations. (4) Public finance, tax and civil affairs authorities at all levels of government shall strengthen collaboration and communication and set up a cross-agency coordination mechanism. ■

MOF published a circular on collecting the special funds for the structural adjustment of industrial enterprises

On January 22, MOF published a circular on collecting the special funds for the structural adjustment of industrial enterprises. (1) The special funds will be collected by the Inspector's Office of MOF in provinces and cities. (2) The special funds will be collected on a monthly basis and paid to the treasury. (3) The special funds will be transferred in full to the treasury, placed under the general public budget management, and catalogued as No. 103029999 "other special revenue" in the accounts of government revenue and expenditure. (4) No locality, unit and individual shall cut, waiver or delay the collection in contravention of this circular. (5) Those obliged to pay the special funds shall pay in time in accordance with the provisions of this circular. ■

MOF published a circular on the business tax policy for employee-based domestic service providers

On January 26, MOF published a circular on the business tax policy for employee-based domestic service providers. The waiver of business tax under the *Circular of MOF and SAT on the Waiver of Business Tax for Employee-based Domestic Service Providers* will remain valid from October 1, 2014 to December 31, 2018. The business taxes that should have been waivered but still paid are allowed to be deducted from the tax payers' future payable business taxes, or refunded to the tax payers if these taxes are not yet fully deducted when the reform that replaces business tax with VAT is implemented. ■

The executive meeting of the State Council identified the measures of promoting financial services to upgrade the industrial sector

On January 28, the executive meeting of the State Council identified the measures of promoting financial services to upgrade the industrial sector. (1) Steering financial institutions to scale up credit supply to high-tech firms and manufacturers of key equipments and parts so as to nurture new engine of growth. (2) Encouraging merger and acquisition financed by funds raised through M&A loans and issuance of preferred shares and convertible bonds so as to retrofit the conventional engine of growth. (3) Cutting and withholding loans to the firms that are perennially loss-making, insolvent, failing the environmental and production safety standards, and with outdated production capacity. (4) Expanding financing channels, promoting direct financing through stock and bond issuance, and developing accounts receivable financing. (5) Continuing to crack down on the irregularities of financial service charging by rescinding or cutting unreasonable charges.■

MOF issued a circular on adjusting the 19th government procurement list for energy saving products

On February 1, MOF issued a circular on adjusting the 19th government procurement list for energy saving products, which provides the following. First, computer equipment and input and output devices on the products list are mandatory items for government procurement. Other products on the list are priority items for government procurement. Second, products that are not included on the list are not mandatory or priority energy saving products for government procurement. Third, when the listed mandatory procurement products are involved in an already negotiated centralized government procurement contract, the centralized procurement agencies should renegotiate the contract with the suppliers based on the adjusted list. Fourth, when a needed product is a mandatory government procurement item, but the current list offers no corresponding detailed classification, or the listed products can not meet the working requirements, then the product can be purchased beyond the list.■

MOF issued a circular on adjusting the 17th government procurement list for environmental labeling goods

On February 1, MOF issued a circular on adjusting the 17th government procurement list for environmental labeling goods, which provides the following. First, the listed products are priority items for government procurement. Second, products that are not included on the list do not belong to priority environmental labeling products for government procurement. Third, government procurement of engineering services and engineering-related products should comply with the priority list for environmental labeling goods. Fourth, the list is applicable for government procurement activities undertaken after the publication of this circular.■

MOF issued the *Management Measures for the Earmarked Central Transfer Payments to Local Governments*

On February 2, MOF issued the *Management Measures for the Earmarked Central Transfer Payments to Local Governments*, which provides the following. First, the establishment of earmarked transfer payments should comply with clear requirements of laws and administrative regulations, performance targets, implementation time lines, etc.. Second, the application for establishing such funds should be submitted to MOF by relevant central authorities or provincial governments. Third, the earmarked funds are automatically terminated after expiration. Fourth, after approval

POLICY UPDATE

of establishing such funds, MOF should develop, together with other central authorities when necessary, management measures for the earmarked funds, so that each fund has its corresponding management measures. Fifth, regular evaluation mechanism for the earmarked funds should be established. Sixth, exit mechanism for the funds should be established. MOF is to handle the funds on a case-by-case basis according to relevant evaluation results. ∎

The Central Committee of the CPC and the State Council issued the *Guidelines for Tackling Poverty and Supporting Development in Old Revolutionary Areas*

On February 2, the Central Committee of the CPC and the State Council issued the *Guidelines for Tackling Poverty and Supporting Development in Old Revolutionary Areas*. First, when implementing mid to long-term programs such as the 13th Five-Year Plan for national economic and social development, staunch support should be given to old revolutionary bases by prioritizing transportation, water, energy and other major engineering projects. Second, the central government should give more support to old poverty areas through providing greater general transfer payments and earmarked funds which focus on people's livelihood. Third, when newly approved construction land in urban and rural areas is designated, priority should be given to supporting development of poor counties in the old areas. Fourth, tap resource advantages on the old poverty areas by enhancing the development of photovoltaic and wind power, so as to foster growth engines in those areas. Fifth, improve pension benefits and regular living allowance standard for entitled groups, such as old revolutionaries and demobilized soldiers. ∎

MOF issued the *Interim Measures for Central State-owned Capital Budget Management*

On February 2, MOF issued the *Interim Measures for Central State-owned Capital Budget Management*, which provides the following. First, the central state-owned capital budget income is to be collected from central departments and central enterprises, and included in the state capital budget management. Second, the central state-owned capital budget expenditures are mainly used to solve the legacy problems of SOE reform and related costs, or provide subsidies and other policy support. Third, the central state-owned capital budget income is to be estimated by MOF based on the annual profitability of central enterprises and policies related to capital gains of central state-owned capital. Fourth, the draft central state-owned capital budget should be reported to the State Council for approval, and then submitted to the NPC for review. Fifth, the central state-owned capital budget income is to be collected by Inspector's Office of MOF, and central departments are responsible for organizing affiliated (owned) central enterprises to turn over the capital gains. ∎

MOF issued the *Management Measures for Assets Verification in Administrative Public Institutions*

On February 3, MOF issued the *Management Measures for Assets Verification in Administrative Public Institutions*. First, administrative public institutions should take stock of their inventory assets. The institutions should submit application to their supervising authorities for the stocktaking, specify the rational of the work, scope of assets for review, and benchmark dates. The institutions may entrust intermediary agencies to conduct a special audit on the stocktaking results when necessary. The inventory should be reported through the commander chain and verified by the supervising authorities. Second, administrative public institutions may entrust legally established accounting firms or other intermediary agencies to conduct special audit on the results of the stocktaking. Third, the stocktaking mainly includes basic assets, financial books, property and the inventory logging system.∎

MOF issued a circular on tax incentives for public rental housing

On February 4, MOF issued a circular on tax incentives for public rental housing. First, the land for public rental housing (including construction land and completed housing) is exempt from urban land-use tax. Second, the managing institutions of public rental housing are exempt from the stamp duty involved in the construction and management of public rental housing. Third, when purchased commercial housing is to be managed as public rental housing, the transaction is exempt from contract tax and stamp duty. Fourth, when enterprises, administrative institutions, social groups or other organizations transfer their old property to be public rental housing, and the increased land value does not exceeding 20% of the deducted value, the property is exempted from land appreciation tax. Fifth, when enterprises, administrative institutions, social groups or other organizations donate their property to be public rental housing, the expenditure relating to the charitable donation which is under 12% of the total annual profit may be deducted when calculating taxable income. Sixth, housing rental subsidies for low-income families are exempt from personal income tax. Seventh, public rental housing is exempt from property taxes. Rental income from the operation of public rental housing is exempt from business tax. ∎

Figure2   The public rental housing

Source: Ministry of Finance of China

POLICY UPDATE

The State Council published several opinions on further advancing the new-type urbanization

On February 6, the State Council published several opinions on further advancing the new-type urbanization. (1) Pushing forward the process of turning rural migrant population into urban residents. The household registration system will be reformed, the residence permit system be enforced, the universal access of urban residents to basic public services be promoted, and incentives be created for rural migrants to become city dwellers. (2) Comprehensively improving the functions of cities. Renewal of urban shanty towns and decrepit houses will be accelerated, urban underground pipe networks be improved, and the level of urban public service be enhanced. (3) Developing small and medium-sized cities and towns with special features. Infrastructure of counties and key towns will be improved, functions of major towns be expanded, towns of special features be promoted, and a batch of small and medium-sized cities be developed. (4) Driving the development of the new countryside. Infrastructure and public service will be extended to rural areas to promote the integrated growth of industries and development of e-commerce, and the relocation of people for the purpose of poverty reduction will be combined with the new-type of urbanization. (5) Innovating investment and financing mechanisms. Cooperation between public and private capitals will be deepened, government input be stepped up, and financial support be strengthened.■

The State Council decided to conduct pilot program for innovative development of trade in services

On February 15, Premier Li Keqiang presided an executive meeting of the State Council, which decided to conduct pilot program for innovative development of trade in services so as to transform the foreign trade and improve the competitiveness of the service sector. According to the meeting: (1) service firms with advanced technology will be eligible for tax incentives, and the scope of eligible firms will be extended from service outsourcing firms to other high-tech and high value-added firms in the service sector. (2) Funds will be created to guide the innovative development of trade in services, and provide financial support for small and medium-sized service firms in the pilot area. Fiscal subsidies will be given to the pilot areas for their imports of R&D, energy-saving and environmental protection services that are urgently needed in China. (3) Financial institutions will be encouraged to innovate supply chain financing and other business, and the certified service firms of advanced technology in the pilot areas will be subject to service outsourcing bonded supervision.■

MOF published several opinions on promoting the stable growth, structural adjustment and efficiency enhancement of the industrial sector through enhanced financial support

On February 17, MOF published several opinions on promoting the stable growth, structural adjustment and efficiency enhancement of the industrial sector through enhanced financial support. (1) Strengthening the monetary and credit policy support and creating an enabling monetary and financial environment. Enhanced financial support will be provided for the supply-side structural reform in the industrial sector, the differentiated industrial credit policy be implemented, the innovation of industrial credit products be accelerated, and the industrial credit management system be improved. (2) Increasing the support of the capital market and insurance market to industrial companies. Support for the direct financing of industrial companies will be strengthened, the capacity of investment funds to support industrial companies be increased, asset securitization be promoted steadily, and the level of industrial insurance service be constantly raised. (3) Advancing the innovation of industrial companies' financing mechanism. Receivable-based financing will be vigorously promoted, and efforts will be made to match industrial companies and financial institutions. (4) Promoting the merger and reorganization of industrial companies. The policy environment and financing channels for such merger and reorganization will be optimized. (5) Supporting industrial companies to "go global". Supportive policies and financing support for the industrial firms that endeavor to "go global" will be improved. ■

MOF published the guidelines on capitalizing government investment funds with fiscal resources to support industrial development

On February 17, MOF published the guidelines on capitalizing government investment funds with fiscal resources to support industrial development. (1) When fiscal resources are injected into government investment funds, it is important to consider the specific issues concerning macroeconomic and industrial development, enhance top-level design of policies, clearly define the functions and determine the appropriate size of those funds, and orderly proceed with the capitalization. (2) Market-based operation and professional management shall be adopted to ensure the well-functioning of those funds. (3) Finance departments, as the authorities that administer fiscal resources, shall earnestly fulfill their duties as the investors that capitalize those funds, strive to meet industrial policy targets, and protect the rights and interests of the investors. (4) Finance departments shall strengthen oversight of those funds, improve institutional arrangement, and foster a sound environment to enable supportive policies to better promote industrial development. ■

The Central Committee of the CPC and the State Council published the *Opinions on Comprehensively Advancing the Work of Making Government Affairs Public*

On February 18, the Central Committee of the CPC and the State Council published the *Opinions on Comprehensively Advancing the Work of Making Government Affairs Public*. (1) Making government affairs transparent. Greater openness is required for government decision making, implementation, management, services, results, and information in key areas. (2) Increasing the public participation in government affairs. It is important to make government data more transparent, enhance the explanation of policies, increase the public participation, respond to public concerns, and give full play to the role of the media. (3) Strengthening the capacity for making government affairs public. Relevant institutional arrangement shall be improved, a negative list for information disclosure be created, IT-application be increased, government websites be refined, and training and education be enhanced. (4) Improving supporting measures. The information disclosure shall proceed in an organized way and the performance be evaluated and supervised. ■

POLICY UPDATE

The Central Committee of the CPC and the State Council issued several opinions on further strengthening the urban planning and construction management

On February 22, the Central Committee of the CPC and the State Council issued several opinions on further strengthening the urban planning and construction management. First, raise building energy efficiency standards, and promote the use of green construction and building materials. Second, on the basis of pilot and demonstration projects, intensify efforts to comprehensively promote energy-saving projects featuring combined heat and power, energy saving by government agencies, and green lighting. Third, deepen the reform on urban housing. The basic housing needs of the disadvantaged groups are mainly to be guaranteed by the government, while the diversified housing demands of the general public are to be addressed mainly by the market. Fourth, gradually push ahead with the development of urban underground pipeline system, with co-ordination of various types of pipe laying. Fifth, improve the public transport system by enhancing the burden-sharing ratio, in order to ease the pressure on urban traffic. Sixth, adhere to the concept of shared development, so the people may share greater benefit in common development.∎

MOF and MOA held a video conference on providing future incentives for ecological protection of grassland

On February 23, MOF and the Ministry of Agriculture (MOA) held a video conference on providing future incentives for ecological protection of grassland, which made targeted adjustment to relevant policy measures. First, the general production subsidies and forage seed subsidies for the herders are removed. The fund for those subsidies is to be combined with additional central fiscal fund to provide compensation for the grazing ban and incentives for balanced livestock raising. Second, financial awards will continue to be provided to areas with outstanding achievements in ecological protection and used by the local government in related efforts. Third, the agro-pastoral subsidies are to be earmarked to the local authorities for grassland protection and development at their own discretion.∎

MOF issued a circular on regulating land reserves and fund management

On February 23, MOF issued a circular on regulating land reserves and fund management. First, when an existing loan for land reserve is identified as local government debt as of December 31, 2014, the loan should be put under the budget management of governmental funds. Second, the funds needed by land reserve institutions in launching additional land reserve projects are to be provided from the state-owned land income fund, the land transfer revenue and other fiscal funds. The funding gap, if any, is to be made up by issuing local government bonds by the provincial government. Third, the land reserve funds are to be used to pay for: the price or compensation relating to requisition, acquisition, priority purchase or recovery of the land; and the necessary pre-development expenses after requisition, acquisition, priority purchase or recovery of the land. Fourth, the land reserve agency should prepare the land reserve budget for the next year, on the basis of local economic development of the third quarter of the current year and overall financial conditions of the previous year.■

The State Council decided to further support the new energy vehicle industry

On February 24, during an executive meeting chaired by the Premier Li Keqiang, the State Council identified further measures to support the new energy vehicle industry. First, the central government is to replace relevant subsidies with financial awards for new energy vehicle manufacturers based on battery performance, sales and other indicators. Second, the local government is encouraged to provide policy incentives based on the charging volume of the vehicle, and reduce fees for charging service. Third, the central government departments, government agencies and public institutions in demonstration cities for new energy vehicle should see to it that the new energy vehicles account for over 50% of their total replaced vehicle of the year. Fourth, access standards should be improved with enhanced quality and safety supervision. Measures should be taken to promote the development of new energy vehicles + the Internet of Things, and make manufacturers accountable for the safety monitoring and dynamic inspection. Fifth, fiscal subsidies and other supporting policies should be improved, and no traffic or purchase restrictions shall be imposed on the new energy vehicles.■

MOF issued the *Work Outlines for 2016 Government Procurement*

On February 26, MOF issued the *Work Outlines for 2016 Government Procurement*. First, strengthen the development of government procurement system. Second, make in-depth study on relevant policies, and improve innovation-supporting measures. Third, improve the government procurement related management and trading system. Central government departments and procurement agencies are encouraged to use the project review system. Fourth, establish an integrated platform for the trading of public resources and design unified trading rules for government procurement. Fifth, strictly design budget and plans for government procurement. The procurement should be managed with sound record-keeping, streamlined approval process and simplified procedure for imported goods. Sixth, organize nationwide and inter-connected supervision and monitoring on delegated procurement agencies, and improve the performance evaluation on centralized procurement agencies. Seventh, step up publicity efforts, and enhance research on deepening the reform of the government procurement system.■

MOF, MOST and SASAC jointly published the *Interim Measures for the Equity and Dividend Incentives of the State-owned Science and Technology Firms*

On February 29, MOF, the Ministry of Science and Technology (MOST) and the State-owned Assets Supervision and Administration Commision of the State Council (SASAC) jointly published the *Interim Measures for the Equity and Dividend Incentives of the State-owned Science and Technology*

POLICY UPDATE

Firms and decided to roll out the trial policies nationwide from March 1, 2016 onwards. The qualified state-owned science and technology firms can distribute to important technical and managerial staff either equity incentives, such as equity sale, equity rewards and equity options, or dividend incentives, including those based on project profits or staff performance. Meanwhile, in distributing the incentives, firms shall proceed in a transparent and fair way in accordance with relevant laws and regulations; take into account the specific circumstances of firms; ensure the benefits are shared and risks are pooled; and enhance accountability and oversight. ■

The State Council published a circular on providing incentives for the areas that have made notable achievements in implementing relevant policy measures

On February 29, the State Council published a circular on providing incentives for the areas that have made notable achievements in implementing relevant policy measures. (1) Disbursing a portion of the 2016 special construction funds to those areas. (2) The central budgetary investment funds that sat idle in 2015 and are taken back in 2016 will be allotted by the provincial development and reform departments to the specific projects in those areas. (3) The idle specific-purpose transfer payment funds taken back in 2016 will be allocated by MOF to the provinces (districts and cities) in those areas. (4) The businesses of those areas can directly submit application documents at the administrative service center of the National Development and Reform Commission (NDRC) if they are to issue corporate bonds. (5) The central government may make advance arrangement of funds to the provinces (districts and cities) in those areas. (6) Rewards in the form of extra land designation for construction projects will be granted to those areas. ■

MOF published a circular on the subsidy standard for gas development and use during the 13th Five-Year Plan period

On March 1, MOF published a circular on the subsidy standard for gas development and use during the 13th Five-Year Plan period. (1) During the 13th Five-Year Plan period, the subsidy standard for gas development and use is raised from 0.2 RMB/m^3 to 0.3 RMB/m^3. In the meantime, MOF will adjust, when appropriate, the subsidy policy in light of the developments in the gas industry and the changes of the extraction costs and the market sales price. (2) Other relevant matters will continue to be governed by the *Opinions of the Ministry of Finance on Implementing the Subsidy for Coal-bed Methane (Gas) Development and Use.* ■

MOF published a circular on further clarifying the issues related to the application of public-welfare social organizations for the invoices of donation for public welfare

On March 1, MOF published a circular on further clarifying the issues related to the application of public-welfare social organizations for the invoices of donation for public welfare. (1) Public-welfare social organizations can apply to the corresponding-level finance authorities for the invoices. (2) The invoices are obtained only when relevant credentials are presented, the number of invoices issued each time is subject to limit, and new invoices can only be acquired when the counterfoils of the old ones are verified. (3) The finance authorities shall strengthen the oversight and inspection over the application (purchase), use and keeping of the invoices by the public-welfare social organizations. (4) The civil affair authorities shall urge the public-welfare social organizations to ensure the invoices are well used. ∎

MOF published a circular on the relevant tax policy issues related to the Insurance Security Fund

On March 1, MOF published a circular on the relevant tax policy issues related to the Insurance Security Fund. (1) The income in forms of statutory insurance security funds contributed by domestic insurance firms, donation proceeds and bank deposit interests shall be exempted from the corporate income tax. (2) The income in forms of statutory security funds contributed by domestic insurance firms, compensation from the liquidated property of the dissolved or bankrupt insurers, and the recourse against the liable parties shall be exempted from the business tax. (3) The capital accounts newly created by the Fund as well as the relending contract signed with the People's Bank of China (PBoC) in the course of risk resolution of insurers shall be exempted from the stamp tax. ∎

MOF published the guidelines on the promotion of green consumption

On March 2, MOF published the guidelines on the promotion of green consumption. (1) Encouraging the consumption and promotion of green products, including energy-efficient electric motors, vehicles and lighting products. (2) Expanding the green consumption market, including facilitating the distribution channels of green products and fostering green distributors such as green wholesale market, green malls, energy-efficient supermarket, water-saving supermarket and goodwill supermarket. (3) Promoting green office, including raising the using efficiency of office equipment and assets, encouraging double-sided printing, advancing the development of information system and data sharing, and creating the paperless office. (4) Improving the green procurement system, including rigorously enforcing the system of priority and mandatory procurement of energy-saving and environmentally friendly products by government, expanding the scope of government's green procurement, putting in place sound standard system and enforcement mechanism, and increasing the size of government's green procurement. ∎

Figure3   the consumption and promotion of green products

Source: Ministry of Finance of China

POLICY UPDATE

MOF and MOT jointly issued the *Guiding Opinions on Promoting Government Procurement of Services in Transport Sector*

On March 10, MOF and the Ministry of Transport (MOT) jointly issued the *Guiding Opinions on Promoting Government Procurement of Services in Transport Sector*: (1) items for procurement. Transport services may be gradually acquired from private service providers through government procurement, except for cases otherwise stipulated by laws and regulations, or involving national security, or relating to services directly obtained from administrative institutions, which are unsuitable for private sectors. (2) The purchaser should establish a sound mechanism for government procurement of highway and waterway transportation services, which should be flexible, regulated, competitive and cost effective. (3) The fund for government procurement of private services is to be included in fiscal budget and allocated from departmental budget or approved earmarked funds. (4) Efforts are to be made to strengthen performance management of government procurement of transportation services, enhance the sense of accountability and efficiency, and improve the performance evaluation mechanism. ∎

MOF published a circular on the harmonization of the old and new *Rules for the Administration of Accounting Files*

On March 14, MOF published a circular on the harmonization of the old and new *Rules for the Administration of Accounting Files*. (1) Where the new rules differ from the old ones in terms of the minimum retention period, the new rules shall prevail. (2) If the files reach the minimum retention period set out in the old rules, they shall be verified under the new rules to decide whether they will be destroyed or kept. (3) The files that do not reach the minimum retention period set out in the old rules shall be reassessed to determine a new retention period as required by the new rules. (4) The accounting documents formed before 2014 shall be filed away and kept according to the old rules. (5) All the entities that retain the files electronically in accordance with the new rules shall, in principle, do so at the start of a complete accounting year. ∎

MOF published a circular on the *2016 Rules for the Administration of the Issuance Quota of Treasury Savings Bonds*

On March 15, MOF published a circular on the *2016 Rules for the Administration of the Issuance Quota of Treasury Savings Bonds*. (1) Before the issuance, MOF and PBoC, in accordance with the circular, shall make pro rata allocation of the basic sales quota among the members of the underwriting syndicate. (2) MOF and PBoC may cut the remaining basic sales quota of the underwriters that are lagging in sales. (3) The competitive sales quota (for electronic bonds) left over and zeroed out on a given day shall not exceed 7% of the basic sales quota of the current bonds. (4) If the sales exceed the allowed quota limit, the sales shall be suspended immediately. (5) After the end of the issuance (of the electronic bonds), the unsold quota shall be zeroed out or suspended; and the China Central Depository and Clearing Co. shall cancel the unsold quota in its system. ∎

MOF published a circular on continuing the preferential tax policies for the operation of the rural drinking water safety project

On March 16, MOF published a circular on continuing the preferential tax policies for the operation of the rural drinking water safety project. (1) The project operating and management agencies shall be exempted from the deed tax when they acquire the land use rights for the project. (2) The project operating and management agencies shall be exempted from the stamp tax when they sign the property transfer documents to acquire land use rights or when they sign construction contracts with the construction companies. (3) The property and land used by the project operating and management agencies for operation and office purposes are exempt from the property tax and urban land use tax. (4) The sales income derived by the project operating and management agencies from supplying tap water to rural residents is exempt from the VAT. (5) Starting from the tax year when the first operating income is generated from the project, the project operating and management agencies shall be exempted from corporate income tax from year 1 to year 3, and have their corporate income tax halved from year 4 to year 6. ∎

MOF issued the *Rules for the Administration of Non-tax Revenues of the Government*

On March 18, MOF issued the *Rules for the Administration of Non-tax Revenue of the Government*. (1) The non-tax revenues can either be levied directly by the finance authorities, or by agencies or institutions commissioned by the finance authorities. (2) All non-tax revenues should be turned over to the treasury. (3) The non-tax revenues should be collected under the centralized single treasury account. (4) Finance authorities at all levels should strengthen the receipt management to ensure the legal and legitimate non-tax revenues are collected to the treasury in full and on time. (5) The receipts of non-tax revenues are to be obtained with required credentials, with regular issuance and value ceiling for each time, and new receipts can only be acquired when the counterfoils of the old ones are verified. (6) The recipient of non-tax revenues should file the counterfoils in sequence and keep them in bound books. (7) The non-tax revenues should be collected, deposited, returned, cleared and audited through the single treasury account system. ∎

MOF issued a circular on the tax policy for railway bond interest income

On March 23, MOF issued a circular on the tax policy for railway bond interest income. (1) For corporate investors, the corporate income tax for interest income generated from railway bonds issued during 2016-2018 is levied with a 50% discount. (2) For individual investors, interest income generated from railway bonds issued during 2016-2018 is recorded at 50% in the calculation of taxable individual income. The bond underwriter is to withhold the tax when the interest is redeemed by the individual investor. (3) Railroad bonds are issued and redeemed by the China Railway Corporation, including debt financing instruments such as the Chinese railway construction bonds, medium-term notes, and short-term financing bonds. ∎

POLICY UPDATE

MOF issued guidance on providing financial services to support poverty reduction

On March 24, MOF issued guidance on providing financial services to support poverty reduction. (1) The financial services should be tailored to support development plans of the poor regions, development of special industries, employment and education of the poor population, and relocation efforts for poverty reduction purposes. (2) Efforts should be made to improve the rural payment system to provide access for villagers and rural households, enhance the rural credit system to better connect credit record and extension of loans, and promote financial literacy to strengthen financial consumer protection in poverty-stricken areas. (3) Development financing and policy financing should be calibrated to serve poverty alleviation initiatives. Measures are to be adopted to improve comprehensive commercial financial services, build a multi-level financial service system in rural areas, strengthen financial counseling and incubation, and make innovation in targeted poverty reduction products and services. (4) Programs of pro-poor re-lending are to be launched. Efforts should be made in strengthening financial and taxation policy coordination and implementing differentiated regulatory policies.∎

China starts to levy import duties on cross-border e-commerce retail products and adjust the parcel tax since April 8

According to the news released on March 24 by MOF, China will start to levy import duties on cross-border e-commerce retail products and adjust the parcel tax since April 8. The imported retail products through cross-border e-commerce are subject to tariffs on imported goods. The value ceiling for each single purchase is raised from the current 1,000 RMB under the parcel tax to 2,000 RMB, and the annual limit for gross transactions by an individual consumer is 20,000 RMB. As long as the purchase doesn't exceed the ceilings, the interim tariff rate is zero, and an import value-added tax and consumption duties will be levied but with a 30% discount. Meanwhile, China will adjust the parcel tax, reducing the current four tax brackets to three. In order to be consistent with the overall tax rate for similar imported goods, the parcel tax brackets for taxable items after the adjustment are 15%, 30% and 60% respectively.∎

MOF issued a circular on the full roll-out of the "replacing business tax with VAT" pilot reform

On March 24, MOF issued a circular on the full roll-out of the "replacing business tax with VAT" pilot reform: starting from May 1, 2016, the pilot VAT reform will be implemented nationwide and across all sectors, covering all business taxpayers in construction, real estate, financial services and consumer services. Local authorities should attach great importance to this initiative by stepping up relative administration and organization, specifying lines of responsibility, adopting measures to make preparations, and conducting monitoring, analysis and public education of the program during the rolling out process, all in a bid to ensure steady, orderly and smooth progress of the reform.∎

The State Council published the *Regulations of the National Social Security Fund*

On March 29, the State Council published the *Regulations of the National Social Security Fund*. (1) The National Council for Social Security Fund (SSF) shall make investment in domestic and foreign markets by following the investment proportion authorized by the State Council. (2) SSF may make entrusted investment or other alternative forms of investment authorized by the State Council. (3) The property of the Fund shall be independent from the property owned by SSF, investment managers and trustees, and shall also stay independent from other property invested by the investment managers and under the custody of the trustees. (4) The Fund is entitled to preferential tax treatments prescribed by the state. (5) Finance authorities and social insurance authorities of the State Council shall fulfill their mandate and exercise supervision over the collection, outlay, management, investment and operation of the Fund. (6) National Audit Office (NAO) shall conduct at least one audit of the Fund in each year and make public the audit results. ∎

The State Council published the opinions on the key tasks required by the *Government Work Report*

On March 30, the State Council published the opinions on the key tasks required by the *Government Work Report*. (1) Improve and stabilize the macroeconomic policies, keep the economic performance within a reasonable range, redouble efforts to implement proactive fiscal policies, and enforce prudent monetary policies in a flexible and appropriate manner. (2) Push forward supply-side structural reforms, enhance the momentum for sustained growth, push ahead deregulation, improve regulation, unlock the potential for entrepreneurship and innovation, cut overcapacity and costs, improve the provision of products and services, deepen SOE reform, and invigorate the non-public economic sector. (3) Tap the potential for domestic demand, expand the room for development, spur economic growth through consumption, maintain steady growth and improve economic structure through leveraging effective investment, advance the new-type urbanization, and optimize the development across regions. ∎

MOF issued a circular on processing application for financial discounts of loan by businesses in their efforts to upgrade the quality of refined oil

On April 6, MOF issued a circular on processing applications for financial discounts of loans by businesses in their efforts to upgrade the quality of refined oil. (1) The discount rate is subject to the annual budget and below the benchmark rate set by PBoC for similar loans during the same period. The discount is applicable for loans incurred during 2015-2017. (2) In the beginning of each year, the applicant business shall present its application to, through the chain of reporting, the home provincial energy and finance authorities, together with relevant credentials such as the contract and receipt of bank loans. (3) The National Energy Administration (NEA) shall commission independent third parties to evaluate the qualification of applications, and publish qualified discount recipients after due process of public comment. (4) The NEA is to conduct supervision and inspection on discount

POLICY UPDATE

recipients in the progress of upgrading the quality of refined oil. ■

MOF issued a circular on tax policy for certain national reserve commodities

On April 6, MOF issued a circular on tax policy for certain national reserve commodities. (1) The commodity reserve and management companies and their direct affiliates are exempted from stamp tax on their financial accounting books as well as on procurement and sales contracts for commodity reserve related transactions. The other parties of the contracts are subject to statutory stamp duty. (2) The commodity reserve and management companies and their direct affiliates are exempted from the property tax and urban land use tax on their real estates and land used for commodity reserve business. (3) For tax levied after January 1, 2016 which is eligible for exemption should be discounted from payable taxes of the taxpayer. (4) Qualified businesses should present relevant credentials to tax authorities for the filing of tax relief procedures based on related requirements. ■

The State Council specified priorities for the medicine and health reform in 2016

On April 6, Premier Li Keqiang chaired an executive meeting of the State Council and identified priorities for the medicine and health reform in 2016. (1) Expand comprehensive piloting reform for urban pubic hospitals from 100 cities to 200 cities. (2) Roll out piloting programs for hierarchical medical system to 70% of prefecture-level cities across the country. In-service or retired attending doctors in public hospitals are encouraged to offer service in grass-roots medical institutions or clinics. (3) Improve the compensation mechanism by removing medicine markups in piloting urban public hospitals. Excessive medical tests are strictly controlled. (4) Promote centralized medicine procurement in public hospitals. Establish traceability mechanism to the factory price of pharmaceuticals by adopting a "double-invoice" regime, i.e. requiring invoice from the manufacturer to wholesale supplier and from the supplier to hospitals and clinics, thus enhancing the transparency of intermediary markups. (5) Encourage pilot cities to design aggregated determination measures for performance-related pay in public hospitals. Incentive income mechanism should be established to link job responsibility with performance. (6) Promote the development of national basic medical insurance network and portable medical billing across regions. ■

MOF issued the *Interim Measures for the Administration of Fiscal Funds for Comprehensive Improvement of Rivers, Lakes and Reservoirs*

On April 8, MOF issued the *Interim Measures for the Administration of Fiscal Funds for Comprehensive Improvement of Rivers, Lakes and Reservoirs*. (1) The earmarked funds are under joint jurisdiction of MOF and the Ministry of Water Resources (MWR). (2) The funds are used for improvement of medium and small rivers, comprehensive renovation of key counties, construction of small reservoirs, and better connectivity among rivers, lakes and reservoirs. (3) The funds are allocated mainly through the multiple factor method. Lump-sum grants are provided to major construction projects approved by the CPC Central Committee and the State Council, and also allocated to certain project-specific outlays. (4) Project-specific funds are to be jointly endorsed by MWR and MOF, with clear specifics for the applicants, types of projects and application terms. (5) MOF and MWR are to conduct joint evaluation on the performance of the funds. The valuation results are important factors in the fund allocation. (6) The budget of the funds is provided through statutory procedures by MOF after consultation with MWR. ∎

MOF published the *Interim Measures for the Performance Assessment of the Special Funds for Urban Pipeline Network*

On April 8, MOF published the *Interim Measures for the Performance Assessment of the Special Funds for Urban Pipeline Network*. (1) MOF, the Ministry of Housing and Urban-Rural Development (MOHURD) and other competent authorities shall be the principal agencies for overseeing the performance assessment exercise. (2) MOF, in conjunction with MOHURD and other ministries, will review the performance targets submitted by the provincial government departments. (3) MOF, in conjunction with MOHURD and other ministries, will develop assessment indicators and standards on the basis of the specific purposes of the special funds. (4) MOHURD will work with relevant government agencies in conducting the performance assessment and make annual assessment when necessary. (5) MOHURD will aggregate the assessment reports and submit the reports, along with its recommendations on the use of the assessment results, to MOF. (6) The assessment results will serve as important basis for rewards and penalties. (7) The provincial-level finance as well as housing and urban-rural development authorities shall enhance their supervision over the use of the funds and develop a provincial-level assessment mechanism with reference to the *Interim Measures*. (8) Finance, housing and urban-rural development authorities and other competent authorities shall strengthen the monitoring over the execution of the budget of the special funds and see to the realization of the performance targets. ∎

MOF published a circular on the 2016 pilot localities for the treasury cash management scheme

On April 12, MOF published a circular on the 2016 pilot localities for the treasury cash management scheme. (1) The pilot localities shall implement the scheme by strictly following the *Measures for the Pilot Treasury Cash Management Scheme in Localities* after completion of record-filing with MOF and PBoC. (2) The pilot localities shall strictly comply with the operational procedures and timely submit their monthly operation plan and detailed information of each operation. The announcement for bids and bidding results shall be made public in time. (3) The pilot localities shall handle pledging in strict accordance with rules. Local government bonds are not subject to the restrictions on issuing entities and can allow for cross-jurisdiction pledging, and pilot localities shall not designate the specific types of pledges. (4) The pilot localities shall take into account the progress of interest rate liberalization, actively control the financing costs, guide financial institutions to determine their bid rate for treasury cash deposit on the basis of costs and risks and within the agreed range in the provincial market, and further improve the mechanism

POLICY UPDATE

for the formation of the bid rate.■

MOF published the explanations to the notes regarding the relevant goods in the *Catalogue of Goods Imported through Cross-border E-commerce Retailing*

On April 13, MOF published the explanations to the notes regarding the relevant goods in the *Catalogue of Goods Imported through Cross-border E-commerce Retailing*. (1) On the notes of "except those that shall be registered in accordance with the *Food Safety Law* but have not been registered" under the item of "formula milk powder". As the formulation of the *Measures for the Formula Registration of the Infant Milk Powder Products* is still in the works, the certificate of formula registration is currently not required for the import of infant formula milk through cross-border e-commerce retailing. (2) On the notes of "except the cosmetics that are imported for the first time" under the item of "cosmetics". From now on, the cosmetics imported through cross-border e-commerce retailing shall be the products that are licensed in accordance with relevant regulations.■

MOF published the *Guiding Opinions on the Appraisal of the Intangible Assets of Cultural Enterprises*

On April 14, MOF published the *Guiding Opinions on the Appraisal of the Intangible Assets of Cultural Enterprises*. (1) The appraisal shall consider the impact on the value of intangible assets brought by the social benefits generated by different types of cultural enterprises, which may manifest in the forms of political guidance, cultural creation and service, audience feedback, social influence, internal institutional and team building. (2) The appraisal is required to highlight the characteristics of cultural enterprises, define the scope and features of different types of intangible assets in cultural industries, and assess all sorts of factors that need to be considered. (3) The *Opinions* will provide guidance on the practice of appraisal and put emphasis on operability. Some of the provisions provide examples to illustrate the classic cases of cultural enterprises, helping provide tailored guidance for the real-world appraisal. (4) The *Opinions* are aligned to the promulgated "1+3" framework of standards for intangible asset appraisal and the recently issued *Guidelines on the Appraisal of Intellectual Property Right Assets*.■

MOF issued a circular on the 2016 application of water connectivity projects among rivers, lakes, and reservoirs

On April 16, MOF issued a circular on the 2016 application for water connectivity projects among rivers, lakes, and reservoirs. (1) The projects for application include: water diversion among rivers, lakes and reservoirs, waterway dredging, construction and revamping of sluices, ecological slope revetment, water ecology system protection and restoration, etc.. (2) The projects under application should be catering to genuine demand, ecologically secure and sustainable, and consistent with the development requirements for relevant drainage basin and region. The projects should be focusing on addressing water-related ecological problems in urban and rural areas, while taking into account the allocation of water resources, water safety and flood control and drainage. The preliminary design report of the projects has been approved. The projects are not included in the overall planning for small and medium river management, and not supported by the central infrastructure fund or other funds. (3) The applicants should be city-level or country-level water administration agencies. The application paperwork is to be strictly reviewed by provincial water authorities in conjunction with finance authorities. ■

MOF released a circular on tax collection requirements before expanding the VAT pilot program

On April 18, MOF released a circular on tax collection requirements before expanding the VAT pilot program. (1) Local authorities should fully recognize the importance of easing tax burden for enterprises in enhancing their indigenous strength. (2) Tax authorities should not adjust levy schedules to make advanced tax collection prior to the existing month or quarter. Deductable input tax or tax returns under VAT should be deducted or returned accordingly. Except for standard procedure, tax-collection campaigns targeting tax arrears should be strictly prohibited. Tax authorities should not ask taxpayers to pay excess or advance taxes before May 1 and then return the tax after May 1, nor deliberately refuse to provide VAT invoice or require redundant invoice procedures, nor collude with enterprises to adjust the financial books. (3) After the roll-out of VAT pilot program, overdue taxes by taxpayers incurred before May 1 should be levied by local tax authorities, and state authorities which take over the jurisdiction over the taxpayers should support the collection of tax arrears. (4) Tax and finance authorities should intensify supervision in conjunction with other competent authorities. ■

The State Council issued the *2016 Guidelines on the Public Disclosure of Administrative Information*

On April 19, the State Council issued the *2016 Guidelines on the Public Disclosure of Administrative Information*. (1) Further promote reform and enhance administrative transparency. Government agencies should further disclose the list of their administrative authorities and responsibilities, enhance transparency of market regulation and supervision, and disclose more public service related information. (2) Promote public disclosure to foster economic development. Economic and social policy related information should be more open and transparent, including negative list for market access, major construction projects with government investment, allocation of public resources, reduction of taxes and administrative fees, and regulation on the operation of state-owned enterprises. (3) Information relating to people's livelihood should be made more public, including poverty reduction efforts, social assistance, incentives for job creation and entrepreneurship, renovation of urban shantytowns and rural dilapidated housing, development of affordable housing, as well as information related to environmental protection, education, health, and food and drug safety. (4) Enhance transparency to boost capacity building of the government. Efforts should be made to promote public disclosure on decision-making, policy implementation and budget designing and final auditing. ■

POLICY UPDATE

MOF issued a circular on measures to further promote shantytown renovation

On April 19, MOF issued a circular on measures to further promote shantytown renovation. (1) Finance authorities at all levels should focus on speeding up the renovation of shantytowns as required by the State Council, actively raise funds and make co-ordinated arrangements to ensure smooth implementation. (2) Strictly implement tax incentives to effectively reduce the cost of shantytown renovation. (3) Provide cash compensation for the relocated residents from shantytowns to accelerate de-stocking of commercial housing. (4)The procurement should strictly follow the rules and procedures of government procurement, in order to prevent black-box operation and corruption. (5) Promote the government procurement of shantytown renovation related services, and coordinate with loan extension for related work. (6) Financially-challenged cities and counties with heavy task load of shantytown renovation should be the main recipients of relevant subsidies. The subsidizing fund is to be raised by provincial governments by issuing bonds on local governments' behalf. (7) Discounted loans are provided to shantytown renovation efforts to attract private capital. (8) The earmarked funds should be used for intended purpose only, no institution or person may obstruct or misappropriate the funds. (9) Performance evaluation is to be carried out to raise the social and economic returns on shantytown renovation.■

MOF issued a circular on phased reduction of the social insurance rate

On April 21, MOF issued a circular on phased reduction of the social insurance rate. (1) Starting from May 1, 2016, provinces (autonomous regions and municipalities) with employers' contribution rate for employees' basic pension of over 20% should lower the rate to 20%; provinces (autonomous regions and municipalities) with the rate of 20% and an accumulated pension fund covering up to 9 months of pension outlays as of the end of 2015 may reduce the employers' contribution rate to 19%. (2) Starting from May 1, 2016, the total unemployment insurance rate, which was already cut by 1 percentage point in 2015, may be further lowered by 1%-1.5%, with individual contribution rate dropping under 0.5%. The reduced rate is temporarily set for the next two year. (3) Various localities should continue to implement the decision of the State Council in 2015 to reduce the average occupational injury insurance rate and maternity insurance rate by 0.25 and 0.5 percentage point respectively.■

The State Council gave guidance on pro-poor transport infrastructure development

On April 21, Premier Li Keqiang chaired an executive meeting of the State Council, which identified the following measures. (1) Launch the program of building one million kilometers of highway in rural areas to provide highway and passenger car connections to all towns and villages, reconstruct dilapidated roads and bridges, and improve transportation system for tourism development in poverty-stricken areas. (2) Launch the program of building 100 expressways, railways and airports, in an effort to connect all the counties with secondary and above highways, and basically cover all municipal (prefecture) administrative centers with railways and highways. Fill the linkage gaps of highway in boundary areas. Increase fiscal and taxation support, emphasize both construction and maintenance, and improve the long term investment and management mechanism. The above-mentioned programs are designed to stimulate investment, create jobs, support poverty alleviation through better transportation, so as to deliver benefits to millions of people.■

The State Council published the opinions on supporting poor counties to make consolidated use of agriculture-related fiscal funds

On April 25, the State Council published the opinions on supporting poor counties to make consolidated use of agriculture-related fiscal funds. (1) The central and provincial finance authorities shall optimize the composition of transfer payment, significantly increase transfer payment to poor regions, and expand the size and proportion of general transfer payment to enhance the fiscal capacity of poor counties. (2) On the basis of the increased poverty reduction funds, the central, provincial and city-level finance authorities shall tilt towards poor counties in disbursing the poverty reduction funds. (3) Poor counties shall align themselves to the national poverty reduction plans and the specific-purpose plans of competent authorities. The funds shall be used to tackle poverty and the effects of poverty reduction shall be the primary consideration for the performance evaluation of the funds. (4) Poor counties shall explore innovative ways for poverty reduction and make full use of fiscal funds to guide and leverage more financial capital and private capital for poverty reduction. (5) Relevant authorities at central, provincial and city-level shall timely revise and improve rules and regulations and scrap the restrictions on the consolidated use of the funds.■

MOF published a circular on comprehensively reforming the "Sannong subsidies"[1]

On April 25, MOF published a circular on comprehensively reforming the "Sannong subsidies". (1) Enhance and conserve the fertility of farming land and better protect the agricultural eco-resources. (2) The subsidies for the appropriately scaled-up crop growing will be financed by the agricultural support and protection funds and will mainly go to the major crop-growers, family farms, farmers' cooperatives, agricultural service providers and others new agribusinesses. Instead of

---

1 Sannong refers to agriculture, rural area and farmer.

POLICY UPDATE

providing subsidies in cash, localities will be encouraged to develop innovative ways to support new agribusinesses, and subsidized loans and subsidies for the dissemination of major techniques will be used to support diversified forms of appropriately scaled-up crop growing by new agribusinesses. (3) The reform of the "Sannong subsidies" will be overseen by provincial governments and implemented by the local finance and agricultural authorities. (4) The central fiscal subsidies for agricultural support and protection will be allotted to provincial finance authorities in proportion to the size of farming land, crop output and appropriately scaled-up farming, while the recipients, ways and standards of subsidies will be determined by provincial authorities on account of local circumstances.■

MOF published a circular on the computation of deed tax, property tax, land VAT and personal income tax after the VAT reform

On April 26, MOF published a circular on the computation of deed tax, property tax, land VAT and personal income tax after the VAT reform. (1) The transaction price used to compute the deed tax shall exclude VAT. (2) In case of property lease, the lease income used to compute property tax shall exclude VAT. (3) The income generated through property transfer by land VAT payer shall exclude VAT. (4) The taxable income for house transfer by individuals shall exclude VAT, the VAT in the house purchase price is included in the property's original value, and the VAT paid in the property transfer is not deductible when computing the transfer income. (5) In case of VAT exemption, the transaction price, lease income and real estate transfer income shall not deduct VAT when it comes to the computation of taxes. (6) In the administration of the above-mentioned taxes, the price or income verified by the tax authorities for tax computation shall exclude VAT.■

The State Council published the *Priority Tasks for Deepening the Reform of Medical and Health System in 2016*

On April 27, the State Council published the *Priority Tasks for Deepening the Reform of Medical and Health System in 2016*. (1) Comprehensively deepen the public hospital reform, including to improve the reform of county-level public hospitals, expand the pilot reform of urban public hospitals, establish a scientific compensation mechanism, enhance the management system of public hospitals, accelerate the establishment of a remuneration system fit for the healthcare industry, curb the unreasonable rise of health costs, push forward the reform of public traditional Chinese medicine hospitals, and provide nearby public-rental housing for qualified staff of public hospitals. (2) Expedite the creation of a tiered diagnosis and treatment system, including to roll out pilot programs and to expand the service of home doctors. (3) Strengthen and improve the universal health insurance system, including to create stable and sustainable fund-raising and benefit-adjustment mechanisms, further unify the urban and rural health insurance schemes, improve the critical illness insurance and medical aid schemes, further reform the models of health insurance payment and promote the development of commercial health insurance.■

The State Council planned to accelerate the development of education in central and western regions

On April 27, Premier Li Keqiang chaired an executive meeting of the State Council which decided on the following measures for accelerating the development of education in central and western regions. (1) Ensure reasonable distribution of teaching centers and standard-based assignment of facilities and teachers. (2) Improve the standard of per-student funding and gradually waiver the tuition and miscellaneous fees for secondary vocational school students. (3) Build and renovate a batch of high schools, improve the schooling conditions in rural high schools, and waiver the tuition and miscellaneous fees for poor high school students. (4) Support the establishment of a batch of high-standard universities and disciplines and give the students in central and western regions more opportunities to access high-quality education. (5) Enhance pre-school education in rural areas and support the development of nurseries and kindergartens, particularly the private ones. (6) Tilt more policy support to ethnic minority areas and strengthen the "bilingual education" to promote the capacity of students in those areas.■

MOF issued a circular on further clarification of full roll-out of VAT pilot reform in the financial sector

On April 29, MOF issued a circular on further clarification of full roll-out of VAT pilot reform in the financial sector. (1) Interest income of financial institutions from pledged repo of financial products or holding policy financial bonds is recorded as interest income from transactions with other financial institutions. (2) In the *Interim Policy Provisions*, the return-of-premium (ROP) life insurance over one-year maturity eligible to VAT exemption includes other types of annuity insurance, which refer to annuities other than pension insurance. (3) Service revenues of rural credit cooperatives and rural banks from at and below county-level outlets may apply the simplified tax bracket of 3% of VAT. (4) For county-level bank branches covered in rural financial reform pilot program in the provinces, autonomous regions, municipalities with independent planning status and Xinjiang Production and Construction Corps, their interest income from loan extensions to farmers, rural enterprises and rural organizations may opt for simplified tax bracket of 3% of VAT.■

The State Council issued the *Transitional Adjustment of Tax Sharing between Central and Local Governments after Full Roll-out of VAT Pilot Reform*

On April 29, the State Council issued the *Transitional Adjustment of Tax Sharing between Central and Local Governments after Full Roll-out of VAT Pilot* Reform. (1) The baseline for tax rebates from the central government and revenues submitted by local governments should be determined based on the 2014 revenue. (2) VAT revenues from all sectors should be shared by the central government and local governments. (3) The central government is entitled to 50% of VAT revenue. (4) The local government is entitled to 50% of VAT revenue from the locality. (5) Additional revenue shared by the central government after full roll-out of VAT pilot reform is to be transferred

POLICY UPDATE

to local governments through tax rebates, so as to ensure stabilized financial resources of the local governments. (6) Increased revenue received by the central government is to be disbursed to local governments through equalized transfer payment, with priorities given to middle and western regions.■

MOF issued a circular on further clarification of tax deduction policies relating to labor dispatch service and toll roads after full roll-out of VAT pilot reform

On April 30, MOF issued a circular on further clarification of tax deduction policies relating to labor dispatch service and toll roads after full roll-out of VAT pilot reform. (1) On labor dispatch service. When the service is provided by the general taxpayer, the sales value is recorded at full service costs and fees, and the VAT is calculated with general taxation formula, or the taxpayer may opt for deducted tax. When the service is provided by the taxpayer with small business size, the sales value is recorded at full service costs and fees, and the VAT is levied at simplified tax bracket of 3%, or the taxpayer may opt for deducted tax. (2) On tax levy and deduction on toll roads. From May 1 to July 31, 2016, tolls paid by the general taxpayer for roads, bridges or toll gates may be recorded at invoice value for deductibles in input tax. For tolls collected by the general taxpayer on first- or second-grade highways, bridges or tolled gates before the launching of VAT pilot, the taxpayer may opt for simplified tax bracket of 5% of VAT.■

MOF issued a circular on the application for the 2016 cultural development special fund

On May 3, MOF issued a circular on the application for the 2016 cultural development special fund. (1) Applicant fund for the special fund should meet the following requirements: the fund is established in China in accordance with relevant laws and regulations, structured as partnership firm or corporation, categorized as cultural investment fund and investing in cultural sectors or relevant fields. The fund should have sound mechanisms in terms of operation, decision-making and risk control. (2) Provincial cultural investment groups applying for the fund should meet the following requirements: the group should have been established for over 2 years, with total assets above 10 billion RMB, net assets over 5 billion RMB and assets-liability ratio under 70%, as of end 2015. The group should have proper license for cultural assets financing business. The group and organizing parties should provide matching funds for the fiscal fund at no less than 3: 1 ratio.■

The State Council decided on the plans to promote deeper integration of manufacturing and the Internet to speed up the upgrading of Chinese manufacturing

On May 4, Premier Li Keqiang chaired an executive meeting of the State Council and made instruction on promoting deeper integration of manufacturing and the Internet to accelerate the upgrading of Chinese manufacturing. (1) Support manufacturers to build Internet-based innovation platforms and encourage local authorities to build showcase innovative zones. (2) Foster tailored and service-oriented manufacturing models, and carry out pilot programs of smart manufacturing solutions. (3) Promote interconnection between small and medium manufacturers and the Internet, so as to strengthen integration among manufacturing, marketing and logistics. (4) Expand market access for new products and new business models, provide greater support in terms of taxation, finance and land use, encourage telecommunications companies to further speed up broadband access and reduce service fees for innovative incubations, and support financial institutions to use innovative platforms to provide "one-stop" systematic financial services. ∎

MOF issued a circular on VAT refund policy for goods and services purchased in China by foreign embassies (consulates) or their staff

On May 6, MOF issued a circular on VAT refund policy for goods and services purchased in China by foreign embassies (consulates) or their staff. (1) Goods and services purchased in China by foreign embassies (consulates) or their staff are eligible to VAT refund. (2) The "goods and services" refer to consumer office stationary and services with VAT and purchased for self-use. (3) Each receipt for purchased goods or services should exceed 800 RMB and 300 RMB, respectively, for VAT refund application. The refundable value should not exceed 120,000 RMB per person annually. (4) The value of refundable VAT is recorded as the face value of the VAT receipt. When the value of refundable VAT is not specified in the receipt, the tax is recorded as exclusive of sale tax and VAT tax. ∎

MOF published a circular on the relevant issues concerning the preferential corporate income tax policy for software and integrated circuit firms

On May 9, MOF published a circular on the relevant issues concerning the preferential corporate income tax policy for software and integrated circuit firms. (1) When making their annual tax calculation and payment, the software and integrated circuit firms that enjoy preferential tax policies shall file records along with required documents to tax authorities. (2) The regular period for tax reduction and exemption shall start from the profit-making year of the software and integrated circuit firms. (3) The software items 38, 41, 42, 43 and 46 in the *Catalogue of the Items Eligible for Preferential Corporate Income Tax Treatment that are Subject to Record-filing Administration (Version 2015)* attached to the *Announcement No. 76 (2015)* of the SAT as well as the preferential corporate income tax policy for integrated circuit firm are no longer administered as the "items entitled to regular period of tax reduction and exemption that are subject to record-filing administration". ∎

POLICY UPDATE

MOF published a circular on issues concerning corporate income tax policy over equity donation for public welfare purposes

On May 10, MOF published a circular on issues concerning corporate income tax policy over equity donation for public welfare purposes. (1) The equity donation made by an enterprise to a public-welfare social organization shall be regarded as equity transfer in accordance with the provisions, and the income from equity transfer shall be determined at the historical cost of the equity donated by the enterprise upon acquisition thereof. (2) After an enterprise donates equities, the amount of such donation shall be determined based on the historical cost of the equities, and shall be deducted before income tax in accordance with relevant provisions of the law on enterprise income tax. Upon receipt of the above equity donation, the public welfare social organization shall issue an invoice for such donation according to the historical cost of the equity provided by the enterprise. ∎

MOF published the *Interim Measures for the Pilot Reform of Water Resource Tax*

On May 10, MOF published the *Interim Measures for the Pilot Reform of Water Resource Tax*. (1) Water resource tax is levied on surface water and ground water. (2) Separate tax standards are determined for surface water and ground water. (3) Minimum tax standard is set for the taking and use of water for purposes other than hydropower generation and tubular-type coal-fired power generation, with an average of no less than 0.4 RMB/cubic meter levied on surface water and no less than 1.5 RMB/cubic meter levied on ground water. (4) Higher tax standard is set for the taking and use of ground water. (5) Higher tax standard is set for the taking and use of water by special industries. (6) Higher tax standard is set for the taking and use of water that exceeds the planned amount or prescribed limit. (7) Lower tax standard is set for the taking and use of water for agricultural production that exceeds the prescribed limit and for the centralized drinking water project that supplies domestic water for rural residents. (8) Lower tax standard is set for the taking and use of water recycled and reclaimed by enterprises from mine drainage and waste water of ground source heat pump. (9) Water resource tax is exempted for the taking and use of water for agricultural production within the prescribed limit and the taking and use of unconventional water resources such as recycled or reclaimed water from sewage treatment. ∎

MOF published a circular on comprehensively advancing the resource tax reform

On May 10, MOF published a circular on comprehensively advancing the resource tax reform. (1) Carry out the pilot reform of water resource tax and gradually expand the collection of resource tax to other natural resources. (2) Levy ad-valorem tax on 21 types of resources listed in the *Table of Resource Tax Items and Tax Rates* as well as other unspecified metallic ores. (3) In the meantime of levying resource tax on the ad-valorem basis, the mineral resource compensation rate of all types of resources will be cut to zero, the collection of price adjustment charges will be suspended and all sorts of local charges and fees on mineral resources that contravene relevant regulations will be abolished. (4) Within the prescribed tax rate range, the provincial government may propose specific applicable tax rate for the approval of MOF and State Administration of Taxation (SAT). (5) Resource tax rate is cut by 50% for the qualified mineral resources that are extracted by using the cut and fill method; and is cut by 30% for the qualified mineral resources extracted from the mines in the exhaustion stage. (6) All the mineral resource tax income derived from this round of reform will go to local governments, while the water resource tax income is still shared by 1:9 between the central and local governments, as is the case with the distribution of the income from the water resource fee.■

The State Council made plans on the upgrading of consumer product industries

On May 11, Premier Li Keqiang chaired an executive meeting of the State Council, which made plans on the upgrading of consumer product industries. The meeting called on greater efforts to: (1) improve market access, scrap unnecessary approval requirements and unreasonable charges, support enterprises to invest more in making creative design and enhancing technological content and products performance, and promote the innovation and effective supply of mass consumer goods. (2) Encourage enterprises to be quality-centered and integrity-focused, and promote the manufacturing of quality and sophisticated products to win more market shares. (3) Foster a fair and competitive business environment and align domestic consumer goods to international standards. (4) Strengthen regulation, roll out the regulatory approach of "randomly selecting inspection targets, randomly dispatching law enforcement officials, and disclosing investigation results", and create schemes of blacklisting firms and imposing punitive sanctions on them.■

The State Council issued guidance on improving compensation mechanisms for ecological protection

On May 16, the State Council issued guidance on improving compensation mechanisms for ecological protection. (1) Raise financing through various channels to increase the compensation for ecological protection. Raise the balancing transfer payment coefficient to gradually increase transfer payments to key ecological functional areas. (2) Further roll out piloting showcase programs of compensation for ecological protection, co-ordinate various compensation funds, and explore comprehensive remedies. (3) Let local governments play the major role in compensation mechanism with the central government providing fiscal support. (4) Accelerate the establishment of compensation standards based on local conditions, ecological output capacities and improved measurement. (5) Study a new mechanism featuring coordinated ecological remedies, ecological trading market and compensation for protection. (6) Take account of both environmental protection and recovery, and explore new solutions to poverty reduction through ecological development.■

MOF issued a circular on tax policy for imported seeds or seedlings during the 13th Five-Year Plan period

On May 17, MOF issued a circular on tax policy for imported seed or seedlings during the 13th

POLICY UPDATE

Five-Year Plan period. (1) Imported seeds or seedlings that are duty-free include seeds (seedlings), breeding stock (poultry) and fish (seedlings) closely related to or directly used for agriculture and forestry production, or plant and wildlife used for research, seeding or breeding. (2) Importers of seed or seedlings should put forward plans to relevant authorities, and MOF is to work jointly with SAT and the GAC to determine the variety and quantity of the annual duty-free imports. (3) Imported seeds or seedlings that are not verified or included in the duty-free annual list are subject to import VAT. (4) The duty-free seeds or seedlings are subject to domestic tax provisions after entering the domestic market. ∎

MOF issued a circular on the use of management system on national bookkeeping agencies

On May 18, MOF issued a circular on the use of management system on national bookkeeping agencies. (1) Provincial finance authorities should enhance leadership, supporting staff and hardware maintenance, strengthen policy awareness and personnel training, so that supervision authorities for qualified bookkeeping agencies may understand and command the functions of the management system as soon as possible, and bookkeeping agencies may get hold of new policy requirements and working procedures as soon as possible. (2) The supervision authorities should follow the requirements of management system and regulate through the management system. (3) The supervision authorities should take stock of the lessons and experience learned, provide suggestions to improve and upgrade management system, and make timely feedback to MOF. ∎

MOF initiated special inspection over earmarked funds for pollution control and biomass power generation projects

On May 18, MOF announced that special inspection over earmarked funds for pollution control and biomass power generation projects is to be carried out by local Inspector's Office of MOF. The inspection covers Beijing, Tianjin, Hebei and others, all together 11 provinces (autonomous regions and municipalities), and is focused on whether the fund is properly allocated or disbursed in time; whether the fund is effectively used to tackle outstanding problems of air pollution or used for biomass power generation projects with additional power tariff subsidies during 2014-2015; and whether the fund is misused or misappropriated. ∎

The State Council decided to promote down-sizing and higher efficiency of the central enterprises, and enhance competitiveness through reform and restructuring

On May 18, Premier Li Keqiang chaired an executive meeting of the State Council, which decided to promote down-sizing and higher efficiency of the central enterprises, and enhance competitiveness through reform and restructuring. (1) Take targeted measures to address difficulties faced by struggling and loss-making enterprises, phase out outdated production capacity of central enterprises in steel and coal industries, and accelerate the restructuring and market clearing. (2) Combine Internet+ initiative and big data development strategy, so as to constantly promote the industrial advancement and competitiveness of their products. (3) Flatten management hierarchy, and strive to reduce management layers in major central enterprises from the current 5-9 to 3-4 layers in 3 years, and cut corporate units by about 20%. Improve supervision and administration over state-owned assets, take innovative supervision approaches, and prevent the impairment of state assets. (4) Strengthen cost control, reduce accounts receivables, inventory stocks and losses, lower debt levels, in an effort to cut costs and increase profits by 100 billion RMB in the next two years. ■

MOF initiated a special inspection on the special central fiscal fund for the improvement of basic schooling conditions for vocational schools

On May 19, MOF announced that a special inspection on the special central fiscal fund for the improvement of basic schooling conditions for vocational schools is to be carried out by local Inspector's Office of MOF. The inspection covers provincial and lower levels of finance and educational authorities and other fund-using institutions in Liaoning, Jilin, Fujian and others, all together nine provinces. The inspection is focused on whether the fund is applied for and allocated properly, whether the budgeting and fund allocation are in time, the capital construction is compliant with due process, the expenditure is within limits, and whether the fund is used for repaying debt or interest, or for investment, or making up the funding gap for other projects. ■

MOF published a circular on the application for insurance premium subsidies of the first set of major technological equipment

On May 23, MOF published a circular on the application for insurance premium subsidies of the first set of major technological equipment. (1) The time of application. To claim the subsidies, the application documents shall be submitted as required before May 25, 2016, and be sent to the Ministry of Industry and Information Technology (MIT) by May 30, 2016 after the verification by the provincial industry and information technology authorities and the central enterprise group. The manufacturing enterprises that purchase insurance in the subsequent years shall submit their application documents before March 15 and send them to MIT by March 30 after the verification by the provincial industry and information technology authorities and the central enterprise group. (2) The major technological equipment that apply to be included in the *Guiding Catalogue for the Promotion and Use of the First Set of Major Technological Equipment* shall meet the requirements of industrial transformation and upgrading, demonstrate visible energy-saving, material-saving and environmentally friendly effects, possess significant economic and social benefits, and are in the phase of market promotion for the first time. ■

POLICY UPDATE

PPP Center of MOF published the project proposal for the Global Infrastructure Facility (GIF)

On May 23, the Public-Private Partnership (PPP) Center of MOF published the project proposal for the Global Infrastructure Facility (GIF). (1) The proposed project shall be climate-friendly and pro-trade infrastructure projects that adopt the PPP model in the GIF priority areas of energy, water and environmental protection, transport, and telecommunication.(2) The proposed projects shall be major and new infrastructure projects that are aligned to the local development strategy and with a schedule that matches the GIF procedures. (3) The project implementing agency can apply for GIF grants for project identification, with the average grant per project amounting to 250,000 USD. (4) The project implementing agency can apply for GIF loans and develop projects with the assistance from GIF technical partners. (5) After the successful project development, the financing support from GIF partners and international institutional investors is also available.∎

MOF published a circular on taking effective measures to further strengthen the management of local treasury cash

On May 23, MOF published a circular on taking effective measures to further strengthen the management of local treasury cash. (1) Performance evaluation of the local treasury cash management will be conducted on a monthly basis. (2) Ad hoc talks will be made with the finance authorities of the bottom six underperforming localities. (3) The mechanism of linking transfer payment with the size of local treasury cash will be strengthened. (4) All levels of finance authorities shall further enhance the management of transfer payment, and work with other parties to promote the implementation of major pro-growth policy projects by accelerating expenditure on those areas. (5) All levels of finance authorities shall improve the accountability of treasury cash management by clearly defining the work assignment and responsibility.∎

The State Council published guiding opinions on deepening the integration of manufacturing and internet

On May 23, the State Council published guiding opinions on deepening the integration of manufacturing and internet. (1) Deepen the reform of streamlining administration, delegating power, improving regulation and enhancing service delivery, ease the market entry for new products and business models, and foster an enabling environment for the integration of manufacturing and internet. (2) Encourage central enterprises to set up the pro-innovation investment fund and direct local industrial investment fund and private capital to support the development of a platform that facilitates the integration of major companies and internet. (3) Leverage central fiscal funds to encourage local governments to create dedicated funds for the integration, and scale up inputs into the key links and areas of the integration. (4) Further expand the scope of corporate VAT deduction and implement the preferential VAT policies in the process of rolling out the pilot VAT reform.∎

The State Council published the *Priorities for the Reform of Streamlining Administration, Delegating Power, Improving Regulation and Enhancing Service Delivery in 2016*

On May 25, the State Council published the *Priorities for the Reform of Streamlining Administration, Delegating Power, Improving Regulation and Enhancing Service Delivery in 2016*. (1) Continue to intensify the delegation of power, and wherever possible, delegate power to lower level governments or abolish the power to give the market and private sector a greater say. (2) Further increase the autonomy of enterprises and revise the government-authorized investment item catalogue. (3) Further cut a batch of vocational qualification licensing and accreditation to reduce 70% of vocational qualifications previously set up by the State Council. (4) Further ease market entry, cut the business registration pre-approvals by one-third in this year to eliminate 90% of pre-approvals and abolish over 50 post-approvals. (5) Strictly enforce all the existing policies that clean up fees and charges, forestall any new charges or charges in disguised forms, and regulate all sorts of accreditation, evaluation, inspection, testing and other intermediary services. (6) Expand the autonomy of universities and research institutes. (7) Further promote the disclosure of government affairs and make sure the government information is open, transparent and available to the people. ■

MOF issued a circular on further improving PPP-related work

On May 30, MOF issued a circular on further improving PPP-related work. (1) Further strengthen public efforts to guide positive public awareness of PPP, which may contribute to sustainable and sound development of PPP. (2) Enhance inter-agency coordination to form policy synergy, which helps to ensure smooth implementation of PPP projects. (3) Strengthen feasibility study of the projects based on thorough research and sound decision-making, so as to ensure reasonable and effective provision of public service and goods. (4) Establish a dynamic and adjustable mechanism of the return on investment according to changes in conditions, environmental and other factors, so as to ensure a fair return to the government. (5) Enhance interaction between the central and local governments, and improve financing environment for PPP project to reduce their financing costs. (6) Put PPP-related laws, administrative regulations, industry standards, technical specifications and other product or service specifications under effective supervision. (7) Ensure timely publication of information to serve investment demands, promote market information symmetry, so as to ensure full and fair competition. ■

MOF issued a supplementary circular on VAT pilot related culture development fees and collections

On May 31, MOF issued a supplementary circular on VAT pilot related culture development fees and collections. (1) Entertainment providers (including entities and individuals) in China are subject to the levy of culture development fees in accordance with relevant rules. (2) The fees should be levied at 3% of the billed sales income from entertainment services. (3) Tax-payers below the VAT threshold are exempted from the culture development fees. ■

POLICY UPDATE

The State Council decided to improve the management measures for central government scientific research funds

On June 1, Premier Li Keqiang chaired an executive meeting of the State Council, which decided the following. (1) The budget allocation power of most projects with direct funds is delegated to project organizers. Project budget surplus at year-end may be carried forward into the following year. The final balance of the funds can be retained by the project organizer based on relevant regulations. (2) The ceiling proportion of performance incentive expenditure to direct cost minus equipment purchase is increased from 5% to 20%. (3) Universities and research institutes supported by central finance may, based on actual working conditions, design the travel expenditure management methods and specify the size and standards for business meetings. (4) Simplify procurement management for research equipment. Universities and research institutes may use their own discretion in making procurement decisions and selecting evaluation experts for the centralized procurement catalog items. (5) Strengthen the decision-making authority of universities and research institutes in infrastructure projects, and simplify land, environmental assessment and other procedures. The projects supported by proprietary funds rather than government investment are regulated by record-filing instead of approval. ∎

MOF issued the *Management Measures of the Central Special Funds for Guiding Local Science and Technology Development*

On June 3, MOF issued the *Management Measures of the Central Special Funds for Guiding Local Science and Technology Development*. (1) The funds will support the infrastructure, capacity building, innovation platform, service providers and demonstration projects for the local science and technology development. (2) The funds that support science and technology infrastructure usually take the form of direct subsidies. (3) Public institutions are not allowed to use the funds to pay for all sorts of fines, donations, sponsorship, investment, debt service or other expenditures prescribed by the state. (4) Provincial finance authorities and science and technology authorities, in line with their mandate, will conduct supervision and inspection on the performance of project implementation. (5) MOF and the Ministry of Science and Technology (MOST), when appropriate, will conduct supervision and inspection on the management and use of the funds. ∎

MOF published a circular on improving the pilot program of providing social services for agricultural production in 2016

On June 3, MOF published a circular on improving the pilot program of providing social services for agricultural production in 2016. (1) Specifying the ways of providing support. The pilot area will adopt government procurement of social services, or alternatively, the government will support the purchase of social services by agricultural producers. The funds arranged by each province for the pilot program shall maintain a certain degree of continuity and concentration, and the funds for each pilot county shall, in principle, be no less than 10 million RMB. (2) Optimizing the supporting mechanisms. The relationship between government and market shall be properly handled. Government shall refrain from intervention in areas where market mechanism can effectively play its role, and fiscal resources shall be mainly used in the key and vulnerable areas where market mechanism can hardly play its role, so as to achieve the policy objectives of delivering social services throughout the agricultural production process and making comprehensive use of livestock manure and waste.■

MOF published a circular on improving the pilot program of adjusting agricultural structure in 2016

On June 3, MOF published a circular on improving the pilot program of adjusting agricultural structure in 2016. (1) The central finance authority will earmark funds to support the adjustment of the agricultural structure. Under the "food crop to feed crop" conversion program, the government support will mainly target the major herbivore livestock farms with large-scale silage storage capacity. Under the "rice to soybean" conversion program, the subsidy standard shall be linked to the break-even point of different crops and be adjusted in a dynamic way. (2) Each province (autonomous region) shall determine the content of its pilot program for agricultural structure adjustment based on local circumstances, and select the pilot counties in a science-based way. (3) Guided by the local agricultural development plan, all levels of agricultural authorities shall, in line with the requirements of agricultural structure adjustment, develop specific technical plans by areas and by crops. (4) Provincial agriculture and finance authorities shall accelerate the establishment of performance evaluation mechanism for pilot counties, enhance the efficiency of fund use, and strengthen the supervision of funds.■

MOF published a circular on improving the implementation of modern agricultural production and development in 2016

On June 3, MOF published a circular on improving the implementation of modern agricultural production and development in 2016. (1) Each province may take into account such factors as local market price of semen or breeding stock when adjusting the subsidy standard, and may disburse subsidies by breeds on the basis of the local supply of fertile female livestock. The carryover funds from 2015 shall be used as soon as possible. (2) The standardized renovation and extension of major farms of livestock, poultry and aquatic products shall be advanced to further improve production conditions, enhance quality and safety control, strengthen the prevention and treatment of non-point source pollution, and promote ecologically-friendly farming methods. (3) A modern industrial system featuring the integration of agriculture, secondary industry and tertiary industry needs to be built to further enhance the quality and efficiency of agriculture, raise farmers' income, create rural jobs and promote rural prosperity and stability.■

MOF published the *Interim Measures for the Collection, Use and Administration of Adjustment Fees on the Gains from the Appreciation of Rural Collective Construction Land*

On June 6, MOF published the *Interim Measures for the Collection, Use and Administration of Adjustment Fees on the Gains from the Appreciation of Rural Collective Construction Land*. (1) The

POLICY UPDATE

adjustment fees are collected by the finance authorities along with the land resource authorities in the pilot counties. (2) The adjustment fees are levied at 20%-50% of the gains from the appreciation of the rural collective construction land that are sold or reassigned. (3) The transaction price of the rural collective construction land that are sold or used for equity financing is marked as market income; and the rent of the land that are leased out is marked as the market income. (4) The specific items and standards of land acquisition costs and land development expenses will be determined by the government of pilot counties based on local circumstances. (5) The pilot counties shall develop a benchmark price system for rural collective land that is unified with the system for the urban state-owned land. (6) All the adjustment fees shall be turned over to the county treasury and be placed under general public budget management. When the pilot program is in implementation, provinces and cities shall not share the adjustment fee incomes. (7) The adjustment fees are incorporated into the general public budget management of the local government, and their use is arranged by the finance authorities of the pilot counties. (8) The expenses arising from the collection of the adjustment fees are covered by the local fiscal budget of the pilot areas.■

MOF issued a circular on initiating the screening process for the third batch of PPP demonstration projects application

On June 12, MOF issued a circular on initiating the screening process for the third batch of PPP demonstration projects application. (1) The applicants should be public service projects suitable for PPP model, and the term of cooperation should be no less than 10 years in principle. (2) Local finance authorities and industrial regulators are to carry out initial screening for local applicant projects and report the results to provincial finance authorities. The qualifiers are to be filed on the national PPP information platform and reported to MOF in writing, and the relevant ministries should be notified as well. (3) To make prompt and professional assessment of the applicant projects, experts will be invited to carry out collective and closed-door evaluation online through the national PPP information platform. (4) The experts are to be recommended by various ministries or be randomly selected from the PPP expert pool. (5) Applicant projects from each province or municipality should be no more than 50 in principle.■

MOF published a circular on strengthening the management of special funds for structural adjustment of industrial enterprises

On June 14, MOF published a circular on strengthening the management of special funds for structural adjustment of industrial enterprises. (1) Each region and locality must strictly follow the provisions of the *Management Rules for the Special Funds for Structural Adjustment of Industrial Enterprises* in managing and using the funds. (2) Local governments are to develop detailed management rules for the earmarked funds, which is to cover the application, allocation, use and evaluation of the funds. (3) The earmarked funds should not be withheld or misappropriated for other purposes, nor should any administrative fees or cost be levied on the funds, nor should local governments use the funds to supplement fiscal resources. (4) Local governments should make rational and proper allocation of the earmarked funds, and publish the allocation information on the local government website. (5) Archive of the whole process of fund disbursement. (6) Provincial governments should shoulder the overall responsibility for the use and management of the funds. Efforts should be taken to improve risk prevention and control, and to identify and resolve potential risks promptly. Local authorities should strengthen supervision and inspection to plug loopholes and prevent fraud.■

The State Council issued guidance on accelerating the development of education in the midwestern region

On June 15, the State Council issued guidance on accelerating the development of education in the midwestern region. (1) Establish a dynamic and adjustable mechanism for compulsory schools, which aims at optimizing the layout of schools, and narrowing the gap between urban and rural areas and among various schools. (2) Encourage social participation in the development of vocational education to improve schooling conditions. (3) Coordinate the development of high schools and vocational schools, optimize the layout of schools, and constantly improve the universal coverage of high school education. (4) Improve overall planning, provide differentiated guidance and adopt management reform, so as to accelerate administrative decentralization, promote reasonable positioning of midwest colleges and universities, and to enhance the capacity of the schools. (5) Promote the development of rural preschool education system through building nurseries and kindergartens, and gradually increase the enrollment rate in rural areas. (6) Adopt special measures to support education for ethnic minorities and ethnic areas. (7) Expand special education resources to enable more people with disabilities to receive education. Improve professional attractiveness for special education teachers to promote inclusive education.■

The State Council decided to invalidate a number of policy documents which are inconsistent with existing laws and regulations

On June 15, Premier Li Keqiang chaired an executive meeting of the State Council, which decided the following: based on earlier efforts of invalidating 489 State Council documents, additional 506 State Council documents were invalidated after rigorous examination. The invalidated documents include: (1) those which are inconsistent with existing laws and regulations, or have no legal basis; (2) those which are not suited to the economic development or have seriously hindered the production and management activities of businesses; (3) those whose jurisdiction has been canceled or decentralized, or imposed repetitive or inconsistent requirement on a certain matter.■

MOF published the *Procurement Standards of Office Equipments and Furniture for Central Administrative Institutions*

On June 20, MOF published the *Procurement Standards of Office Equipments and Furniture for Central Administrative Institutions*. (1) The central administrative institutions shall follow the requirements of the *Government Procurement Law of the People's Republic of China*, procure safe,

POLICY UPDATE

durable, compatible, energy-efficient and easy-to-maintain equipment, and shall not procure high-end equipment. (2) The Standards will be adjusted when appropriate according to the changes of social and economic development and market prices. (3) The central administrative institutions shall arrange the procurement of their office equipment and furniture within the quantity limits of the Standards. (4) The procurement standards of office equipment and furniture for diplomatic missions are governed separately by other documents. (5) The Standards goes into effect on July 1, 2016.■

MOF published a circular on soliciting public comments on the *Interim Measures for the Administration of Occupational Annuities*

On June 21, MOF published a circular on soliciting public comments on the *Interim Measures for the Administration of Occupational Annuities*. (1) The occupational annuities are managed in the way of centralized and entrusted investment and operation. (2) The agents of occupational annuity schemes, in the name of trustors, will enter into trusteeship management contract with trustees, and trustees will then enter into entrusted management contract with custodians and investment managers. (3) Central and provincial governments will establish committees to select and change occupational annuity management agencies through tendering. (4) For the same occupational annuity scheme, the trustee and custodian, as well as the custodian and the investment manager shall not be the same institution. (5) The property of occupational annuities is independent from the inherent property or other property managed by other organizations. (6) The property of occupational annuities does not fall under the category of liquidation property. (7) The debt claims of the property of occupational annuities shall not be offset against the liabilities of the inherent property of other organizations. (8) The human resource and social security authorities as well as the finance authorities shall supervise the management of the occupational annuities.■

MOF published a circular on further clarifying the VAT policies related to reinsurance, real estate lease and non-degree education

On June 21, MOF published a circular on further clarifying the VAT policies related to reinsurance, real estate lease and non-degree education. (1) The reinsurance services that are provided by domestic insurers for foreign insurers and that are completely consumed abroad shall be exempted from VAT. (2) The reinsurance services provided by the taxpayers are subject to the same VAT policies as those governing the original insurance services. (3) The general taxpayers among the property developers, when renting out old property projects developed on their own, can choose to use the simplified tax calculation method and calculate the payable tax amount at 5% tax rate. (4) The general taxpayers that provide non-degree educational services can choose to use the simplified tax calculation method and calculate the payable tax amount at 3% tax rate. (5) The security guard services provided by taxpayers are regulated by the same policies as those applied to the labor dispatch services. (6) The membership fees collected by parties, CPC youth leagues, trade unions and intergovernmental organizations are exempted from VAT as they are non-for-profit activities.■

MOF published a circular on the pilot program of innovative models for high-standard farmland development for the purpose of comprehensive agricultural development

On June 22, MOF published a circular on the pilot program of innovative models for high-standard farmland development for the purpose of comprehensive agricultural development. (1) The pilot program shall meet the requirement of "integrated development of the whole-industry-chain", and, under the condition of transforming the operational approach, shall focus on farmland infrastructure development while concurrently promoting the supporting industries. (2) The fiscal funds for a single pilot program, in principle, shall be capped at 30 million RMB, and over 60% of them shall be used for high-standard farmland infrastructure development. (3) The pilot provinces shall put the pilot program high on their agenda and strengthen the organization of the program. (4) The program shall be broken down to every specific task to ensure the program is well implemented and proceeds in an orderly way. (5) The pilot provinces shall closely watch and follow the program implementation, take stock of experiences and lessons, and report to the National Office for Comprehensive Agricultural Development. (6) Performance evaluation shall be enhanced and positive incentives be strengthened.■

MOF published a circular on disbursing the 2016 fiscal subsidies for comprehensive agricultural development

On June 23, MOF published a circular on disbursing the 2016 fiscal subsidies for comprehensive agricultural development. (1) Provinces (districts and cities), after receiving the fiscal subsides from the central government, shall disburse, within 30 days, the funds to the relevant government agencies at their level and to finance authorities above the county level, and make available the required local fiscal funds. (2) The finance authorities of provinces (districts and cities) shall work with the competent authorities that oversee the projects to design, review and report the project performance targets, and guide and urge the relevant government agencies at the lower level to manage and use the funds, implement performance targets, and conduct performance management in strict accordance with rules.■

MOF published a circular on invalidating several policy documents relating to vocational qualification examination fees

On June 27, MOF published a circular on invalidating several policy documents relating to vocational qualification examination fees. (1) Invalidating 40 policy documents, including the *Circular by NDRC and MOF on Teaching Qualification Examination Fees and Related Issues* and other documents. (2) Invalidating the provisions relating to vocational qualification examinations fees in the *Circular by NDRC and MOF on Reducing Certain Administrative Fees*. (3) When local examination authorities collect charges on exam-takers, the fees should be strictly verified by the provincial pricing authority and finance authority in accordance with relevant rules and exam costs. (4) Local pricing authorities should work together with relevant agencies to clean up vocational exam fees based on this circular, and promptly abolish regional policy documents inconsistent with national provisions.■

POLICY UPDATE

MOF published a circular on pilot program of integration of financial expenditure for agriculture to support the development of poor counties

On June 29, MOF published a circular on pilot program of integration of financial expenditure for agriculture to support the development of poor counties. (1) Agricultural development agencies at all levels should tap their own advantages and resources to overcome difficulties and foster innovation-driven growth, and actively support the pilot program in poverty-stricken counties. (2) Implement the decision by the State Council and MOF to pool funds for pilot programs in poverty-stricken counties, enhance support and allocate a specific proportion for poor villages. (3) Actively guide poverty-stricken counties to develop plans for the pilot program to provide timely technical support for industrial development and establish a sound management system. (4) Take initiative to strengthen cooperation with the poverty alleviation and development leading group and relevant departments, establish smooth communication and coordination mechanisms, and work together to jointly promote the pilot program in poverty-stricken counties.∎

MOF issued the *Measures on the Administration of Subsidies and Funds for Supporting and Safeguarding Agricultural Development*

On June 29, MOF issued the *Measures on the Administration of Subsidies and Funds for Supporting and Safeguarding Agricultural Development*. (1) Subsidies and funds for supporting and safeguarding agricultural development are earmarked funds from the central fiscal budget. The funds and subsidies are used for preserving the fertility of cultivated land and the appropriate size of grain production, as well as for other national policy objectives. (2) The funds and subsidies are allocated by MOF in conjunction with MOA. (3) The funds used for preserving the fertility of cultivated land are to be granted to agricultural farmers with contractual right of the land. (4) The funds and subsidies are green-oriented. (5) Provincial authorities are to design the subsidizing standards, requirements and approaches of using the funds based on local conditions, so as to ensure policy consistency and stability. (6) The funds and subsides are to be disbursed in accordance with relevant provisions of the centralized treasury payment system. When the funds are subject to government procurement management, relevant government procurement laws and regulations should be followed.∎

The State Council made plans to promote the revitalization and development of revolutionary base areas in Sichuan and Shaanxi Province

On June 30, Premier Li Keqiang chaired an executive meeting of the State Council, which made plans to promote the revitalization and development of revolutionary base areas in Sichuan and Shaanxi, and support their efforts in building a moderately well-off society. The meeting decided the following. (1) Enhance indigenous growth engines of the revolutionary base areas through deeper reform, wider opening-up, and closer regional cooperation. (2) Accelerate the construction of a number of key water conservancy projects, strengthen the electricity, gas and other energy security, and improve the transport network and other infrastructure. (3) Actively develop agro-forestry, new materials, high-end equipment manufacturing, trade and logistics, tourism and other industries, and upgrade traditional industries such as textile and clothing. (4) Step up poverty alleviation efforts by increasing compensation for relocation and micro-loans, and explore ways to support capital income. Operating assets from fiscal input are to be converted into shares and allocated to poor households. (5) Eastern provinces and economically advanced cities and counties of provinces should help revolutionary base areas, so as to promote the new urbanization and coordinated development between urban and rural areas. (6) Gradually increase the size of the central transfer payments, and encourage financial institutions to increase credit support. ∎

MOF published a supplementary circular on the VAT policies concerning inter-financial institution transactions

On July 1, MOF published a supplementary circular on the VAT policies concerning inter-financial institution transactions. (1) The interest income from the inter-financial transaction related to deposit, loan, payment, outright repo, financial bonds, and certificates of deposit is classified as the inter-financial institution interest income as stated in the *Regulations on the Transitional Policies Concerning the Pilot Program of Replacing Business Tax with VAT*. (2) The transactions related to the commercial banks' purchase of central bank notes, as well as currency swap and cross deposit with the central bank shall fall under the fund transfer transaction between financial institutions and PBoC as stated in the *Regulations on the Transitional Policies*. (3) The fund transfer transactions between domestic banks and their overseas headquarters and parent companies, as well as between domestic banks and their overseas branches and wholly-owned subsidiaries belong to the inter-bank branch transaction as stated in the *Regulations on the Transitional Policies*. (4) The income from the securities buying and selling done by domestic companies entrusted by RMB qualified foreign institutional investors, as well as the income gained by the PBoC-accredited foreign institutional investors from the inter-bank local currency market is recognized as the financial goods transfer income as stated in the *Regulations on the Transitional Policies*. ∎

MOF published guiding opinions on strengthening the internal control management of government procurement activities

Figure4 The process of government procurement

On July 4, MOF published guiding opinions on strengthening the internal control management of government procurement activities. (1) Define the duties to ensure earnest fulfillment of responsibilities. Centralized management will be implemented, the rights and obligations of principal and agent will be clarified, and internal supervision will be enhanced. (2) Arrange the job posts in a reasonable manner and strengthen the accountability. The job description will be better defined, incompatible duties be separated,

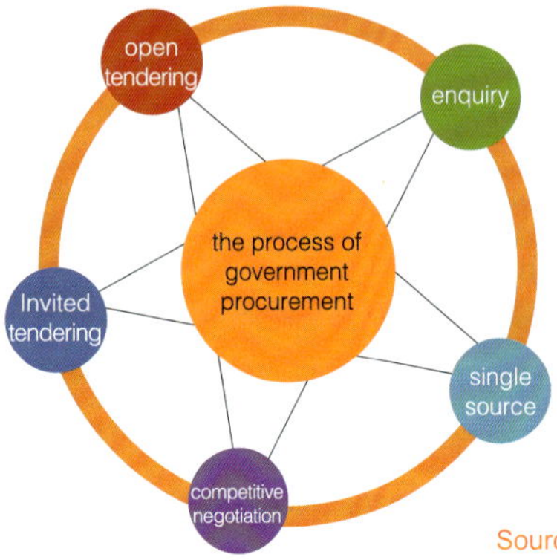

Source: Ministry of Finance of China

more people be involved in relevant operations and regular rotation of post be conducted. (3) Delegate authority by levels and promote science-based decision-making. The management of affiliated agencies will be strengthened, decision-making mechanism be improved, and internal review and approval mechanism be refined. (4) Optimize procedures and enhance the management of key links. The procurement will be better planned, the management of key links be strengthened, the time limit be specified, the conflict of interest be better managed, and the archives management be improved.■

MOF published the *Measures for the Administration of Earmarked Funds for National Key Archives*

On July 5, MOF published the *Measures for the Administration of Earmarked Funds for National Key Archives*. (1) The earmarked funds will be spent on the catalogue structure, development, and establishment of regional protection centers for national key archives. (2) The earmarked funds are allocated by using the factor method and the project method. (3) The provincial finance and archive authorities shall organize archives centers to conduct the project application in their jurisdictions in accordance with the project management requirements. (4) No budget request by localities is required for the catalogue structure development. (5) Localities are required to submit budget requests on the basis of their implementation plans and needs for the development of key thematic programs identified and organized by the state. (6) The disbursement of earmarked funds shall be governed by relevant regulations on treasury centralized payment, and where government procurement is involved, relevant laws and regulations on government procurement shall apply. (7) Where the fixed assets purchased by the earmarked funds fall under the state-owned assets, relevant regulations on state asset management shall apply to prevent the loss of state assets.■

MOF published a circular on the recommendation of funds for equity investment by the National Venture Capital Fund for Emerging Industries

On July 6, MOF published a circular on the recommendation of funds for equity investment by the National Venture Capital Fund for Emerging Industries. (1) The Fund will mainly invest in the venture capital fund for emerging industries capitalized by local governments and leading enterprises. (2) The plan on recommended funds for equity investment drawn up by local government agencies shall be submitted by the provincial (autonomous region, municipalities directly under the central government and cities with independent planning status) development and reform commission and finance department (bureau) to NDRC and MOF. (3) The total size of the recommended funds shall be no less than 200 million RMB; the fund management institutions shall complete business registration beforehand and contribute no less than 1% of the fund's capital; the shareholder structure of the funds shall be clear and exhaustive disclosure be made; the major initiators and custodian banks of the funds shall be basically determined, relevant agreements concerning the funds be signed, and the requirements on project pipeline be met.■

MOF published the *Opinions on Advancing the Reform of Health Service Prices*

On July 7, MOF published the *Opinions on Advancing the Reform of Health Service Prices*. (1) The pricing, health, social security, and finance authorities of all localities shall steadily advance the reform according to the requirements of the Opinions. (2) All localities are required to follow the principle of "cost control, structural overhaul, price adjustment and phased implementation", take into account the affordability of all parties, determine and adjust health service prices in a reasonable manner, gradually rationalize health service prices, and concurrently implement policies to improve health insurance payment and control health expenses to prevent the increase of the overall burden of expenses on people. ∎

MOF issued a circular on the application of PPP promotion projects in the field of water pollution prevention and control

On July 11, MOF issued a circular on the application of PPP promotion projects in the field of water pollution prevention and control. (1) Priority promotion projects include integrated environmental management in drinking water sources areas, and protection and monitoring system for water environment. (2) The provincial finance and environmental protection authorities are responsible for organizing the application of relevant PPP promotion projects within their own jurisdiction. The number of projects for promotion should be under 10 for each province, and the specific number of projects should be determined by the provincial authorities. The projects for promotion should be existing ones under the PPP comprehensive information management platform. (3) The provincial finance and environmental protection authorities should jointly report (formal document with seal) to MOF and Ministry of Environmental Protection (MEP). (4) MOF and MEP will jointly promote those projects. ∎

The central government increased support for occupational training for farmers by allocating 1.386 billion RMB for 2016 farmers' training funds

On July 12, MOF announced that the central government has recently allocated 1.386 billion RMB for 2016 farmers' training funds to support occupational training for farmers. (1) Focus on the needs of farmers to improve the quality of training and public awareness, and motivate farmers to participate in the training programs. (2) Identify key training groups, and establish trainees' pool to include business leaders of new agricultural business and modern farms. (3) Establish and improve the training mechanism to enhance diversity. The mechanism is to be administrated by agricultural authorities, and participated by science and technology education and training centers for farmers and other various market players. (4) Strengthen performance management. A multi-layered performance appraisal system is to be established, with the central government supervising the province; the provincial authority supervising the county; and the county authority supervising the training institutions. ∎

POLICY UPDATE

MOF issued a circular on the application of PPP promotion projects in municipal public utility area

On July 12, MOF issued a circular on the application of PPP promotion projects in municipal public utility area. (1) Priority projects include urban water supply, sewage treatment and garbage disposal. (2) The provincial finance, housing and urban construction authorities are responsible for the projects application in the province, and the number of applicant projects should be under 10. (3) The provincial finance and housing and urban construction authorities should jointly report (formal document with seal) to MOF and MOHURD. (4) Application documents should be electronically submitted to MOF and MOHURD by July 15, 2016. (5) MOF and MOHURD will jointly promote those projects.■

MOF issued the *Measures on the Administration of Conference-related Expenses by the Central Government and Ministries*

On July 13, MOF issued the *Measures on the Administration of Conference-related Expenses by the Central Government and Ministries*. (1) All agencies should strictly control the size of the meeting. (2) The format of the meeting should be improved by making full use of DVC, Internet conference and other modern means of information technology, so as to reduce meeting costs and raise efficiency. (3) When the meeting participants are mainly Beijing-based, the meeting should not be held outside Beijing. Meetings should not be held in scenic areas specified as off-limits by the CPC and the State Council. (4) The conference expenses include conference accommodation, meals, venue rental, transportation, document printing and medical fees. (5) The conference expenses should be put under comprehensive quota management, with leeway for adjustment among various subcategory expenses. (6) The expenses of the first-class conference is supported by earmarked funds from the departmental budget, while the expenses of the second, third and fourth-class fees are arranged as administrative fees of the departmental budget. (7) The expenses should be verified and reimbursed promptly after the meeting. (8) The payment and disbursement of the expenses should strictly follow the relevant provisions of the centralized treasury payment system and official business card management system, with settlement made through official bank card or bank transfers. (9) Conference organizers should provide internal public notification on or access to the name, contents, the number of participants and expenses incurred of the meeting, or disclose relevant information to the general public, as appropriate.■

MOF published the *Implementing Plan for the Development of Public Finance through the Rule of Law*

On July 18, MOF published the *Implementing Plan for the Development of Public Finance through the Rule of Law*. (1) Give full play to the role of public finance in accordance with law. The fiscal and tax reform should be comprehensively deepened, the fiscal management be constantly strengthened, the fiscal risks be effectively controlled, the fiscal resources be optimally allocated, and the provision of basic public services be further improved. (2) Improve the legal system for public finance. The quality and level of fiscal legislation should be comprehensively enhanced and a sound legal system for public finance be basically put in place to provide institutional guarantee for the promotion of fiscal and tax reform and the law-based administration. (3) Promote science-based, democratic and law-based decision making of major fiscal matters. (4) Strictly regulate the administration and law enforcement of public finance. (5) Strengthen the restraint and supervision over the exercise of finance authority. (6) Resolve social tension and disputes in accordance with law. (7) Raise the legal awareness and legal compliance of public finance officials. ■

MOF published the *Measures for the Administration of Funds Earmarked for Precautions and Emergency Response on Work Safety*

On July 19, MOF published the *Measures for the Administration of Funds Earmarked for Precautions and Emergency Response on Work Safety*. (1) The earmarked funds are tentatively designed to last for 3 years, and are subject to adjustment or cancellation based on the assessment by MOF and the State Administration of Work Safety (SAWS). (2) The earmarked funds shall only be used for the intended purpose and be specifically managed. (3) The earmarked funds shall be administered by finance authorities and work safety authorities. (4) SAWS shall determine the overall plan and objectives of the funds. (5) On the basis of the overall plan and the objectives, SAWS will make proposal on the allocation of the funds, and MOF will disburse the funds on account of the request for funds and the size of annual budget. (6) Local finance authorities, after their receipt of funds, shall determine the recipients of the funds among government agencies, public institutions and businesses. (7) The payment of the earmarked funds shall follow the rules and regulations of the fiscal treasury management. (8) The Inspector's Office of MOF shall conduct budget oversight in accordance with the requirements of MOF. ■

The State Council endorsed the national special plan for science and technology innovation in the 13th Five-Year Plan period

On July 20, Premier Li Keqiang chaired an executive meeting of the State Council which endorsed the national special plan for science and technology innovation in the 13th Five-Year Plan period. The Plan identified the following tasks: (1) strengthen the original innovation capacity, improve the basic and cutting-edge research, consolidate and optimize resource allocation, and focus on the pioneering and strategic fields. (2) Develop first-mover advantage, capitalize on the comparative advantage, and focus on the areas with national strategic significance and with potential for improving people's wellbeing. (3) Make use of the platform of mass entrepreneurship and individual innovation, strengthen the primary role of businesses in science and technology innovation, and forge an efficient and synergistic chain for innovation. (4) Accelerate the reform of science and technology system, fully incentivize the science and technology personnel, and improve the policies on the use of research funds and on the distribution of rights to research findings. ■

POLICY UPDATE

MOF published a circular on further regulating the bank confirmation request and the banker's confirmation

On July 21, MOF published a circular on further regulating the bank confirmation request and the banker's confirmation. (1) The certified public accountants shall select among the formats attached to this circular the appropriate bank confirmation request that suits their needs and shall ensure the integrity and effectiveness of the request. (2) The operational, legal and reputational risks caused by the misrepresentation of the bank confirmation request shall be effectively prevented.(3) All banks are encouraged to create a centralized mechanism for processing the confirmation requests to ensure the quality and efficiency of the confirmation. (4) Financial regulatory agencies shall strengthen regulation and hold the banks legally accountable for their acts of dishonesty in confirmation.■

MOF issued the *Administration Measures on the Management of Earmarked Funds for Basic Research at Central-level Public Research Institutes*

On July 27, MOF issued the *Administration Measures on the Management of Earmarked Funds for Basic Research at Central-level Public Research Institutes*: (1) the basic research funds should be used to support research institutes to carry out research projects that provide public services, explore scientific frontier, and with strategic view. (2) MOF is to make dynamic adjustment on the annual funding allocation for the research institutes based on their budget implementation. (3) The basic research funds should be put under unified financial management by custodian agencies, subject to independent accounting and auditing, and used for earmarked purposes. (4) The annual budget and expenditure plans for the basic research funds should be verified and approved by MOF. (5) The research institutes shall, within three months after the end of each year, submit an annual report on the use of the funds to the competent authorities. (6) The basic research funds can be used by the research institutes to carry out joint researches with other institutions or agencies. (7) Expenditure relating to conferences, travel, printing and laboratory tests covered by the funds should be disbursed or settled by official bank card. Advisory fees or services costs should be disbursed through bank transfer. Cash payment should be strictly restricted. (8) Fund allocation should be made in accordance with relevant provisions of the centralized treasury payment system. If relevant operations are within the scope of government procurement, they should be implemented in accordance with the relevant provisions of government procurement.■

MOF issued a circular on real estate registration fees

On July 27, MOF issued a circular on real estate registration fees. (1) When real estate registration agencies offer services relating to the ownership rights for housing or buildings, and using rights for construction land, homestead or waters, including first time registration, as well as registration of change, transfer, correction, or objection, real estate registration fees should be charged. (2) The real estate registration fees should be paid by the real estate registration applicants. (3) The real estate registration fee is standardized and charged by the piece of registration. (4) The real estate registration fee includes the cost for one copy of the estate ownership certificate. (5) The specific standard for the real estate registration fee is to be set by the NDRC and MOF in a separate notice. (6) After the implementation of the circular by the real estate registration agency, all former fees charged by relevant agencies should be canceled. (7) The real estate registration fees collected by the Ministry of Land Resources shall be turned over to the central treasury and subject to the central budget management. ■

The State Council specified measures to strengthen targeted financial services for small and micro enterprises

On July 27, Premier Li Keqiang chaired an executive meeting of the State Council which specified measures to strengthen targeted financial services for small and micro enterprises. (1) Growth rate of loans targeting small and micro enterprises should be on par or above the average growth of loans, and the recipients and extension-to-application ratio of the targeted loans should not be below the numbers of the same period of last year. (2) The loan maturity for small and micro enterprises should be reasonable to ensure liquidity, without sudden withdrawal, repression or cutting-off of the loans. Loan renewal with only interest payment should be promoted. Debt burdens of enterprises should be relieved through revolving credit, installment of payment, etc.. (3) Unreasonable fees during the financing process should be strictly removed. Financing guarantee institutions are encouraged to optimize their performance evaluation system. (4) Financial institutions are encouraged to offer new products of certificates of deposit, convertible notes, collective of bonds, etc.. ■

MOF published a circular on adjusting the 18th phase of the list of environmental labeling products for government procurement

On July 29, MOF published a circular on adjusting of the 18th phase of the list of environmental labeling products for government procurement. (1) The products that are not on the list of environmental labeling products shall not be prioritized in government procurement. (2) Government procurement projects and the procurement of goods related to them shall give precedence to environmental labeling products. (3) Government procurement activities undertaken after the publication of the circular shall abide by this list. (4) Relevant enterprises whose products are on the list shall ensure stable supply during the implementation of this list. ■

MOF published the *Measures for the Performance Evaluation of Financial Cooperations*

On July 29, MOF published the *Measures for the Performance Evaluation of Financial Cooperations*. (1) The performance indicators include profitability, business expansion, asset quality and solvency. (2) The weight of each indicator is determined by the indicator's importance and relevance. (3) The performance evaluation is based on the following data: annual financial statements of financial cooperations, audit reports presented by accounting firms, and notes on the operation of financial cooperations or financial analysis reports. (4) On the basis of reports submitted by centrally

POLICY UPDATE

administered financial cooperations and provincial finance authorities, MOF will screen the data of financial cooperations, eliminate the inappropriate data, retain the data that meet the criteria, and establish a sample database. (5) MOF will calculate the standard level of performance by industry on the basis of the performance evaluation data of financial cooperations. (6) MOF will set the industry adjustment index by industry on the basis of the documents submitted by financial cooperations. ∎

The State Council published guiding opinions on advancing the structural adjustment and restructuring of central SOEs

On July 29, the State Council published guiding opinions on advancing the structural adjustment and restructuring of central SOEs. (1) For the central SOEs that undertake key national special projects, the investment of state capital in them must be guaranteed, and the equity holding of non-state capital be supported. In the areas involving the reserve of materials of national strategic importance, the SOEs must be wholly state-owned or controlled. In the areas of national defense and military, SOEs must be wholly state-owned or absolutely controlled by the state. (2) Revamp the state capital investment and operating companies, explore effective operating models for them, strengthen research and development, step up fundamental research, improve the R&D system, remove the technological bottlenecks and enhance the independent innovation capacity of firms, facilitate the efforts of firms along the value chain to join hands in going global, promote the international production capacity cooperation, boost the cooperation between industrial firms and financial firms, and advance the cross-border takeover. (3) Properly move ahead with the restructuring of firms in the fields of equipment manufacturing, building, electricity, steel, non-ferrous metal, shipping, building material, tourism and aviation services. (4) Take strong measures to resolve excess capacity, phase out perennially loss-making and low-efficient firms, withdraw from the non-core business with no development potential, and move faster to strip the firms off social functions and resolve their historical legacy problems. ∎

The CPC Central Committee and the State Council published the *Several Opinions on Further Improving the Administration of Central Fiscal Funds for Science Research Projects*

On August 1, the CPC Central Committee and the State Council published the *Several Opinions on Further Improving the Administration of Central Fiscal Funds for Science Research Projects*. (1) Simplify budget compilation and delegate the authority for budget adjustment. (2) Increase the proportion of indirect expenses and intensify performance incentives. (3) Specify the scope of service expenses and refrain from imposing limits on their proportion. (4) Improve the management of surplus and carryover funds. (5) Require enhanced self-discipline of horizontal expenses. (6) Improve the management of travel expenses by the faculty and research staff of central-level universities and research institutes. (7) Improve the conference management of central-level universities and research institutes. (8) Improve the government procurement of central-level universities and research institutes, require record-filing by them when they purchase imported equipments and facilities, and allow for the tax exemption when the imports are intended for teaching and research. (9) Increase the authority of central-level universities and research institutes over their capital projects. (10) Simplify the approval procedures of the capital projects of central-level universities and research institutes.■

MOF published a circular on the application by cities for the pilot program of industrial-financial cooperation

On August 2, MOF published a circular on the application by cities for the pilot program of industrial-financial cooperation. (1) The pilot program is mainly about strengthening information sharing and creating platforms for industrial-financial cooperation; actively innovating financial products and services; exploring new models for the cooperation among all sorts of funds; developing innovative models for the effective interaction between public finance and financial sector; and improving the financial services for the industrial chain. (2) The applicants shall be the cities that possess conditions such as solid industrial base, distinctive industrial features, rich financial resources and high importance attached by the local government to the program. (3) Provincial industry and information technology authorities, in conjunction with finance departments (bureaus), branches of PBoC and branches of the China Banking Regulatory Commission (CBRC), shall improve institutional arrangement, follow the requirements of this circular, carefully screen and select the pilot cities, and jointly write and submit the reports.■

MOF published the *Measures for the Reduction of Patent Fees*

On August 3, MOF published the *Measures for the Reduction of Patent Fees*. (1) Patent applicants or patent holders may request the reduction of application fees, patent review fees, annual fees and re-examination fees. (2) If patent applicants or patent holders are individuals or entities, they are eligible for 85% reduction of the fees prescribed in article 2 of the Measures. (3) Patent applicants or patent holders can only request the reduction of fees that are not yet due. (4) If applicants are individuals, they shall present their income level of the previous year in the application forms, and submit the annual income certification provided by their employers. (5) After the grant of their reduction request, patent applicants or patent holders shall still pay the required amount of remaining fees within the prescribed deadline.■

Three ministries decided to expand the selective pilot tariff programs for domestic sales of goods produced in special customs zones

On August 5, MOF, GAC and SAT jointly issued the *Circular on Expanding the Selective Pilot Tariff Programs for Domestic Sales of Goods Produced in Special Customs Zones*, which provides the following: starting from September 1, the selective pilot tariff programs are to be extended to other special customs areas (except bonded zones and bonded logistics park) of the four piloting FTA areas, i.e. Tianjin, Shanghai, Fujian and Guangdong provinces (municipalities), and five special customs areas, i.e. the comprehensive bonded zone of Xinzheng, Henan Province, export processing zone of Wuhan, Hubei Province, comprehensive bonded zone of Yongxi, Chongqing, hi-Tech comprehensive

POLICY UPDATE

bonded zone of Chengdu, Sichuan Province, and export processing zone of Xi'an, Shaanxi Province. In the selective pilot tariff programs, goods produced or processed in special customs zones and then sold in domestic market are subject to tariffs, based on the information of imported raw producing materials reported by the producers, or the site examination results, are also subject to import VAT and consumption tax. When the producer chooses to submit the tariff based on imported raw materials, the delayed tax interest of tariff should also be paid. ∎

The central fiscal fund to safeguard the basic living of orphans

According to the news released on August 8 by MOF, in order to ensure basic living of orphans, the central government has allocated additional 700 million RMB, apart from advance disbursement of 1.24 billion RMB. Up to now, 1.94 billion RMB of basic livelihood guarantee for orphans arranged by the central budget in 2016 has been fully disbursed, which has effectively guaranteed the basic living for over 500,000 orphans and HIV-infected children. ∎

The State Council issued a circular on providing fiscal support for rural migrant population to become urban citizens

On August 8, the State Council issued a circular on providing fiscal support for rural migrant population to become urban citizens. (1) Protect the equal education rights for rural migrant children. Local governments should provide fiscal guarantee to cover compulsory education for rural migrant workers' and other permanent residents' children. (2) Support the development of innovative medical insurance system for both urban and rural areas. Accelerate the reform of portal medical insurance and remote medical billing settlement, unify basic medical insurance system for urban and rural residents, and implement a unified urban and rural medical assistance system. (3) Speed up the unification of urban and rural social security system. (4) Increase fiscal support for the urban employment of rural migrant workers. When providing special funds to support employment, the central and provincial governments should take into account of urban employment for rural migrant population. The funds should be allocated based on the number of permanent urban residents and newly added urban jobs, each with proper weighting. (5) Establish fiscal grants to reward efforts that facilitate the shift of rural population to urban residents. (6) The balancing transfer of payment should give due consideration to rising local spending resulted from basic public service provided to new residents. (7) The basic financial guarantee mechanism at the county level should take into account of migrant population holding a residence permit. (8) When designing local economic and social programs, urban-rural development plans and urban infrastructure construction plans, local governments should incorporate the effort of facilitating rural population to become urban residents. (9) When rural population become urban residents, their rights on contracted land, homestead and bonus from collective income should be preserved. (10) Increase fiscal support for rural migrants to become urban residents, and create a dynamic adjustment mechanism for relevant funds. ∎

MOF issued a circular on the inquiry and use of credit records in government procurement

On August 11, MOF issued the *Circular on the Inquiry and Use of Credit Records in Government Procurement*, which provides the following. (1) Finance authorities and relevant agencies at all levels should, in accordance with the *Government Procurement Law* and relevant implementation regulations, keep record of misconduct of the suppliers, procurement agencies and evaluation experts who are participating in government procurement, and incorporate the information into the unified credit recording system. (2) Finance authorities at all levels should strengthen the development of government procurement information system, step up related technical support, establish a data-sharing mechanism for the credit information platform, in a bid to gradually achieve automatic submitting, receiving, inquiry and application of the information. (3) Following the above requirements, various localities and authorities should enhance the dissemination and application of credit information during government procurement, actively design the operational procedures and measures based on local conditions, forcefully implement the relevant requirements, and give timely feedback to MOF. ∎

MOF published a circular on the tax policy concerning the import of supplies by animation enterprises for the development and production of animation

On August 16, MOF published a circular on the tax policy concerning the import of supplies by animation enterprises for the development and production of animation. (1) The animation enterprises that meet the criteria of this circular may apply to the Ministry of Culture (MOC) before the end of September of each year, and the MOC, along with MOF, and SAT will review and approve the eligibility of the animation enterprises for import tariff exemption. (2) The eligible animation enterprises shall be subject to annual review undertaken by the MOC. (3) The eligible animation enterprises are exempted from the import tariffs and VAT when they import the goods on the *List of the Imported Supplies by Animation Enterprises for the Development and Production of Animation*. (4) The import-tariff-free goods used for developing and producing direct animation products shall not be transferred, collateralized, pledged and used for other purposes without the authorization and approval of the customs authorities. ∎

The State Council planned to organize a nationwide inspection on the tackling of excess capacity in the steel and coal industries

On August 16, Premier Li Keqiang chaired an executive meeting of the State Council. The meeting decided to organize a nationwide inspection on the tackling of excess capacity in the steel and coal industries. In the inspection, emphasis will be put on the actual exit of excess capacity, the clean-up of projects that are illegal or violate regulations, control of new capacity, resettlement of employees, and the mobilization and use of funds as rewards and incentives. Localities will be urged to enhance law enforcement and inspection of compliance in environmental protection, quality, work safety, energy efficiency, and the operation of land and mines. Enterprises will be encouraged to engage in

POLICY UPDATE

merger and acquisition and upgrade themselves. Law-based and market-oriented approaches will be adopted to accelerate the exit of backward capacity. The public disclosure mechanism will be established to prevent fraud and deception as well as the resurgence of excess capacity. The incentive and disincentive mechanisms will be implemented, and experiences and lessons will be summed up. The poor implementation, slow progress and increase of new capacity that violate the regulations will be publicly reprimanded, questioned and held accountable so as to ensure that the binding annual task of resolving excess capacity can be accomplished. ∎

Figure5 excess capacity in the steel industries

Source: Ministry of Finance of China

MOF published a circular on continuing implementing the relevant tax policy for college student apartments and cafeteria

On August 17, MOF published a circular on continuing implementing the relevant tax policy for college student apartments and cafeteria. (1) From January 1, 2016 to December 31, 2018, the college student apartments are exempted from property tax; the apartment rental contracts signed with the college students are exempted from stamp tax. (2) From January 1 to April 30, 2016, the revenues derived from the boarding fees charged from the college students in accordance with national standards are exempted from business tax; and starting from May 1, 2016, those revenues are also exempted from VAT during the implementation of the VAT reform. (3) From January 1 to April 30, 2016, the revenues derived from the provision of catering services by cafeteria to college faculty and students are exempted from business tax; and starting from May 1, 2016, those revenues are also exempted from VAT during the implementation of the VAT reform. (4) The property tax and stamp tax already paid but should have been exempted as prescribed in this circular will be offset against the tax payer's future payable property tax and stamp tax or be returned; the business tax already paid but should have been exempted shall be returned; the VAT already paid but should have been exempted will be offset against the tax payer's payable VAT in the months to come or be returned. ∎

MOF published the *Interim Measures for the Administration of Final Account for the Completion of Capital Projects*

On August 18, MOF published the *Interim Measures for the Administration of Final Account for the Completion of Capital Projects*. (1) After the projects are completed and operationalized or after they are proved to be well-functioning in the trial period, the final account for completion of the works shall be prepared within three months. (2) Before the compilation of the final account, the contractor shall provide all the necessary documents and check and verify the assets and properties to ensure that the accounts are truthful and accurate. (3) The final account of the central-level projects shall follow the review and approval system and operational procedures formulated by MOF. (4) MOF and competent authorities will first review and then approve the final account, and may entrust the budget evaluation bodies or the specialized private agents to do the review. (5) In the review of the final account, if the budgetary estimate turns out to exceed the verified amount, the difference will be returned to the investors in proportion to their investment. (6) MOF will conduct spot check on the final account of the central-level projects approved by competent authorities. ■

MOF published the *Regulations for Administering the Construction Costs of Capital Projects*

On August 18, MOF published the *Regulations for Administering the Construction Costs of Capital Projects*. (1) The project construction and management expenses of public institutions are subject to a limit and shall be truthfully reported by year. (2) The project construction and management expenses of the government-funded state-owned or state-controlled enterprises shall be regulated by the article 1. In case less than 50% of the capital of the commercial projects of state-owned or state-controlled enterprises is government-funded, their project construction and management expenses may not follow the article 1. (3) For the projects commissioned by governments through invitation of bidding, the project management expenses will be included into the project construction costs by the finance authorities in accordance with the project construction requirements and be accounted at a level no higher than the standard set out in the Regulations. (4) The net loss due to scrapped project is included into the deferred investment expenses. ■

MOF issued a circular on the registration of identification and credit record of the government procurement suppliers

On August 22, MOF issued a circular on the registration of identification and credit record of the government procurement suppliers. (1) When registering serious defaults or breaches of contract of government procurement suppliers, local finance authorities at various levels should keep file of one of the following identification codes of the supplier: social credit code, organization code, business registration number, or tax registration number. (2) When organizing the on-line registration of local government procurement agencies, the provincial finance authority should require the agencies to file their identification code. (3) The provincial finance authority should ensure the integrity and accuracy of credit information and provide related support. ■

POLICY UPDATE

MOF issued a circular on further cultivating high-skilled personnel

On August 23, MOF issued a circular on further cultivating high-skilled personnel. (1) The Ministry of Human Resources and Social Security and MOF will disburse central subsidies for promoting local employment in mid-June each year. Local finance authorities at various levels should increase investment in cultivating high-skilled personnel, and ensure the implementation of related projects. The implementing agency should also provide necessary funding for the projects. (2) The finance and human resources and social security authorities of the provinces (autonomous regions and municipalities) should determine the size, quantity and lay-out of the training center projects and master studio projects. (3) The work mechanisms should be improved by enhancing review, management, oversight and evaluation of the projects. ∎

The State Council issued the *Work Plan on Reducing Costs for Enterprises of the Real Economy*

On August 23, the State Council issued the *Work Plan on Reducing Costs for Enterprises of the Real Economy*. (1) Reduce the tax and fees on enterprises properly by fully implementing the VAT reform and R&D expense deduction policies. (2) Effectively reduce financing costs by maintaining adequate liquidity and reducing the intermediary financing costs. (3) Reduce institutional transaction costs by breaking up the geographical segmentation and industrial monopolies, and strengthening the building of a level playing field. (4) Reduce labor cost properly by reducing the social security contribution rate for employers and improving the housing fund system. (5) Further reduce the energy and land-using costs for businesses by accelerating the reform of the energy and power sectors. (6) Substantially reduce logistics costs by promoting the development of new forms of transports and setting proper road tolls. (7) Enhance the business cash flow efficiency by promoting operating asset securitization of the real economy and properly regulating the depository funds of the construction sector. ∎

The State Council made plans to enhance the quality and standards of consumer goods

On August 24, Premier Li Keqiang chaired an executive meeting of the State Council, which made plans to enhance the quality and standards of consumer goods, so as to strengthen effective supply of goods made in China, and to facilitate the upgrading of consumption demand. The meeting decided to: (1) accelerate the development of a number of mandatory national standards to strengthen quality and safety requirements for consumer products; (2) give guidance to enterprises to enhance the quality, brand and marketing awareness, implement sophisticated quality management, and improve capacity in on-line quality monitoring, control and life-cycle traceability; (3) develop new approaches in standards implementation and quality oversight by conducting spot check on enterprises, products and institutions, and developing public service platform that crosses agencies and industries on the quality of consumer goods; and (4) establish quality and safety traceability system for major consumer products, and strengthen consumer rights protection. ∎

The State Council issued opinions on the establishment of an accountability system on operational and investment violations of SOEs

On August 24, the State Council issued opinions on the establishment of an accountability system on operational and investment violations of SOEs. (1) When a SOE manager violates laws, regulations or internal business management procedures, or fails to perform his duties properly, which may cause loss of state-owned assets in business and transaction management, or other adverse consequences, the person should be held accountable. (2) When loss occurs for state-owned assets in the process of SOE operation and investment, it should be recognized based on investigation and verification. (3) When the failure to fulfill duties properly caused loss of state assets or other serious adverse consequences, the person in question should be held accountable. ∎

MOF issued a circular on further implementing VAT policy for photovoltaic power generation

On August 25, MOF issued a circular on further implementing VAT policy for photovoltaic power generation (PV): from January 1, 2016 to December 31, 2018, the taxpayer is eligible to 50% discount of VAT for the sales of self-produced PV. For already collected tax eligible for the discount, it should be used to offset VAT payable later or be refunded. ∎

MOF issued a circular on the tax policy for technology business incubators

On August 25, MOF issued a circular on the tax policy for technology business incubators. (1) From January 1, 2016 to December 31, 2018, the property tax and urban land-use tax are exempt for the property and land used for qualified incubators, including self-owned, freely transferred and leased property and land of the incubators. From January 1, 2016 to April 30, 2016, revenues from housing and property leasing and incubation-related services to the incubators are exempt from the sales tax, and eligible for VAT exemption during the VAT pilot program. (2) Qualified NGO incubators are eligible for discounted business VAT. (3) Provincial technology authorities should conduct regular inspection on the incubators to check their eligibility under this circular, and submit relevant reports to MOST for approval. ∎

The State Council issued guiding opinions on promoting the reform of the way powers and expenditure responsibilities are shared between the central and local governments

On August 25, the State Council issued guiding opinions on promoting the reform of the way powers and expenditure responsibilities are shared between the central and local governments. (1) The boundaries between the central and local governments in fiscal powers should be redefined.

POLICY UPDATE

The fiscal power in the central government should be properly expanded, and local governments' fiscal resources should be guaranteed. The areas where the central and local authorities overlap should be narrowed and properly regulated. A dynamic mechanism for the adjustment of fiscal boundaries should be established. (2) The boundaries between the central and local governments in spending responsibilities should be improved. The central fiscal power should cover the central spending responsibility, while local fiscal power should be used to meet the local spending demand. The overlapping areas should be resolved on case-by-case merit. (3) The boundaries in fiscal powers and expenditure responsibilities below the provincial level should be clarified in time. Provincial governments are to properly assign the fiscal powers among lower authorities according to the principle of boundary-setting between the central and local governments.■

MOF and other government agencies jointly published the *Plan on the Development of the National Demonstration Zone for the Sustainable Development of Agriculture*

On August 30, MOF and other government agencies jointly published the *Plan on the Development of the National Demonstration Zone for the Sustainable Development of Agriculture*. (1) Adjust and optimize industrial structure, strengthen infrastructure development, and promote the coordinated advancement of industrial development, resource conservation and environmental protection. (2) Strictly protect farmland, improve farmland quality, develop water-efficient farming, and undertake ecological protection of grassland and wetland. (3) Improve rural environment, develop leisure farming, protect cultural heritage of agriculture, and build beautiful and livable villages.■

MOF published a circular on the declaration of state-owned capital gains by the central-level cultural enterprises for 2016

On August 30, MOF published a circular on the declaration of state-owned capital gains by the central-level cultural enterprises for 2016. (1) The central-level cultural enterprises included in the central state-owned capital operating budget shall declare their state-owned capital gains as required by this circular. (2) The content of declaration shall include profits payable, state-owned stock dividend, the income from the transfer of state-owned property rights, and the income from the enterprise liquidation. (3) The profits payable are 10% of the wholly-state-owned enterprises' net profits belonging to owners of parent company, as presented in the consolidated financial statements of 2015 audited by CPAs. (4) The wholly-state-owned enterprises that adjust the annual loss and profits of previous years shall hand over the profits or offset against the profits payable for 2016.■

MOF published the *Measures for Administering the Fiscal Subsidies for Ending the Provision of Public Utilities Services by Central SOEs to the Residences of Their Employees*

On August 31, MOF published the *Measures for Administering the Fiscal Subsidies for Ending the*

Provision of Public Utilities Services by Central SOEs to the Residences of Their Employees. (1) The central finance authorities will extend subsidies to end the provision of public utilities services by central SOEs to their employees. (2) The central SOEs will be eligible for subsidies equivalent to 50% of the expenses of ending the public utilities services, while the central SOEs that were bankrupt due to policy reasons will be eligible for subsidies equal to 100% of the expenses of ending those services. (3) The central SOEs that have signed the agreement or framework agreement on ending the public utilities services may apply for the subsidies in advance. (4) The companies affiliated to the group corporation shall submit to the latter the documents on their application for the subsidies. (5) SASAC will review the application for subsidies and give its comments to MOF before September 15, 2016. (6) After examination of the SASAC'S comments, MOF will determine the amount of subsidies to be extended. (7) In accordance with annual budgetary arrangement and the regulations of treasury management, MOF will disburse the subsidies to the group corporation.■

MOF published opinions on the exemption of tuition and fees for the documented poor high-school students

On September 1, MOF published opinions on the exemption of tuition and fees for the documented poor high-school students. (1) Starting from the fall semester of 2016, the tuition and fees of documented poor students of public high schools will be exempted. (2) The criteria for the exemption will follow the standards of tuition and fees approved by provincial governments and their price and public finance authorities. (3) The schools that suffer from losses due to the exemption of tuition and fees will be eligible for subsidies determined by MOF in accordance with the number of exempted students and the standards of exemption so as to ensure the normal functioning of the schools. (4) The central finance authorities will verify, every three years, the subsidy standard for exemption in each province.■

MOF and other ministries jointly issued the *Guidance on Developing Leisure Agriculture*

On September 5, MOF and other ministries jointly issued the *Guidance on Developing Leisure Agriculture*, which identified measures to: (1) encourage tailored development plans based on rural conditions and consolidation of various regulations; (2) encourage the development of rural leisure farms, rural hotels and featured inns; (3) support the construction of clusters of featured villages, parks and cooperatives of leisure agriculture, and improve service facilities; (4) support the poor households in developing leisure agriculture cooperatives, small farmhouses and picking gardens; (5) carry out general survey of agricultural heritages, strengthen dynamic supervision on identified agricultural heritages, and revive traditional Chinese craftsmanship; (6) strengthen efforts to protect traditional villages and houses by improving the protection and management mechanisms; and (7) put emphasis on building a series of leisure agriculture brands.■

POLICY UPDATE

The State Council made plans to address weaknesses in key areas and weak links

On September 5, Premier Li Keqiang chaired an executive meeting of the State Council, which identified measures to: (1) accelerate the implementation of overarching, fundamental and strategic projects outlined in the 13th Five-Year Plan, actively resolve excess capacity, and eliminate outdated production capacity; (2) further liberalize investment restrictions in infrastructure, and allow equal treatment in market access, professional accreditation and social security for private and public institutions in education, medical service, elderly care and other areas relating to people's livelihood; (3) adopt innovative approaches to make use of precipitated funds. The central budget is to increase investment in water conservation projects and urban waterlogging prevention facility, especially through PPP projects; (4) Adopt further measures to attract FDI, including rapid roll-out of experience learned in the FTA pilot, introduction of negative list for foreign investment and the policies to facilitate the shift of processing trade to the Midwest; (5) Adopt incentive and disincentive mechanisms in weakness areas.■

MOF and the State Oceanic Administration jointly issued the *Circular on Fiscal Support for Demonstrative and Innovative Development of Marine Economy during the 13th Five-Year Plan Period*

On September 6, MOF and the State Oceanic Administration jointly issued the *Circular on Fiscal Support for Demonstrative and Innovative Development of Marine Economy during the 13th Five-Year Plan Period*. The two ministries will focus on shoring up weak links, fostering new development engines and nurturing regional comparative advantages in the marine industry. Measures will be taken in several selected cities to cultivate demonstrative and innovative development of marine economy, foster collaborative innovation in the industrial chain and cluster innovation in industrial incubators, support marine enterprises to make innovation in technology, management and business models, and encourage key industries to extend industrial chain and enhance core competitiveness. The objective is to, after several years of efforts, produce a number of internationally competitive niche products, and foster a number of leading and innovative enterprises, SMEs and industrial clusters in marine economy. With an advanced industrial structure and the shift to efficient and quality marine economy, we strive to build a healthy marine economy with balanced structure, speed, quality and efficiency in its development.■

MOF issued a circular on the additional urban maintenance tax and education fees relating to remote and advance VAT payments

On September 6, MOF issued a circular on the additional urban maintenance tax and education fees relating to remote and advance VAT payments. (1) When a taxpayer provides construction service, or sells or rents a real estate in a location other than his home residence, advance VAT payments should be made in the location where the construction service is provided or the real estate is located. The additional urban maintenance tax and education fees relating to the advance VAT should be calculated based on the amount payable, and be collected in the location where the service is provided or the transaction is occurred. (2) When advance VAT taxpayers declare the paid VAT at their resident location, the additional urban maintenance tax and education fees relating to the advance VAT should be calculated based on the amount actually paid, and be collected in the resident location.■

MOF issued a circular on VAT, property tax, urban land-use tax incentives for heating providers

On September 7, MOF issued a circular on VAT, property tax, urban land-use tax incentives for heating providers. (1) From January 1, 2016 to the end of the heating season in 2018, the income of heating providers from residential heating services is exempt from VAT. (2) From January 1, 2016 to December 31, 2018, residential heating providers' plants or properties used to generate the heating service are exempt from property tax and urban land-use tax, while the plants or properties of the heating provider for other purposes are subject to standard property tax and urban land-use tax.■

MOF published the *Measures for Administering the Funds and Projects for National Comprehensive Development of Agriculture*

On September 9, MOF published the *Measures for Administering the Funds and Projects for National Comprehensive Development of Agriculture*. (1) The funds necessary for comprehensive agricultural development will be arranged by the central finance authorities in their annual budget in view of the related targets and tasks, while the matching fiscal resources from the local finance authorities shall also be in their annual budget. (2) The allocation of the central fiscal funds for comprehensive agricultural development will mainly follow the factor method. (3) Grants, subsidies, and other forms of support can be used to catalyze private capital for comprehensive agricultural development. (4) The National Office for Comprehensive Agricultural Development will determine the proportion of self-financing by considering the project nature and the recipients of support. (5) The funds for comprehensive agricultural development will prioritize land management projects. (6) The funds for comprehensive agricultural development shall be used for farmland irrigation and drainage, land leveling and soil improvement. (7) County governments are required to keep accounts of the funds for comprehensive agricultural development by following the regulations of the centralized treasury payment system. (8) The surplus funds for comprehensive agricultural development shall be returned to the corresponding level of finance authorities as required.■

MOF published a circular on the central fiscal support for the demonstration of innovative development of maritime economy during the 13th Five-Year Plan period

On September 9, MOF published a circular on the central fiscal support for the demonstration of innovative development of maritime economy during the 13th Five-Year Plan period. (1) The demonstration cities shall push forward innovation on multiple fronts such as technology, management and business model, and foster new drivers of industry development. (2) A combination of subsidized loans, rewards, and equity investment shall be used to support innovative industries and more funds shall be channeled to strategic and emerging industries in the maritime sector. (3) The work targets shall be quantified, verifiable and operable. (4) Trial and exploratory efforts shall be made and relevant experiences be summed up.■

China will make tariff concession on 201 IT products as of September 15

According to the news released by MOF on September 14, China will make tariff concession on 201 IT products as of September 15. These products cover 480 tariff numbers in Chinese tax code, including new generation of multi-component integrated circuits, touch screens, semi-conductors and their manufacturing equipment, audiovisual products, medical equipment and apparatus, and components and raw materials required for making IT products. The tariff cut is aimed at implementing the negotiation outcomes of the expansion of WTO Information Technology Agreement. On December 16, 2015, 24 participating parties, including China, jointly issued the *Ministerial Statement on the Expansion of Trade in Information Technology Products* in Nairobi, Kenya, and pledged to eliminate tariffs on 201 products.■

MOF published a circular on the mid-term assessment of the *Plan for Promoting High-standard Farmland and Comprehensive Development of Agriculture*

On September 19, MOF published a circular on the mid-term assessment of the *Plan for Promoting High-standard Farmland and Comprehensive Development of Agriculture*. (1) The provinces that have completed the tasks set out in the Plan or are close to complete those tasks shall present relevant data and specify the focus of local agricultural development and the direction of fund use going forward. (2) The provinces that implement the Plan as scheduled shall sum up experiences and take stock of their existing problems. (3) The provinces that implement the Plan behind schedule shall get to the bottom of the problems, pursue a problem-oriented approach, and take the initiative to work out the problems while taking into account of the local circumstances.■

The State Council published the *Interim Measures for Administering the Sharing of Government Information*

On September 20, the State Council published the *Interim Measures for Administering the Sharing of Government Information*. (1) NDRC will be responsible for drafting the *Guidelines for Compiling the Catalogue of Government Information*. (2) All government agencies shall compile and maintain the catalogue of government information as required. (3) The government information falls into three types: unconditional sharing, conditional sharing, and prohibited sharing. (4) NDRC will oversee the establishment of a national platform for the sharing of government information as well as a nationwide system for this purpose. (5) The government agencies that use the shared information shall do so in accordance with their mandates. (6) The government agencies that supply the shared information shall timely maintain and update the information. (7) The government agencies that use the shared information shall do so in accordance with their mandates and by following the relevant laws and regulations, and strengthen due oversight throughout this process.■

MOF published a circular on the tax policy concerning the science and technology parks of national universities

On September 20, MOF published a circular on the tax policy concerning the science and technology parks of national universities. (1) From January 1, 2016 to December 31, 2018, the real estate and land that the eligible parks use by themselves or provide for the incubated firms free of charge or through rental shall be exempted from property tax and urban land use tax; from January 1 to April 30, 2016, the revenues from renting premises and buildings to the incubated firms or from providing incubation services for them shall be exempted from business tax; during the VAT reform, those revenues shall be exempted from VAT as well. (2) The revenues of the parks that meet the criteria of non-profit organization shall be eligible for preferential corporate income tax treatment according to the corporate income tax law and relevant tax policy.■

MOF published a circular on improving the income tax policy concerning equity incentives and technology invested as capital stocks

On September 22, MOF published a circular on improving the income tax policy concerning equity incentives and technology invested as capital stocks. (1) Tax deferral can be applied to the stock options, equity options, restricted stocks and equity rewards of eligible non-public firms. (2) The stock options, restricted stocks and equity incentives of public firms are eligible for the extension of tax deadline. (3) Selected preferential tax policies can be applied to technology invested as capital stocks. (4) Individuals who obtain stocks (equities) from their employers below market fair price shall pay individual income tax if they fail to meet the criteria for tax deferral. (5) After individuals have obtained equities through equity incentives or technology invested as capital stocks, in case of non-public firms going public on domestic exchange, the prevailing tax regulations on restricted shares shall govern the disposal of tax-deferred equities. (6) The transfer of equities by individuals is regarded as eligible for the preferential policy of tax deferral. (7) During the period of holding the tax-deferred equities, the revenues from converting capital reserve into shares and from reinvesting those equities into non-monetary assets shall be liable for taxes.■

MOF issued a circular on enhancing transparency of budget and final accounts for local governments

On September 24, MOF issued a circular on enhancing transparency of budget and final accounts

POLICY UPDATE

for local governments, which included requirements to: (1) further enhance accountability; (2) strengthen guidance for and coordination of the disclosure; (3) improve the basic work related to the disclosure; (4) improve relevant assessment and evaluation; (5) strengthen supervision and inspection; (6) take noncompliance accountable; (7) take corrective measures; (8) verify the implementation in 2016; and (9) make early arrangement for 2017. ∎

MOF issued the *Implementation Plan on Differentiated Assessment for Various Types of Central Enterprises Based on Their Functions*

On September 27, MOF issued the *Implementation Plan on Differentiated Assessment for Various Types of Central Enterprises Based on Their Functions*, which stipulates the following. (1) For central enterprises with main business in areas of fully commercial competition, the assessment is to focus on the economic efficiency, capital return ratio and market competitiveness of the enterprises, and to urge the enterprises to raise operation efficiency and profitability. (2) For central enterprises in key industries and fields relating to national security and vital for national economy, or undertaking important and designated tasks, the assessment is to focus on their performance to serve national strategy, safeguard national security and economy, foster strategic industries, and complete major special tasks. (3) For central enterprises for public welfare, the assessment is to focus on the quality of public products or services provided, cost control, operational efficiency and safeguarding capabilities. ∎

MOF issued the *Measures on the Project Administration for the National Social Science Fund*

On September 28, MOF issued the *Measures on the Project Administration for the National Social Science Fund*, which provides the following. (1) Project expenses of the Fund refer to spendings incurred during project implementation which are related to the research and covered by the Fund. There are direct and indirect expenses. (2) The indirect expenses are under the management of the project organizer. (3) The project organizer should prepare fact-based budget, and explain the use of direct expense and the underlying rationale. (4) The project budget is to be submitted to and approved by the National Social Science Planning Office. The budgets rejected by the Office should be adjusted as required before re-submission. (5) Projects with joint sponsors and requiring external allocation of funding should be separately listed in the project budget. The amount of externally allocated funding should be determined by the project organizer and its partner for the research project. ∎

MOF issued the *Standard Accounting Treatment for Financial Operation Relating to Cutting Overcapacity and Excess Inventory, Deleveraging, Reducing Costs and Strengthening Pointes of Weakness*

On September 28, MOF issued the *Standard Accounting Treatment for Financial Operation Relating* to Cutting Overcapacity and Excess Inventory, Deleveraging, Reducing Costs and Strengthening Pointes of Weakness, which provides the following. (1) When an enterprise acquires the control of a designated enterprise, it should be recorded as "long-term equity investment" in the debit entry, and "capital accumulation (capital premium)" in the credit entry, at the amount verified by regulatory authorities of state-owned assets, on the date of acquisition. (2) The acquiring enterprise is to prepare consolidated financial statements, including the balance sheet, income statement, cash flow statement and the statement of changes in owners' equity. (3) When an enterprise loses the control of a designated enterprise, it should be recorded as "long-term equity investment" in the credit entry, and "capital accumulation (capital premium)" in the debit entry, at the book-value of the long-term equity investment of the designated enterprises. (4) The consolidated financial statements should not cover the enterprise which has been taken over by other enterprises.■

MOF issued the *Measures on the Administration of Earmarked Funds for Inclusive Financing*

On September 29, MOF issued the *Measures on the Administration of Earmarked Funds for Inclusive Financing*, which provides the following. (1) The Fund is to provide certain incentives for qualified county-level financial institutions. (2) For the agriculture-related loans above annual growth of 13%, finance authorities may provide rewards of under 2% of the loan balance. (3) The incentives are to be disbursed in the following year and included as incomes of the county-level financial institutions. (4) The Fund is to provide subsidies for new types of rural financial institutions and financial or banking outlets in western regions. (5) The subsidies are to be disbursed in the following year, and included as income of the financial institutions. (6) In the eastern, middle and western regions, rural financial institutions (outlets) are eligible for the subsidies for certain period of time. (7) The Fund is to provide certain discount to qualified secured loans for start-up companies. (8) For secured loans for start-ups and small and micro businesses, the finance authority may offer interest discount according to national standards. (9) The Fund is to provide guarantee loans with discounted interest for start-ups initiated by individuals. The loan ceiling is 100,000 RMB, with the term of under 3 years.■

MOF published a circular on further regulating the recovery and payment of central fiscal funds for comprehensive agricultural development

On September 30, MOF published a circular on further regulating the recovery of central fiscal funds for comprehensive agricultural development. (1) If the central fiscal funds lent to a local government become due in 2016 or beyond, MOF will recover the funds by deducting the given amount from its year-end financial settlement with the local government. (2) Upon the receipt of transfer payment for comprehensive agricultural development, local finance authorities shall recover the central fiscal funds for the officially terminated projects. (3) The transfer payment funds involved in corruption cases shall be recovered by the local finance authorities if those cases were found out by the local agricultural authorities or relevant government agencies; and if those cases were discovered by National Office for Comprehensive Agricultural Development or relevant central government agencies, the provincial finance authorities shall carry out the recovery of the funds, and MOF will

POLICY UPDATE

recover the money by deducting the given amount from its year-end financial settlement with the local government. ■

The State Council published guiding opinions on accelerating the "internet+ government service"

On September 30, the State Council published guiding opinions on accelerating the "internet+ government service". (1) Optimize and reinvent government services. It is important to regulate online services, optimize the procedures of online services, promote the online provision of services, innovate online service models, and fully disclose information on the services. (2) Integrate and upgrade the platforms and channels. More efforts should be made to regulate the online government service platforms, integrate physical government service center with online service platforms, and ensure seamless connection between community service centers and online service platforms. (3) Strengthen the basic groundwork. Greater emphasis should be placed on advancing the sharing of government information, accelerating the development of smart cities, improving the relevant standards and system, beefing up the network infrastructure, and enhancing the protection of network and information security. (4) Enhance institutional capacity, including the leadership, accountability and training. ■

Figure6 internet+government service

Source: Ministry of Finance of China

MOF published the *Rules on the Operation of Market-Making Support for Treasury Bonds*

On September 30, MOF published the Rules *on the Operation of Market-Making Support for Treasury Bonds*. (1) Tools such as random buying and selling will be deployed in market-making support. (2) The market-making support will be carried out on the platform dedicated for such purpose. (3) MOF and PBoC, in light of the forecast of treasury balance and the liquidity in the banking system, will determine the date and amount of the operation of market-making. (4) The condition for market-making is that the participating institutions shall be no less than 5 and the total quotation shall be no less than 200 million RMB. (5) The treasury bonds that are reissued according to the issuance plan and are receiving market-making support shall be classified as the bonds suited for random selling. (6) The maximum amount for random buying at a time is 2 billion RMB. The cumulative amount of random buying for a given treasury bond shall not exceed 10% of the bond's balance. (7) The market-making shall be priced at a single price. (8) After the market-making is finished, MOF will announce the results of the operation on its official website. ■

MOF published a circular on promoting PPP in the area of public service

On October 12, MOF published a circular on promoting PPP in the area of public service. (1) Finance authorities shall work with relevant government agencies in enforcing the latest requirements of the supply-side structural reforms. (2) Pilot programs shall be carried out in the public service areas supported by central public finance. (3) All sorts of private capital will be encouraged to participate in the projects. (4) The pre-feasibility study of the projects shall be conducted in a sound way. (5) Finance authorities shall work with relevant government agencies in studying the project cycle, charging mechanism, investment return and other factors to make science-based design of the implementation plan for PPP projects. (6) Finance authorities shall work with relevant government agencies in promoting the well-regulated implementation of PPP demonstration projects. (7) The project management system shall be improved by taking into account of the local circumstances. (8) The public funds, assets and resources shall be arranged in a holistic way to balance the public burden with the private capital's pursuit of profits and to create a mechanism of reasonable return for PPP projects. (9) Deregulation needs to be advanced to unleash the potential of market players. (10) Fiscal support shall be further stepped up. (11) The role of PPP information portal shall be given full play.■

The State Council published the *Plan on Helping 100 Million People Obtain Urban Hukou*

On October 12, the State Council published the *Plan on Helping 100 Million People Obtain Urban Hukou*. (1) Further ease the criteria of urban Hukou. The restrictions on urban Hukou shall be lifted across the board for key groups of people, and the Hukou policy in major cities and mega cities shall be adjusted and improved. (2) Develop and implement the supporting policies. Specifically, step up and dynamically adjust the fiscal support to the rural migrants who become urban residents, provide fiscal funds for infrastructure investment in cities that absorb large number of rural migrants, link the increase of the supply of urban construction land to the number of rural migrants that cities absorb, improve the financing mechanism of urban infrastructure, protect the legitimate rights of farmers who get urban Hukou, fully enroll the farmers with urban Hukou in the urban social housing schemes, enroll the farmers with urban Hukou in the basic urban health insurance schemes, give the children of farmers with urban Hukou equal access to education, and ensure that all urban residents without urban Hukou will be covered by the residence permit scheme.■

MOF published the *Interim Measures for the Administration of Occupational Annuity Fund*

On October 13, MOF published the *Interim Measures for the Administration of Occupational Annuity Fund*. (1) The public institutions that offer occupational annuity schemes shall declare their payment

POLICY UPDATE

of annuities to the social insurance providers that manage their pensions. (2) When employees of public institutions retire or emigrate, any changes of the payment shall be reported to the finance authorities of the same level. (3) The management and investment of occupational annuities shall follow the principle of prudence and risk diversification. (4) The occupational annuities shall only be invested domestically. (5) The occupational annuities in every investment portfolio shall be managed by one investment manager. (6) The relevant regulatory agencies shall adjust the scope and proportion of the investment in accordance with the changes of the financial market and the operation situation of the investment. (7) With the exception of stock index futures, the transaction of securities related to occupational annuity shall be in the form of spot transaction or other forms prescribed by the state.∎

MOF and other ministries jointly issued a circular on accelerating the implementation of the third batch of PPP demonstration projects

On October 13, MOF and other ministries jointly issued a circular on accelerating the implementation of the third batch of PPP demonstration projects. (1) 516 projects including the expressway surrounding Beijing, with a total planned investment of 1.1708 trillion RMB, were identified as the third batch of demonstration projects. (2) Finance authorities and competent authorities of the provinces, autonomous regions and municipalities where the projects are located shall pay high attention to the projects and work closely with each other. (3) Finance authorities shall earnestly fulfill their duties and create conditions for the speedy implementation of projects. (4) Finance authorities shall work with competent authorities to ensure the demonstration projects are implemented as scheduled. (5) The land for PPP projects shall meet the overall plan or annual plan of land use, and go through the approval procedures in accordance with law.∎

MOF issued the *Measures on the Administration of Loans and Grants from International Financial Organizations and Foreign Governments*

On October 17, MOF issued the *Measures on the Administration of Loans and Grants from International Financial Organizations and Foreign Governments*, which provides the following. (1) As the overarching authority for the administration of external government debts, MOF is responsible for the overall administration of external loans and grants. (2) The external loans and grants should adhere to the philosophy of innovative, coordinated, green, open and sharing development, follow the guidelines of national economic and social development strategies, and be compliant with medium-term fiscal plans. The loans and grants should be used as public finance resources and promote sustainable development. (3) The administration of loans and grants should under unified planning. The resources should be used in a proper size, with categorized regulation, clearly defined responsibilities, performance targets and risk control. (4) In terms of differentiated repay responsibilities of the government, the loans are divided into liable ones and guaranteed ones. (5) Grants are included under the budget management of the central government. (6) MOF may disburse loans to provincial governments or relevant departments of the State Council.∎

The State Council issued the *Implementation Measures for the Accountability System on Poverty Reduction*

On October 18, the State Council issued the *Implementation Measures for the Accountability System on Poverty Reduction*. (1) The CPC Central Committee and the State Council are responsible for the design of overarching guiding policies for poverty reduction. (2) The State Council Leading Group for Poverty Alleviation and Development is responsible for the nationwide coordination of poverty alleviation efforts, and establishing and improving performance evaluation mechanisms for poverty reduction. (3) The State Council Leading Group for Poverty Alleviation and Development will establish a mega-data platform for targeting poverty, an information sharing mechanism among ministries, and a poverty reduction related statistical and monitoring system in rural areas. (4) Relevant central and state agencies should tap industry resources to facilitate poverty alleviation. (5) The Central Commission for Discipline Inspection is to hold relevant authorities accountable for poverty reduction efforts. (6) The provincial Party committees and governments are accountable for poverty eradication in the local jurisdiction, and to ensure accountability at all levels. (7) The provincial Party committees and governments should improve the structure of fiscal expenditure and establish a mechanism to ensure growing funding for poverty alleviation. ■

The CPC Central Committee Organization Department, MOF and the Ministry of Education jointly issued the *Circular on Further Standardizing and Strengthening the Training for the Medium to Long-term Management of Central Enterprises*

On October 18, The CPC Central Committee Organization Department, MOF and the Ministry of Education (MOE) more jointly issued the *Circular on Further Standardizing and Strengthening the Training for the Medium to Long-term Management of Central Enterprises*, which provides the following. (1) Under the centralized HR management mandate, competent units or the Party Committee of the central enterprises and their HR departments should organize training programs for key management members. (2) The training should be properly designed to facilitate reform and development in the enterprises, and cultivate the capacity to tackle difficulties in the long term. (3) Separate training courses should be organized for the middle and senior management of central SOEs. (4) The training fees should be reasonable, so as to ensure cost-benefit efficiency. ■

MOF issued the *Guideline for Accounting Reform and Development During the 13th Five-Year Plan Period*

On October 18, MOF issued the *Guideline for Accounting Reform and Development in the 13th Five-Year Plan Period*, which required efforts in the following. (1) Strengthen the legal framework related to accounting. Efforts should be made to improve accounting legislation, enhance legal awareness, and strengthen supervision and inspection. (2) Speed up accounting reform for the government and non-profit organizations. The government accounting system is to be established, and the accounting system for NGOs be improved. (3) Enhance the accounting standards for enterprises. It is necessary

POLICY UPDATE

to further pursue the convergence international of accounting standards, strengthen implementation and improve external consultation mechanisms. (4) Promote the extensive application of management accounting. Efforts should be made to strengthen the guidance of management accounting system and promote its application. (5) Improve the internal control system, especially on the enforcement of rules. (6) Strengthen the information system related to accounting. Efforts should be made to promote effective implementation of the general classification standards for enterprise accounting standards, and further improve the information system. ∎

MOF issued a circular on random checks and information disclosure for the inspection of government procurement

On October 19, MOF issued a circular on random checks and information disclosure for the inspection of government procurement. (1) The inspection of government procurement is to be conducted in accordance with random check list published by MOF and the approved annual inspection plan. The inspection should follow due procedures and be conducted in a fair, efficient, open and transparent manner. (2) The inspection should establish law enforcement inspectors' directory and examinees' directory. (3) The inspection may take directional or non-directional sampling. Major procurement or issues with high public attention may become a directional sampling target. (4) Before the inspection, MOF will randomly identify the inspector and the target for inspection through the unified information platform, and randomly select the whole-process record for review. (5) The sampling ratio is 10% -30% for those on the directory of checklist. ∎

MOF issued the *Training Program Plan for National Accounting Elites*

On October 20, MOF issued the *Training Program Plan for National Accounting Elites*. (1) Every year, a number of financial and accounting managers or their deputies from large and medium-sized enterprises, listed companies or other enterprises are enrolled in the elite training course. (2) Every two years, a number of financial and accounting managers or deputies from administrative institutions or important agencies are enrolled in the elite training course. (3) Every year, a number of internationally accredited CPAs and experienced practitioners are selected to join the course. (4) Every two years, the program is open to academic accounting elites with promising potential. (5) The training program is to provide tailored courses to enhance the professional capacity of the trainees in all aspects, and make them qualified leaders of the accounting profession. ∎

MOF issued the *Interim Measures for the Financial Management of Public and Private Partnership Projects*

On October 21, MOF issued the *Interim Measures for the Financial Management of Public and Private Partnership Projects*. (1) For PPP projects ready to be implemented, the project owners are to improve the execution plan based on value-for-money evaluation and fiscal input evaluation, and submit to the government of the same level for review and approval. (2) The project owners should give priority to competitive procurement of social capital through open bidding and competitive negotiation. (3) The government's capital commitment beyond the year in the PPP contract is to be covered in the medium-term fiscal plan, reviewed and consolidated by the finance authority and submitted to the government at the same level for examination and approval. (4) When a PPP project is covered by the medium-term fiscal plan at the consent of the people's government at the same level, the industrial regulator of the project is to incorporate the fiscal input of contract under its budget management. (5) Financial authorities at various levels should work together with other government agencies to ensure the management of PPP related state-owned assets. (6) The transfer of state-owned assets or equity in PPP projects should undergo due assessment procedures to prevent misappropriation of state-owned assets. ∎

The CPC Central Committee and the State Council published the *Opinions on Establishing and Improving the Mechanism for the Implementation of the 13th Five-Year Plan*

On October 24, the General Office of the CPC Central Committee and the General Office of the State Council published the *Opinions on Establishing and Improving the Mechanism for the Implementation of the 13th Five-Year Plan*. (1) Properly handle the relationship between government and market. Allow market to play a decisive role in resource allocation and government to better play its role, and make sure market and government can fulfill their respective role in an effective way. (2) Unleash the incentives of both the central and local government, ensure nationwide coordination, and properly handle the relationship between regional interests and overall interests. (3) Push forward the overall work while seeking breakthrough in key areas, and ensure the two are mutually reinforcing. (4) Enhance the guiding and binding effects of the Plan, as the Plan integrates the Party's position with the will of the state and the people, and is the guiding document for China's economic and social development in the next 5 years. ∎

MOF published a circular on the application for the national comprehensive agricultural development projects for 2017

On October 25, MOF published a circular on the application for the national comprehensive agricultural development projects for 2017. (1) Provide interest subsidies and other subsidies to catalyze private capital, cultivate new types of agri-business, develop agricultural industries with local advantages, and support the projects on developing special base for forestry, plantation and breeding. (2) Simplify the application procedures for interest subsidies, and allow the scope of subsidies to be determined before they are disbursed. (3) The projects that receive fiscal subsidies shall be aligned to the local plan for the comprehensive agricultural development and the fostering of agricultural industries with local advantages, help address the weaknesses in agricultural industry, and raise the overall capacity and competitiveness of the agricultural industry. (4) The criteria for assessing the project applicants shall be objectively determined. ∎

POLICY UPDATE

The State Council published opinions on unleashing the vitality of the key groups of people to drive the increase of income for urban and rural residents

On October 25, the State Council published the opinions on unleashing the vitality of the key groups of people to drive the increase of income for urban and rural residents. (1) Deploy both material and spiritual incentives and use all sorts of incentives including remuneration and enhanced protection of rights to unlock the motivation and creativity of different groups of people. (2) Take multi-pronged approach to increase the income of people, particularly the intangible income related to salary and commercial operation and the property-related income. (3) Effectively reduce the social insurance contribution rate and other institutional barriers that raise labor costs and impede the flow of workforce, and erase the burden of all sorts of market entities. (4) Encourage people to get rich while making efforts to narrow the income gap. (5) Set the targets and take the policy measures that both meet the expectation of the society and ensure financial affordability and sustainability by taking into account country circumstances, development stage and economic cycle.■

MOF published the *Rules Governing the Random Check of the Asset Appraisal Industry*

On October 26, MOF published the *Rules Governing the Random Check of the Asset Appraisal Industry*. (1) MOF will establish a unified information portal on random check as well as set up and maintain a directory of the inspected people. (2) MOF will also set up a directory of the law enforcement staff and inspectors in the asset appraisal industry, and the directory will be updated on a dynamic basis according to the changes of the personnel. (3) Before the annual inspection, the information portal shall be used to randomly determine the inspector and the inspected. (4) The random check can be done in a targeted or non-targeted way and the proportion and frequency of the check shall be reasonably determined. (5) An inspection team shall be formed for each inspection task and a team leader shall be designated. (6) The list of items subject to random check shall be available on the information portal and be timely disclosed to the general public.■

MOF published the *Measures for Administering the Funds for Basic Science Research in Central Universities*

On October 27, MOF published the *Measures for Administering the Funds for Basic Scientific Research in Central Universities*. (1) The funds for basic science research are to be allocated by using the factor method which considers factors including the research needs and capacity of faculty and students as well as the state of research activities in central universities. (2) Central universities shall finish the application, review, selection and prioritization of the next year's research programs and make the annual budget arrangement by the end of November in each year. (3) The central universities shall make sound budget arrangement according to the proposed research programs. (4) The scope of usage and the spending standards of the science research funds shall be determined by the central universities in light of their specific circumstances and in accordance with the state regulations. (5) The science research funds shall not be used to finance the salary, bonus, allowances and benefits of the staff; shall not be used to purchase apparatus and equipments with prices exceeding 400,000 RMB; and shall not be used to fund the administration and operation of the university. (6) The disbursement of the science research funds shall be done through the centralized treasury payment system.∎

The CPC Central Committee and the State Council issued the *Opinions on Improving the Separation of the Ownership Right, Contractual Right and Operational Right of Rural Lands*

On October 31, the General Office of the CPC Central Committee and the General Office of the State Council issued the *Opinions on Improving the Separation of the Ownership Right, Contractual Right and Operational Right of Rural Lands*, which specified tasks in the following: (1) identify the entity with the contractual, ownership and operational rights of the land, confirm the entity's rights and interests, so as to stabilize the land contracting relationship. (2) Regulate the transfer of land operational right, improve market operating regulations, strengthen the contract management, and improve the regulation and risk prevention mechanism for the land leasing for commercial purposes. (3) Improve the supporting incentives of fiscal subsides, credit insurance, land use and project facilitation for new operation entities. (4) Actively carry out compensated termination of land contractual right, land operational right-backed mortgage loans, equity participation of land operational right in agricultural business, and other pilot projects. Speed up the legislative revision on land contract-related laws.∎

The State Council confirmed implementation details for enhancing the disclosure of government affairs

On October 31, Premier Li Keqiang chaired the Executive Meeting of the State Council, which decided the following: (1) proper procedures should be ensured in the whole administrative process, including decision-making, enforcement, regulation, services provision and evaluation of policy impacts. (2) Principle officials in the central and local authorities should take the lead in disclosing official information. At the same time, experts and scholars should make correct interpretation on policies to enhance public awareness. (3) Information disclosure should be responsive to social concerns, especially on those which may affect the interests of the general public, market expectations and public emergencies. Relevant central and local authorities should take the initiative to provide information to the public. (4) Make use of multiple media platforms to expand the coverage and public influences of administrative information, including through the building of governmental portals. (5) Broaden the channels for public participation in policy design, implementation and supervision.∎

MOF issued a circular on further integrating agriculture-related funds in poor counties

On November 1, MOF issued a circular on further integrating agriculture-related funds in poor counties, which specified the following tasks: (1) speed up the plan-making for consolidating

POLICY UPDATE

agriculture-related funds in poor counties according to the poverty alleviation strategies of the county, and submit the plan to the provincial Poverty Alleviation and Development Leading Group for record-keeping. (2) Provincial authorities should guide the poverty-stricken counties to make coordinated use of the funds, and speed up the design of specific measures in this regard. (3) Funds will be allocated to the county level in time. The funds allocated to the poverty-stricken counties should not grow slower than the overall increase of the earmarked funds. (4) Give full play to the coordination role of the Poverty Alleviation and Development Leading Group in policy explanation and communication, so as to promote the consolidation process. (5) Select a number of priority poverty-stricken counties as showcase counties. (6) Establish a progress notification system. ∎

The State Council published the *Work Plan on Controlling the Green House Gas Emission during the 13th Five-Year Plan Period*

On November 7, the State Council published the *Work Plan on Controlling the Green House Gas Emission during the 13th Five-Year Plan Period*. (1) Strengthen the control of the carbon emission targets, enhance energy conservation, accelerate the development of non-fossil fuel, and optimize the use of fossil fuel. (2) Expedite the structural adjustment of industries, curb the emission from industrial sectors, develop low-carbon agriculture, and increase the carbon sink of eco-system. (3) Build low-carbon cities and rural areas, develop low-carbon transport system, enhance the reuse and low-carbon treatment of wastes, and advocate low-carbon lifestyle. (4) Control carbon intensity, develop pilot regions for low-carbon development, and support the low-carbon development of poor regions. (5) Establish a nationwide carbon trading system, launch a nationwide carbon trading market, and strengthen the infrastructure for nationwide carbon trading. (6) Enhance the basic research on climate change, accelerate the research and development as well as demonstration of low-carbon technology, and step up the application of low-carbon technology. (7) Improve the legal framework for combating climate change, enhance the accounting and data collection of green house gas emission, and strengthen the institutional building and development of talents. (8) Deeply participate in the global climate governance, promote practical cooperation, and enhance the fulfillment of agreement. ∎

The CPC Central Committee and the State Council published the *Several Opinions on Implementing the Distribution Policy Aimed at Increasing Knowledge Value*

On November 8, the General Office of the CPC Central Committee and the General Office of the State Council published the *Several Opinions on Implementing the Distribution Policy Aimed at Increasing Knowledge Value*. (1) Gradually increase the income of researchers and give full play to the role of public research funds as important incentives. (2) Encourage research institutes and universities to adopt the distribution policies that reflect their characteristics, improve the incentive mechanisms that fit with the features of teaching posts in universities, allow research institutes greater autonomy, and emphasize the performance evaluation of medium and long-term targets of research institutes and universities. (3) Use the public research funds as incentives in the distribution of knowledge value, and improve the fund management system for research projects at research institutes and universities, especially the projects concerning philosophy and other fields of social sciences. (4) Enhance the accountability of research institutes and universities for the commercialization of science and technology findings as important incentives, improve the management system for the equity ownership by the leaders of research institutes and universities in the commercialization of findings, improve the medium and long term incentive mechanism for researchers in state-owned enterprises, and improve the tax policies related to equity incentives. (5) Allow researchers to engage in part-time work to obtain legitimate incomes and allow university teachers to get legitimate incomes by teaching in different places.■

MOF published a circular on the formulation of plans for land treatment projects

On November 10, MOF published a circular on the formulation of plans for land treatment projects. (1) Implement the strategy of raising crop yield through soil and technology improvement, make the improvement of comprehensive agricultural production capacity the basic target, prioritize the sustainable development of agriculture, focus on the appropriately scaled-up operation and upgrading of agriculture, consolidate resources, increase input, optimize the development plan, strive for high-standard farmland development, and ensure the implementation of the *High-standard Farmland Development Plan for the National Comprehensive Development of Agriculture (2011-2020)*. (2) Support the comprehensive ecological treatment to provide green guarantee for the development of ecological civilization. (3) Encourage new types of agri-businesses to participate in projects, promote the appropriately scaled-up operation of farmland, catalyze financial and private capital, enhance the integration of primary, secondary and tertiary industries, and gradually build the pilot areas for comprehensive agricultural development into the pillar zones for national food security, demonstration zones for modern agriculture and exemplary zones for institutional innovation.■

MOF published a circular on the exemption of tax for the imported materials used for coal bed methane exploration and development during the 13th Five-Year Plan Period

On November 10, MOF published a circular on the exemption of tax for the imported materials used for coal bed methane exploration and development during the 13th Five-Year Plan period. (1) From January 1, 2016 to December 31, 2020, during the process of domestic exploration and development of coal bed methane projects by the China United Coal Bed Methane Corporation, its import of directly-used materials that domestic market can neither produce nor meet the required standards, and that are on the *List of Tax Free Materials*, shall be exempted from the import tariffs and import VAT. (2) Other domestic agencies that engage in coal bed methane exploration and development shall submit application in accordance with due procedures to MOF before declaring their import of materials. (3) The import of qualified materials on the List and under the exploration and development projects in the circular is allowed to be exempted from import tariffs and VAT. (4) The rental of qualified imported materials on the List and under the exploration and development projects in the circular is allowed to be exempted from import tariffs and VAT, and the rental of imported materials that are not on the List shall be taxed according to relevant regulations.■

POLICY UPDATE

MOF issued a circular on the pre-tax deduction of corporate income tax for deposit insurance premiums of banking financial institutions

On November 11, MOF issued a circular on the pre-tax deduction of corporate income tax for deposit insurance premiums of banking financial institutions, which provides the following. (1) When banking financial institutions get deposit insurance premiums based on relevant provisions of deposit insurance regulations and with insurance rate under 1.6, the income is eligible for pre-tax deduction. (2) The pre-tax deductible= deposit insurance premium × deposit insurance rate. The basis of the premium shall be verified by the People's Bank of China. (3) The pre-tax deductible does not include surcharge for overdue tax. (4) The banking financial institutions refer to deposit taking institutions established in China in accordance with the *Deposit Insurance Regulations*, such as commercial banks, rural cooperative banks and rural credit cooperatives.∎

MOF issued a circular on the income tax policy for high-tech service business in newly listed demonstrative cities for service outsourcing

On November 14, MOF issued a circular on the income tax policy for high-tech service business in newly listed demonstrative cities for service outsourcing: in the ten newly established demonstrative cities for service outsourcing, i.e. Shenyang, Changchun, Nantong, Zhenjiang, Fuzhou, Nanning, Urumqi, Qingdao, Ningbo and Zhengzhou, high-tech service business is eligible for corporate income tax credit, according to the circular which was jointly issued by MOF, the State Administration of Taxation (SAT), the Ministry of Commerce (MOFCOM), the Ministry of Science and Technology (MOST) and NDRC.∎

The State Council issued the *Contingency Plans for Addressing Local Government Debt Risks*

On November 14, the State Council issued the *Contingency Plans for Addressing Local Government Debt Risks*, which provides the following. (1) Local governments should establish an emergency working mechanism for addressing risks, which is to initiate rapid responses, adopt differentiated and targeted measures, and take coordinated and appropriate actions. The bottom line is to prevent systemic regional risks. (2) When taking contingency measures, there should be clear accountability assigned to each level of authority, prompt response, and legally-compliant treatment. (3) Differentiated treatment should be applied to different types of debts. Local governments shall bear full repayment responsibility for local government bonds. Government backed or guaranteed debts should be replaced by government bonds, with local governments shouldering the responsibility for repayment. (4)

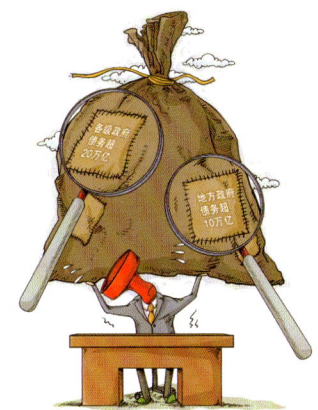

Figure7 local government debt risks

Source: Ministry of Finance of China

Establish accountability mechanisms for local government debts. (5) Provincial governments take overall responsibility for emergency response to local government debt risks.■

MOF issued a circular to task central ministries for self-evaluation on expenditure performance

On November 15, MOF issued a circular to task central ministries for self-evaluation on expenditure performance. (1) Ministries should take responsibility for the budget performance, including the authenticity and timeliness of the self-evaluation. (2) Ministries should organize their departments and subordinate units to carry out self-assessment of budget performance, to ensure 100% coverage. (3) The self-evaluation should ensure accuracy and objectiveness. False results are strictly prohibited.■

The State Council adopted the *National Key Poverty Alleviation Plans for the 13th Five-Year Plan Period*

On November 15, Premier Li Keqiang chaired an executive meeting of the State Council, which decided the following. (1) Establish targeted supporting mechanisms to link industries to households, including fostering feature industries and competitive products for each poor county, township and village through market forces, and carrying out hydropower, mineral development and other pilot programs. (2) Enhance infrastructure development in poverty-stricken areas, and promote the one-million -kilometers-rural-road project and small water conservancy projects. (3) Carry out relocation of poor population in an orderly manner by integrating urbanization, to promote the construction of supporting facilities, provision of public services, and industrial development in resettlement areas. (4) Ensure basic social security in poor areas, including pension, health care and education. (5) Increase fiscal, investment, financial, land and other policy support, promote innovations in government procurement of services, poverty alleviation and cooperation between eastern and western regions, and between enterprises and social organizations.■

The State Council issued the *Detailed Rules for Comprehensively Promoting Open Government*

On November 16, the State Council issued the *Detailed Rules for Comprehensively Promoting Open Government*. (1) Efforts should be made to promote public disclosure of decision-making, enforcement, management, service, and enforcement results. Official documents and conference organization should be included in the disclosure. A dynamic directory should be established for informing the public of relevant information. The information should be updated and reviewed regularly. The requirements should also be enforced at grassroots agencies. (2) The information disclosure should promote policy awareness, including major policies of the State Council, various ministries and local authorities. (3) Open government should be responsive to public concerns, identify accountability, and design solutions. (4) Platform development should be strengthened through government portal building and management, better collaboration among official websites and interaction with the media. (5) The public should be engaged more broadly in administrative affairs, through standardized participation and better channels.∎

MOF issued a circular on improving the management of government procurement budget of central ministries and the R&D equipment procurement by universities and research institutes

On November 17, MOF issued a circular on improving the management of government procurement budget of central ministries and the R&D equipment procurement by universities and research institutes. (1) Central government ministries and agencies should integrate the government procurement budget into the department budget preparation. The government procurement budget should be filed and recorded based on actual procurement projects, and should not be deliberately reduced to circumvent government procurement requirements and open tender. (2) Universities and research institutes supported by central budget can procure research equipment based on their own decisions. (3) Imported research equipment procured by universities and research institutes should be tagged and filed. (4) The procurement models of science research equipment by universities and research institutes should be simplified. (5) Universities and research institutes can choose research equipment evaluation experts by themselves. (6) The internal control is to be strengthened for the procurement of research equipment.∎

The State Council published a circular on increasing the incentives and support to the localities which work diligently and make notable achievements

On November 18, the State Council published a circular on increasing the incentives and support to the localities which work diligently and make notable achievements, which provides the following. (1) Provinces (regions and municipalities) that overshoot the targets of reducing excess capacity in steel and coal sectors will receive tiered rewards and subsidies when the earmarked funds used as incentives and grants for structural adjustment of industrial enterprises are allocated. (2) Provinces (regions and municipalities) that achieve notable outcomes in improving the basic conditions for science research, optimizing the environment for science and technology innovation, and implementing major national policies for the development of science and technology will be prioritized, based on the results of performance evaluation, when the earmarked funds provided by the central government for the local science and technology development are allocated. (3) Provinces (regions and municipalities) that cultivate a financial ecology of ethics and integrity and maintain a sound financial order will be prioritized, other conditions being equal, when they apply for the pilot financial reform zone, and the supportive relending and rediscount for them will also be intensified in relevant areas. (4) Cities (prefectures) and counties (cities and districts) that achieve notable outcomes in promoting the PPP model and where private capital participation is active will be prioritized when the earmarked subsidies for the pre-work of PPP projects financed by the central government are allocated.∎

MOF published the Operational Procedures for the Disclosure of Local Government Budget and Final Accounts

On November 21, MOF published the *Operational Procedures for the Disclosure of Local Government Budget and Final Accounts*, which provides the following. (1) The local government budget and final accounts shall be disclosed to the society within 20 days after the approval of the local People's Congress or its standing committee. The departmental budget and final accounts shall be disclosed to the society within 20 days after the approval of local finance authorities. (2) With the exception of national confidential information, the general public budget, government fund budget, state capital operating budget and social security fund budget shall be disclosed by all levels of local finance authorities. (3) When disclosing government budget and final accounts, all levels of local finance authorities shall make explanations and interpretations on the arrangement of transfer payment, borrowing of government debt, status of the work of performance-based budgeting and other important matters. (4) The local departmental budget, final accounts and financial statements approved by local finance authorities, including the receipt and expenditure of the fiscal appropriations and the department as a whole, shall be disclosed. (5) If local finance authorities and departments have their own portal websites, they shall disclose and permanently keep the budget and final accounts information on their websites.■

MOF published a circular on conducting dynamic monitoring of the performance of government procurement by central budgetary units

On November 22, MOF published a circular on conducting dynamic monitoring of the performance of government procurement by central budgetary units, which provides the following. (1) Promote the dynamic monitoring of the performance of government procurement by central budgetary units. Through the Chinese Government Procurement Website, government procurement planning and management system and other information system, MOF checks and verifies the data and information related to the budgeting and planning of procurement projects, pre-review disclosure of single-source procurement, procurement notice, bid-winning notice and contract-awarding notice, and conducts dynamic monitoring of the performance of procurement by central budgetary units. (2) The dynamic monitoring is mainly about the budgeting and planning of procurement, the review and approval of procurement, and the disclosure of procurement information.■

MOF published a circular on the continued implementation of the VAT policy for the purchase of equipment by R&D institutions

On November 23, MOF published a circular on the continued implementation of the VAT policy for the purchase of equipment by R&D institutions, which provides the following. (1) The domestic-funded and foreign-funded R&D institutions to which the policy of full VAT refund for the purchase of China-made equipment is applicable include: the national engineering research centers jointly verified by NDRC, MOF, the General Administration of Customs (GAC) and SAT, and the business technology centers jointly verified by NDRC, MOF, GAC and SAT. (2) The foreign-funded R&D

POLICY UPDATE

institutions established on September 30, 2009 and earlier shall concurrently meet the criteria of having no less than 90 dedicated R&D staff and no less than 10 million RMB of cumulative original equipment costs of equipment purchased since establishment. (3) The foreign-funded R&D institutions established on October 1, 2009 and later shall concurrently meet the criteria of having no less than 150 dedicated R&D staff and no less than 20 million RMB of cumulative original equipment costs of equipment purchased since establishment.∎

MOF published a circular on the exemption of corporate income tax for the enterprises that produce and assemble special products for the wounded and disabled

On November 24, MOF published a circular on the exemption of corporate income tax for the enterprises that produce and assemble special products for the wounded and disabled. From January 1, 2016 to December 31, 2020, the enterprises that meet the following criteria will be exempted from corporate income tax. (1) The special products produced and assembled by the enterprise are on the list of the *Catalogue of Special Products for the Wounded and Disabled in China*. (2) The annual income derived from the sales of special products for the wounded and disabled shall account for over 60% of the enterprise's total income. (3) The enterprise has sound accounts and documents, and is able to accurately and completely provide tax payment documents to the tax authorities. (4) The enterprise shall have no less than 1 professional with qualification certificate for making prosthetic limbs and orthotic devices. (5) The enterprise shall have the special-purpose equipment and tools that fit with its business of producing and assembling the special products, for example, equipment and tools for measurement, casting, and model processing. (6) The enterprise shall have independent reception room, room for making prosthetic limbs or orthotic devices, and prosthetic training room, with a usable floor space of no less than 115 square meters.∎

MOF published a circular on the work of departmental final accounts for 2016

On November 24, MOF published a circular on the work of departmental final accounts for 2016, which provides the following. (1) Central departments shall urge the budgetary units affiliated to them to cooperate with local inspector's offices in the review process of the budgetary units' final accounts. While submitting their final accounts to competent authorities, the budgetary units at level II or below shall also copy the final accounts to local inspector's offices. Before March 20, 2017, they shall present the aggregated departmental final accounts, reporting instructions and analysis report, status report on the analysis and evaluation of the final accounts, as well as the electronic data to the MOF departments that oversee departmental budgets for their review, and adjust the final accounts according to the comments of the MOF departments. (2) Local finance authorities shall complete the review and aggregation of the departmental final accounts by April 20, 2017, and in accordance with the notice on the joint review of departmental final accounts, bring the aggregated departmental final accounts, reporting instructions, analysis report and other documents for the joint review organized by the treasury Department of MOF.∎

The State Council decided to implement a flat VAT refund to protect local fiscal resources

On November 29, Premier Li Keqiang chaired an executive meeting of the State Council, which identified the following: since the full roll-out of the VAT pilot reform on May this year, four new pilot sectors, which are financial sector, construction, real estate and services, have witnessed increased tax reductions over the months. As the end of October, the accumulative tax cut was 96.5 billion RMB. Coupled with earlier tax reductions of the pilot in other sectors, the total annual tax reduction was more than 500 billion RMB. In the next steps, we should closely follow the progress of the pilot program, and carry out third-party assessment of operational effects. For the problems reflected by the financial, construction and other pilot sectors, we should study and design a clear policy path forward. Relevant measures should be improved based on risk control and institutional fairness, so as to further reduce tax burdens. At the same time, in order to further improve the tax-sharing fiscal system, the meeting decided that starting from 2016, the central government is to provide a flat VAT refund to local governments, so there will no longer be additional deduction in the refund for VAT growing regions or further refund for VAT declining regions. In arranging future balancing transfer payments and other types of financial assistance, we will take into account the actual situation in eastern, central and western regions, resolve the financing gap in difficult areas, and gradually shore up the fiscal capacity of local financial authorities.■

MOF further simplified and optimized the review and approval process for central budgetary unit to change government procurement models and procure imported products

On November 29, MOF issued a *Circular on Simplifying and Optimizing the Review and Approval Process for Central Budgetary Unit to Change Government Procurement Models and Procure Imported Products*, which provides the following. (1) The change of government procurement models should be applied and reviewed in a basket. The budgetary authority should strengthen the management of such changes of its subordinate agencies, submit the application for changes to MOF in a basket on a regular basis, and MOF is to review the application in a basket. (2) Procurement of imported goods should be analyzed and reviewed in a centralized manner. The central budgetary supervisory authority should combine the procurement requests of its subordinate agencies annually, organize experts to conduct professional analysis on those requests, and report to MOF. MOF is to review the application in a basket. (3) The efficiency of application and review process is to be enhanced. For the applications by the central budgetary units, MOF has a deadline for the review and feedback process. For qualified applications, MOF should complete the approval process within 5 working days upon receiving the application.■

MOF issued the *Management Measures for the Administration of Urban and Rural Compulsory Education Subsidy Funds*

On November 30, MOF and the Ministry of Education jointly issued the *Management Measures for the Administration of Urban and Rural Compulsory Education Subsidy Funds*, which provides the

POLICY UPDATE

following: urban and rural students enrolled in compulsory education (including private school students) are exempt from miscellaneous fees and provided with free textbooks. Students from financially challenged families are eligible for living subsidies. Urban and rural compulsory schools are provided with standardized subsidies based on per-students expenses, which are to be shared by the central and local governments at proportion. Efforts should be made to improve the safety and security of rural compulsory school buildings and establish a long-term mechanism, and support the maintenance and reconstruction, earthquake-prevention reinforcement, and the expansion of campus and ancillary facilities of public schools. Living allowances are to be provided for teachers working in poor villages.∎

A circular on relevant tax policies for the Shenzhen-Hong Kong Stock Connect Pilot was issued

On December 1, MOF, SAT and China Securities Regulatory Commission (CSRC) jointly issued the *Circular on Relevant Tax Policies for the Shenzhen-Hong Kong Stock Connect Pilot*, which provides the following: when mainland individual investors receive income from the transactions in HK stock exchange through the Shenzhen-HK Stock Connect Pilot, the income is exempt from individual income tax from December 5, 2016 to December 4, 2019, and exempt from VAT during the VAT pilot period. When mainland institutional investors receive income from the transactions in HK stock exchange through the Shenzhen-HK Stock Connect Pilot, the income is to be included in total income, and subject to corporate income tax, but is exempt from VAT during the VAT pilot period. When HK investors (both institutional and individual) receive income from the transactions in Shenzhen stock exchange through the Shenzhen-HK Stock Connect Pilot, the income is temporarily exempt from individual income tax, and from VAT during the VAT pilot period.∎

MOF issued the *Management Measures for the Administration of General Budgetary Debt of Local Governments*

On December 2, MOF issued the *Management Measures for the Administration of General Budgetary Debt of Local Governments*, which provides the following: the general debt generated income should be used for the capital expenditure of public welfare services, not for recurrent spending. There should be plans for repaying general debts and a stable financing source underpinning the plans. The principal of general debts should be re-paid by budgetary income or through issuance of general bonds. The interest of general debts should be re-paid by budgetary income, but not through issuance of general bonds. The general debts other than bonds should be swapped to general bonds within the timetable set by the State Council. Local governments should strengthen information capacity building relating to debt management, in order to bring the revenue and expenditure of general debts into the information system of fiscal budget management at the local level, and bring the general debts management into the unified national information system. MOF is to formulate other measures for the administration of the external debt and related credit loans.∎

 ### MOF issued the *Management Measures for the Administration of Special Budgetary Debts of Local Governments*

On December 2, MOF issued the *Management Measures for the Administration of Special Budgetary Debts of Local Governments*, which provides the following: the management of the income, spending, payment of principal and interest, and issuance costs of special budgetary funds is brought into the budgetary management of government funds. The income of special debt is to be generated from special bonds, which is to be issued by provincial, autonomous regional or municipal governments, and operated by the provincial financial department. The special debts generated income should be used for the capital expenditure of public welfare services, not for recurrent spending. There should be plans for repaying special debts and a stable financing source underpinning the plans. Special debt income and expenditure should be balanced by the corresponding government fund incomes and special incomes. Government funds across different categories cannot be re-allocated. If the government fund revenue corresponding to the special debt is not enough to repay the principal and interest, it can be supported by the special income from corresponding public welfare project units. The special debts other than bonds should be swapped to special bonds within the timetable set by the State Council. Local governments should strengthen information capacity building relating to debt management, in order to bring the revenue and expenditure of special debts into the information system of fiscal budget management at the local level, and bring the special debts management into the unified national information system.■

 ### MOF published a circular on administering the budget execution of the central budgetary units in 2017

On December 5, MOF published a circular on administering the budget execution of the central budgetary units in 2017, which provides the following. (1) The time, content, approval, adjustment and other matters related to the submission of the budgetary units' spending plan are still governed by the existing regulations. (2) Basic expenses are carried over by budget items and project expenses are carried over by budgeted projects. (3) When using the funds, the budgetary units can choose for themselves the payment method according to the criteria provided by MOF. (4) The payment method for the surplus funds of the treasury centralized payment in 2016 shall be re-determined by following the new criteria. (5) Some budgetary units, such as the secondary and primary schools affiliated to central universities funded by public finance, shall be covered in the administration of centralized treasury payment. Unless authorized or approved by MOF, budgetary units shall not transfer funds from their zero-balance accounts to the funded accounts of themselves or other bodies affiliated to them.■

 ### MOF published a circular on the tax policies for imported seeds and provenances during the 13th Five-Year Plan Period

On December 5, MOF published a circular on the tax policies for imported seeds and provenances during the 13th Five-Year Plan period, which provides the following. (1) The scope of tax exemption covers the seeds (seedlings), breeding stock (poultry), fish seeds (fry) and wild fauna and flora

POLICY UPDATE

provenances that are closely related to agriculture and forestry and are directly used for or serve agriculture and forestry production. (2) For their tax-free imports, seeds and seedlings shall be both on the list of tax-free goods and used for or serve agriculture and forestry production. (3) For their tax-free imports, wild fauna and flora provenances shall be both on the list of tax-free goods and be used for science research, breeding or reproduction. (4) MOF, GAC and SAT and other government departments will monitor and inspect the policy enforcement when appropriate.∎

MOF published a circular on implementing supportive tax policies to reduce enterprise leverage

On December 6, MOF published a circular on implementing supportive tax policies to reduce enterprise leverage, which provides the following. (1) The enterprises that carry out equity (asset) acquisition, merger and other restructuring consistent with the tax laws will be eligible for deferred payment of income tax. (2) The enterprises that invest with nonmonetary assets will be allowed to pay income tax in installments within 5 years. (3) In case of bankruptcy and liquidation, the relevant liquidation expenses as well as the salary, social insurance and indemnity of employees are eligible for pre-tax deduction. (4) The loss suffered by enterprises as creditors, if consistent with the tax laws, can be deducted when the payable income tax is calculated. (5) The loan loss provision drawn by financial enterprises, if consistent with the tax laws, can be deducted before the corporate income tax. (6) The transfer of goods, real estate and land use rights involved in the transfer of physical assets, wholly or partially, to other entities and individuals in the process of corporate restructuring, if consistent with relevant regulations, can be exempted from VAT. (7) The land value-added tax, deed tax and stamp tax arising from the corporate restructuring, if consistent with relevant regulations, will be eligible for preferential policies. (8) Tax payers that meet the conditions for credit asset securitization are eligible for relevant preferential policies.∎

MOF published the *Measures for Administering the Calculation and Payment of Correspondent Banking Service Fees for the Centralized Treasury Payment*

On December 7, MOF published the *Measures for Administering the Calculation and Payment of Correspondent Banking Service Fees for the Centralized Treasury Payment*, which provide the following. (1) The service fees are calculated on the basis of the service type, business volume and annual evaluation results of the correspondent bank. (2) The head office of the correspondent bank shall calculate the relevant fees in January by following the stipulated standards and submit them to MOF by January 15 2017. (3) On the basis of the documents submitted by the head office of each correspondent bank, MOF calculates the amount of annual service fees of each correspondent bank by considering the actual services provided by it, the business volume and the payment standards. (4) MOF determines the service quality rating of the correspondent bank in accordance with the annual evaluation results, and verifies the finalized amount of annual service fees to be paid to each correspondent bank. (5) MOF pays service fees to the head office of each correspondent bank before April 10 of each year.∎

The State Council published several opinions on improving policies to support the continued income increase of farmers

On December 7, the General Office of the State Council published several opinions on improving policies to support the continued income increase of farmers, which provide the following. (1) Improve pro-agriculture system and tap the potential of income growth within the agricultural sector. Increase investment in agricultural infrastructure, revamp policies of agricultural subsidy, improve agricultural structural adjustment policies, reform the price formation mechanism of agricultural products, improve supportive policies for new agri-businesses, strengthen rural financial services, develop innovative agricultural insurance products and services, and explore new modalities to leverage financial resources to support agriculture. (2) Strengthen pro-employment and pro-entrepreneurship policies, and expand the channels of income increase for farmers. Enhance the training of the new-type and professional farmers, ensure equal employment conditions for urban and rural laborers, support business start-up of farmers, encourage industrial and commercial capital to invest in rural areas and agriculture, and improve the benefits-linking mechanism of the industrial chain. (3) Build a long-term mechanism for the integrated development of urban and rural areas and unlock the potential for income increase of farmers. Deepen the reform of the collective property right system in rural areas, unleash the vitality of rural resources and assets, and maximize the catalytic effects of the new-type of urbanization. ■

MOF published the *2016-2020 Plan for the Development of Intelligent Manufacturing*

On December 8, MOF published the *2016-2020 Plan for the Development of Intelligent Manufacturing*, which provides the following. (1) Accelerate the development of intelligent manufacturing equipments, and focus on the key areas of sensing, control, decision making and enforcement. (2) Enhance the innovation of key generic technologies, and provide technology support for the transition towards intelligent manufacturing equipments and process. (3) Develop a standard system for intelligent manufacturing. (4) Build a validation platform and identification system for industrial internet and promote the upgrading of intranet. (5) Develop pilot programs on the new modalities of intelligent manufacturing in the key regions and areas with favorable conditions and urgent needs. (6) Promote smart transformation of the ten key areas identified in the *Made in China 2025*. (7) Advance the smart development of SMEs. (8) Cultivate an ecosystem for intelligent manufacturing. (9) Develop the clustering of industries for intelligent manufacturing equipments, promote differentiated development of intelligent manufacturing across regions, and strengthen the synergy of intelligent manufacturing resources in different regions. ■

MOF issued the *Measures for Administration of Water Conservancy Funds by the Central Government*

On December 12, MOF issued the *Measures for Administration of Water Conservancy Funds by the Central Government*, which provides the following. (1) The administration of water conservancy funds is jointly managed by MOF and the Ministry of Water Resources(MWR). (2) The funding

POLICY UPDATE

expenditure covers farmland water conservancy development and comprehensive management of groundwater overdraft area. (3) MOF and MWR are to jointly prepare the three-year rolling planning and annual budget for the water conservancy funds. (4) The central finance authority is to mainly use the factor approach when allocating the water conservancy funds. (5) Local water conservancy authorities at various levels should work together with local finance authorities to disburse the funds to projects, through competitive selection of projects and improved project pool. (6) The incentives from the water conservancy funds are to be provided after the completion of projects, in the form of awards rather than subsidies, and to support private projects. (7) Finance authorities at various levels are to work jointly with water conservancy authorities to make consolidated use of the funds. (8) The funds are to be disbursed in accordance with the provisions of the centralized treasury payment system. (9) Finance authorities at various levels are to work jointly to improve the budget performance of the water conservancy funds.∎

MOF issued a circular on the standards for real estate registration fees

On December 13, MOF issued a circular on the standards for the real estate registration fees. (1) When real estate registration agencies above the county level register the rights of real estates, the fees should be varied in accordance with different circumstances. (2) When real estate registration agency levies registration fees in accordance with provision, the first real estate ownership certificate is free of charge, while each additional certificate is charged for 10 RMB. (3) Fees for the application of correction and disputed registration of real estate are levied at a discount. (4) The real estate registration fee is charged by piece, not proportionate to the space, size or price of the real estate. (5) The real estate registration fee is to be paid by the registration applicant.∎

MOF issued guiding opinions on poverty alleviation through employment support

On December 13, MOF issued guiding opinions on poverty alleviation through employment support, which provided the following. (1) Local poverty-relief authorities should, based on record filing, further collect basic employment information on the poor population. (2) Local authorities should work hard to create additional job opportunities for nearby workforce in poverty. (3) Local authorities should make good use of the cooperation mechanism between eastern and western regions and the inter-provincial assistance mechanism, carry out inter-provincial labor cooperation, and actively promote labor cooperation between economically advanced regions and poverty-stricken areas. (4) Relevant authorities should actively organize regular, pre-job, tailored and skills-upgrading training for poor laborers, and improve the relevance and effectiveness of the training programs. (5) Efforts should be taken to safeguard the rights and interests of poor labors by urging enterprises to enter into formal labor contracts and contribute to social insurance.∎

MOF issued the *Accounting Treatment Provisions for VAT*

On December 14, MOF issued the *Accounting Treatment Provisions for VAT*. (1) VAT payers are subject to VAT payable, unpaid VAT and pre-paid VAT under the tax item of tax payable. (2) At the end of each month, enterprises should transfer the unpaid or over-paid VAT of the month from the item of VAT payable to unpaid VAT of the month. (3) Small and micro enterprises, when qualified for VAT exemption, should transfer VAT payable to current profits and losses. (4) At the beginning of the month when covered into the VAT pilot program, the former general VAT payers are eligible to tax deductibles which are used to exclude output VAT for sales of services, intangible assets or real estate.■

MOF issued a circular on reducing consumption tax for vehicles of and under 1.6 L emissions

On December 15, MOF issued a circular on reducing consumption tax for vehicles of and under 1.6 L emissions. (1) From January 1 to December 31, 2017, the consumption tax for vehicles of and under 1.6 L emissions is levied at a reduced rate of 7.5%. Starting from January 1, 2018, the vehicle consumption tax is to restore to the statutory rate of 10%. (2) The date of vehicle purchase is taken as specified on the *Standard Invoice for Motor Vehicle Sales* or the *Special Certificate for Tariff Payment*. (3) The consumption tax of new energy vehicles is administrated by the *Notice on the Exemption of consumption Tax for New Energy Vehicles*, which was jointly issued by MOF, SAT and the Ministry of Industry and Information Technology.■

The State Council published a circular on the lump-sum rebate of VAT to local governments

On December 16, the State Council published a circular on the lump-sum rebate of VAT to local governments. In order to further improve the tax-sharing regime and implement the interim scheme that adjusts the division of VAT revenue between the central and local governments after the full roll-out of VAT reform pilot, the State Council decided that starting from 2016, the previous practice of VAT rebate to local governments will be adjusted. Specifically, the baseline for rebate is shifted from the VAT method established in 1994 when the tax-sharing regime was enforced to the lum-sum method established in 2015, and the regions that have seen increase or decrease of VAT will not get corresponding amount of VAT rebate or deduction. The specific baseline of rebate will be determined by MOF.■

MOF published a circular on the work of financial final accounts of central cultural enterprises in 2016

On December 19, MOF published a circular on the work of financial final accounts of central cultural enterprises in 2016. (1) Improve the management of financial final accounts, refine the

POLICY UPDATE

working mechanism, develop innovative working methods, and strengthen the financial foundation. (2) Enhance operation management and improve the functions of financial final accounts. The competent authorities and central cultural enterprises shall give full play to the functions of financial final accounts, comprehensively take stock of the assets of those enterprises, strengthen the analysis of financial final accounts, and utilize the outcomes of the work related to final accounts. (3) Enhance the rectification of problems and give full play to the role of audit oversight. The competent authorities and central cultural enterprises shall strengthen audit oversight, seriously address the problems identified by audit, select accounting firms according to rules, improve the audit quality of financial final accounts, and enhance the rectification of problems identified by audit. (4) Regulate the review of final accounts and submit final accounts report and other documents on time.■

MOF published the *Interim Measures for the Local Government Debt Oversight by the Inspector's Office Affiliated to MOF*

On December 20, MOF published the *Interim Measures for the Local Government Debt Oversight by the Inspector's Office Affiliated to MOF*. (1) Provincial finance authorities are responsible for the management of local government debt, and the Inspector's Office will exercise daily oversight over local government debt in accordance with relevant regulations and requirements of MOF. (2) The oversight of the Inspector's Office covers the debt limit management, budget management, risk warning and contingency response of local government debt as well as the borrowing by local governments and financing vehicles. (3) The Inspector's Office shall establish regular oversight mechanisms for local government debt. (4) Oversight shall be strengthened in high-risk areas and risks be periodically assessed. (5) Local finance authorities shall cooperate with the Inspector's Office by timely providing relevant information, documents and data and ensuring their truthfulness, accuracy and completeness.■

The State Council published the *Plan on the Development of National Strategic and Emerging Industries during the 13th Five-Year Plan Period*

On December 20, the State Council published the *Plan on the Development of National Strategic and Emerging Industries during the 13th Five-Year Plan Period*. (1) Pursue innovation-driven development by implementing the "Made in China 2025" strategy. (2) Get China better connected to the Internet and accelerate the development of "digital China". (3) Promote breakthroughs in high-end equipment and new-material industry and move towards new progress in China's manufacturing industry. (4) Advance the precise and personalized healthcare and expedite the transformation to highly efficient precision agricultural breeding. (5) Promote rapid expansion of the new-energy vehicles, new energy and energy-efficient and environmentally friendly industries, and build a new model for sustainable development. (6) Promote the development of cultural and creative industry by deploying digital technology and advanced ideas. (7) Keep fostering new industries with a focus on the key areas related to space, sea, IT and internet. (8) Promote the clustering of strategic and emerging industries and the coordinated development of industries. (9) Implement the strategy of opening-up and development, and build a new mechanism for international coordination of strategic and emerging industries. (10) Improve institutional mechanism and policy framework and foster a new ecology for development.■

MOF published a circular on further strengthening the equity management of state-owned financial enterprises

On December 21, MOF published a circular on further strengthening the equity management of state-owned financial enterprises. (1) All finance authorities shall strengthen the oversight of state-owned financial assets and improve the basic management system. (2) Equity management of the state-owned financial enterprises shall follow the principle of unified policy and tiered management, and be subject to the oversight of the central and local finance authorities. (3) The equity management covers the incorporation, change of share nature, and the increase or decrease of capital and share. (4) All finance authorities shall strictly regulate the procedural and transactional behaviors such as the certification and registration of financial assets. (5) All finance authorities shall strengthen the regulation of the capital and share increase of the state-owned financial enterprises. (6) The centrally managed financial enterprises and local finance authorities shall establish and improve the reporting system on the state-owned equity management of financial enterprises. (7) Local finance authorities may formulate the detailed rules for managing the equity of the local state-owned financial enterprises in accordance with the requirement of this circular and in light of the local circumstances. ■

MOF published a circular on clarifying the VAT policy for finance, real estate development and educational support services

On December 21, MOF published a circular on clarifying the VAT policy for finance, real estate development and educational support services. (1) The non-principal-guaranteed return derived from the financial products during the holding period is exempted from VAT. (2) The asset managers shall pay VAT incurred in the process of operating asset management products. (3) The compensation for demolition and relocation paid by the general taxpayers of real estate developers to other units or individuals when they acquire lands for real estate development is also eligible for deduction in the calculation of their sales value. (4) The take-away food sold by the tax payers that provide catering services shall pay VAT according to the rules under the "catering services". (5) The educational support services provided by the general tax payers may follow the simple calculation method to calculate and pay VAT at 3%. (6) The armed guard and escort services provided by tax payers shall pay VAT according to the rules under the "security protection services". (7) The home-decorating services offered by property-service providers to home owners shall pay VAT according to the rules under the "building services". ■

MOF issued a circular on adjusting tariffs for some import and export items starting from January 1, 2017

On December 23, MOF issued a circular on adjusting tariffs for some import and export items starting from January 1, 2017: the provisional tax rate will be reduced for the imports of IC testing and sorting devices, as well as for hydraulic actuator of aircrafts. Import tariffs will be reduced for consumer goods such as tuna and arctic shrimp, and for anti-cancer drug ingredients such as yew balk and branches. Export tariffs will be removed for commodities such as nitrogen fertilizer,

POLICY UPDATE

phosphate fertilizer and natural graphite, while those for NPK compound-fertilizer, billet steel and ferrosilicon will be reduced. Negotiated tariffs will continue to be applied to certain imports from 25 countries or regions, and those negotiated with South Korea and Australia will further be reduced. ∎

MOF issued a circular on adjusting the management requirements for designated accounts at central budgetary units

On December 26, MOF issued a circular on adjusting the management requirements for designated accounts at central budgetary units, which provides the following. (1) For central SOEs, their affiliates and central units with both commercial and public functions which receive no budgetary fiscal funding, the finance authority will no longer conduct approval and record-filing on the designated accounts, and the accounts should be put under the supervision of the units. (2) The accounts for regular deposit, foreign exchange and special deposit are continue to be approved and managed by the finance authority, while the record-filing requirement for the loan-to-deposit account is changed to independent management by the units. (3) The annual inspection for the accounts is to be replaced by a biannual inspection cycle, during which 50% of the accounts is to be put under review each year. (4) A sampling inspection mechanism is to be established for the bank accounts at central units. ∎

MOF issued the *Provisions for the Account Treatment on Business Bankruptcy Liquidation*

On December 27, MOF issued the *Provisions for the Account Treatment on Business Bankruptcy Liquidation*, which provides the following. (1) When an enterprise is declared bankrupt by court, the initial confirmation of its assets should be measured in net terms on the date of bankruptcy. (2) The assets of the bankrupt enterprise recognized during the liquidation process shall be measured in net terms and add to the initial confirmation. (3) In case of assets disposal during the liquidation process, the difference between the disposal proceeds and the book value of the disposed assets, deducting direct disposal costs, should be recorded under liquidation gains and losses. (4) Costs occurred or proceeds gained during the liquidation process should be directly included into the liquidation gains and losses. (5) During the liquidation process, if the bankrupt enterprise is required to pay income tax, the tax payable shall be calculated and included in the liquidation gains and losses. ∎

MOF issued guidance on supporting the development of social organizations through government procurement of services

On December 29, MOF issued guidance on supporting the development of social organizations through government procurement of services, which provides the following. (1) There are qualification requirements for social organizations to provide government procured services, but no specific requirements for their length of existing. (2) Based on procurement needs and professional strengths of social organizations, local governments and relevant authorities should specify priorities for supported government procurement. (3) Working procedures should be improved to enhance efficiency, including project application, budget preparation, procurement organization, project supervision and performance evaluation. (4) Social organizations should strictly fulfill the contracts under the supervision of procurement authorities. (5) Training and demonstrative platform for social organizations to provide government purchased services should be strengthened.∎

MOF issued guiding opinions for reforms of government procurement of services in public institutions

On December 29, MOF issued guiding opinions for reforms of government procurement of services in public institutions, which provides the following. (1) By the end of 2020, services which are provided by category II public institutions and can be outsourced should be obtained through government procurement rather than using fiscal resources. (2) Fiscal and human resource arrangements should be explored for supporting government procurement of services. (3) Services which are currently provided by public institutions and can be outsourced should be included into the catalog of government procurement of services. (4) Incomes of public institutions from providing services to government procurement should be included into the budget accounting of the institutions, and eligible to relevant tax credits.∎

FACTS & FIGURES

01 China's PMI stood at 49.7% in December 2015

According to the data released on January 1 by the National Bureau of Statistics (NBS), China's PMI in December 2015 was 49.7%, 0.1 percentage point higher month on month. In terms of various business sizes, PMI of large enterprises was 50.9%, a decline of 0.3 percentage point month on month; for medium enterprises, the PMI was 49.6%, an increase of 1.3 percentage points; and PMI of small businesses was 44.9%, up by 0.1 percentage point. In terms of sub-index, the production index was 52.2%, up by 0.3 percentage point; new orders index was 50.2%, increasing by 0.4 percentage point. Employment index was 47.4%, down by 0.2 percentage point; raw materials inventory index was 47.6%, an increase of 0.5 percentage point; and the supplier delivery time index was 50.7%. ∎

02 China's lottery sales in November 2015

According to the data released on January 5 by MOF, the total lottery sales were 30.63 billion RMB in November 2015, down by 3.487 billion RMB year on year, or 10.2%. In breakdown, the welfare lottery sales were 17.022 billion RMB, down by 1.205 billion RMB year on year, or 6.6%; the sports lottery sales were 13.608 billion RMB, decreasing by 2.282 billion RMB, or 14.4%. From January to November, the total lottery sales were 333.764 billion RMB, down by 12.462 billion RMB year on year, down by 3.6%. In the first 11 months, the welfare lottery sales were 182.298 billion RMB, decreasing by 4.11 billion RMB, or 2.2%; the sports lottery sales were 151.466 billion RMB, decreasing by 8.352 billion RMB, or 5.2%. ∎

03 China's final verified GDP in 2014 was 63.591 trillion RMB

The data published by NBS on January 7 showed that China's final verified GDP at current price in 2014 was 63.591 trillion RMB, down by 22.9 billion RMB compared with the initially verified figure, registering an increase of 7.3% over 2013 in constant price terms. In breakdown, the GDP for the primary industry was 5.8336 trillion RMB, up by 4.1% over 2013; 27.1764 trillion RMB for the secondary industry, up by 7.3% over 2013; and 30.581 trillion RMB for the tertiary industry, up by 7.8% over 2013. ∎

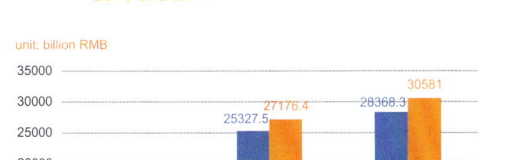

Figure1 The comparison of China's final verified GDP between 2013 and 2014

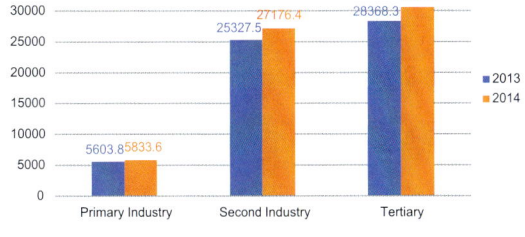

Source: National Bureau of Statistics of China

04 China's CPI rose by 1.6% year on year in December 2015

The data published by NBS on January 9 showed that China's CPI rose by 1.6% year on year in December 2015, among which, the CPI rose by 1.7% in urban areas and 1.5% in rural areas; 2.7% for food and 1.1% for non-food; 1.5% for consumer goods and 2.1% for services. Overall CPI in 2015 edged up by 1.4% over 2014. Nationwide consumption price level of residents in December also went up by 0.5% month on month, among which, the figure rose by 0.5% in both urban and rural areas; increased by 1.5% for food and stayed flat for non-food; went up by 0.7% for consumer goods and stayed flat for services. ∎

05 300 billion RMB of tax relief was offered to encourage entrepreneurship and innovation in 2015

According to the data released on January 18 by SAT, over 300 billion RMB of tax relief was provided in 2015 to support mass entrepreneurship and individual innovation. Throughout the year, near 100 billion RMB of tax cut was offered to small and micro enterprises and individual industrial and commercial households through raising the tax threshold, and cutting the corporate income tax by half for small firms. Over 140 billion RMB of high-tech related tax incentives was implemented. An additional 18 billion RMB of tax credit was provided to promote the employment of college graduates, the unemployed, the disabled, dependents of soldiers, dis-mobilized soldiers and retired soldiers. ∎

06 China preliminary GDP figures for Q4 and 2015

According to the data released on January 20 by NBS, China's GDP for the fourth quarter of 2015 stood at 18.9372 trillion RMB, up by 6.8% year on year. In breakdown, the output of primary industry was 2.1965 trillion RMB, an increase of 4.1%; the secondary industry was 7.6405 trillion RMB, an increase of 6.1%; the tertiary industry was 9.1002 trillion RMB, an increase of 8.2%. The annual GDP for 2015 was 67.6708 trillion RMB, an increase of 6.9% over 2014. In breakdown, the primary industry was 6.0863 trillion RMB, an increase of 3.9% compared with 2014; the secondary industry was 27.4278 trillion RMB, an increase of 6.0%; the tertiary industry was 34.1567 trillion RMB, an increase of 8.3%. ∎

07 China lottery sales in December 2015

According to the data released on January 21 by MOF, a total of 34.121 billion RMB of lottery was sold in December 2015, down by 2.032 billion RMB year on year, or 5.6%. In breakdown, the welfare lottery sales were 19.214 billion RMB, down by 347 million RMB year on year, or 1.8%; sports lottery sales were 14.907 billion RMB, down by 1.685 billion RMB year on year, or 10.2%. Through the whole year of 2015, the total lottery sales were 367.884 billion RMB, down by 14.494 billion RMB, or 3.8%. In breakdown, the welfare lottery sales were 201.511 billion RMB, contracting by 4.457 billion RMB, down by 2.2%; sports lottery sales were 166.373 billion RMB, down by 10.037 billion RMB, or 5.7%. ∎

FACTS & FIGURES

The performance of Chinese SOEs in 2015

The data published by MOF on January 25 showed that the operating income of SOEs totaled 45.47041 trillion RMB in 2015, down by 5.4% year on year, among which, the figure for central SOEs was 27.1694 trillion RMB, down by 7.5% year on year, and the figure for local SOEs was 18.30101 trillion RMB, down by 2.3% year on year. The operating costs of SOEs totaled 44.51961 trillion RMB, down by 4.8% year on year, among which, the figure for central SOEs was 26.24076 trillion RMB, down by 6.9% year on year, and the figure for local SOEs was 18.27885 trillion RMB, down by 1.6% year on year. The profits of SOEs totaled 2.30275 trillion RMB, down by 6.7% year on year, among which, the figure for central SOEs was 1.61489 trillion RMB, down by 5.6% year on year, and the figure for local SOEs was 687.86 billion RMB, down by 9.1% year on year. The payable tax of SOEs totaled 3.85987 trillion RMB, up by 2.9% year on year, among which, the figure for central SOEs was 2.97314 trillion RMB, up by 3.1% year on year, and the figure for local SOEs was 886.73 billion RMB, up by 2.1% year on year. As of the end of December 2015, the assets of SOEs totaled 119.20488 trillion RMB, up by 16.4% year on year; the liabilities totaled 79.06706 trillion RMB, up by 18.5% year on year; and the owners' equity totaled 40.13782 trillion RMB, up by 12.6% year on year.■

Figure2 The performance of Chinese SOEs in 2015
unit: billion RMB

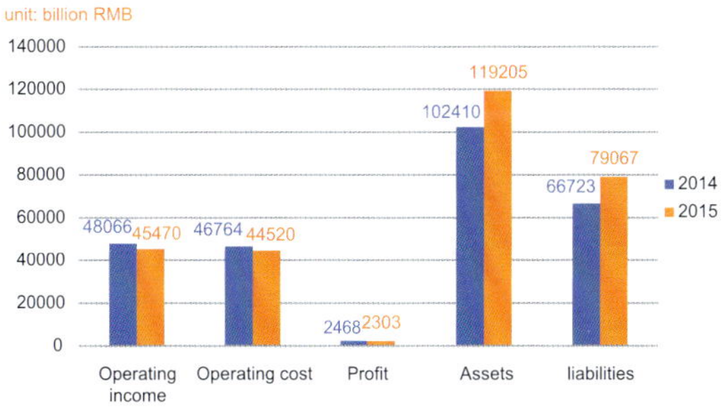

Source: Ministry of Finance of China

The total profits of industrial enterprises above designated size in China fell by 2.3% year on year in 2015

The data published by NBS on January 27 showed that the profits of industrial enterprises above designated size in China totaled 6.3554 trillion RMB in 2015, down by 2.3% year on year; and the profits generated by main business totaled 5.86402 trillion RMB, down by 4.5% year on year. In a breakdown of the profits of the major industrial enterprises, the profits stood at 1.0944 trillion RMB for state-owned ones, down by 21.9% year on year; 50.75 billion RMB for collectively-owned ones, down by 2.7%; 4.29814 trillion RMB for joint-stock ones, down by 1.7%; 1.57261 trillion RMB for foreign and Hong Kong, Macau and Taiwan invested ones, down by 1.5%; and 2.32216 trillion RMB for private ones, up by 3.7%. As of the end of 2015, the assets of industrial enterprises above designated size totaled 99.97411 trillion RMB, up by 6.9% over the last year; the liabilities totaled 56.15603 trillion RMB, up by 5.6%; and the owners' equity totaled 43.81808 trillion RMB, up by 8.8%.■

Fiscal balance in 2015

According to the data released on January 29 by MOF, the general public budget income was 15.2217 trillion RMB in 2015, up by 8.4% over the previous year. In breakdown, the budget revenue of the central level was 6.9234 trillion RMB, an increase of 7.4%; the revenue of the local level was 8.2983

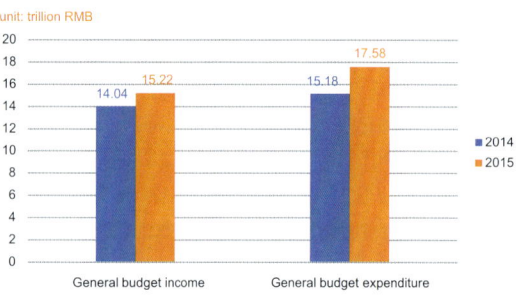

Figure3 China's general public budget income and expenditure in 2015

Source: Ministry of Finance of China

trillion RMB, an increase of 9.4%. The national tax revenue was 12.4892 trillion RMB, up by 4.8% year on year; the non-tax revenue was 2.7325 trillion RMB, an increase of 28.9%. The public budget expenditure in 2015 was 17.5768 trillion RMB, an increase of 15.8% over the previous year. The central level expenditure was 2.5549 trillion RMB, up by 13.2%. The local expenditure from using local revenue, tax refund from the central government, transfer payment and carried forward surplus funds totaled 15.0219 trillion RMB, an increase of 16.3%. ∎

PMI stood at 49.4% in January

According to the data released on February 1 by NBS, the PMI was 49.4% in January, down by 0.3 percentage point month on month. In terms of various sizes of businesses, PMI of large enterprises was 50.3%, down by 0.6 percentage point month on month; PMI for medium-sized enterprises was 49.0%, a decline of 0.6 percentage point; PMI for small businesses was 46.1%, an increased 1.2 percentage points. In terms of various indexes, the production index was 51.4%, down by 0.8 percentage point; new orders index was 49.5%, a decline of 0.7 percentage point. Employees index was 47.8%, an increase of 0.4 percentage point; raw materials inventory index was 46.8%, down by 0.8 percentage point; the supplier delivery time index was 50.5%. ∎

China's total imports and exports dropped by 23.9% month on month in January

The data released by GAC on February 15 showed that in January China's exports amounted to 1.143741 trillion RMB, down by 19.8% month on month, or 6.6% year on year; imports reached 737.537 billion RMB, down by 29.6% month on month, or 14.4% year on year. Total imports and exports were 1.881278 trillion RMB, down by 23.9% month on month, or 9.8% year on year. ∎

China's CPI rose by 1.8% year on year in January

The data released by NBS on February 18 showed that in January China's CPI rose by 1.8% year on year, among which, the price of food, tobacco and alcohol increased by 3.6% year on year; the price went up by 2.9% for health care, 1.9% for apparel, 1.7% for education, culture and entertainment, 1.4% for living, and 0.6% for consumer goods and services; and the price dropped by 1.6% for transport and telecommunication, and 0.4% for other goods and services. ∎

FACTS & FIGURES

14 ▶ Non-banking private financing in China in January

According to the data released by the People's Bank of China (PBoC) on February 23, as of the end of January, China's existing non-banking private financing stood at 141.57 trillion RMB, up by 13.1% year on year. In breakdown, the outstanding RMB loans to the real economy was 95.29 trillion RMB, up by 14.9% year on year; the foreign currency-denominated loans to the real economy was equivalent to 2.87 trillion RMB, down by 17.8%; the balance of entrusted loans was 11.23 trillion RMB, an increase of 19.1%; the balance of trust loans totaled 5.51 trillion RMB, up by 2.9%; undiscounted bankers' acceptance notes amounted to 5.99 trillion RMB, down by 15.8%; the balance of corporate bonds stood at 14.98 trillion RMB, increasing by 25.3%; the stock of domestic non-financial enterprises was 4.67 trillion RMB, up by 22.3%. ∎

15 ▶ China's manufacturing PMI in February was 49.0%

The data published by NBS on March 1 showed that China's manufacturing PMI in February was 49.0%, down by 0.4 percentage point month on month. In a breakdown of enterprises, PMI was 49.9% for large-sized ones, down by 0.4 percentage point month on month; 49.0% for medium-sized ones, staying flat month on month; and 44.4% for small-sized ones, down by 1.7 percentage points month on month. In specific terms, the production index was 50.2%, down by 1.2 percentage points month on month; the new order index was 48.6%, down by 0.9 percentage point month on month; the employee index was 47.6%, down by 0.2 percentage point month on month; the raw material inventory index was 48.0%, up by 1.2 percentage points month on month; and the supplier delivery time index was 49.8%. ∎

16 ▶ China's CPI in February rose by 2.3%

According to the data released on March 10 by NBS, China's CPI in February rose by 2.3% year on year. In breakdown, CPI rose by 2.3% in cities and 2.2% in rural areas; food prices increased by 7.3%, non-food prices went up by 1.0%; consumer goods prices rose by 2.6%, and services prices grew by 1.8%. On month-on-month terms, the CPI rose by 1.6% month on month. It went up by 1.6% in cities and 1.6% in rural areas; food prices rose by 6.7%, non-food prices edged up by 0.3%; consumer goods prices rose by 2.2%, and services prices grew by 0.5%. ∎

17 ▶ China's lottery sales in January

According to the data released on March 11 by MOF, China's lottery sales in January totaled 32.641 billion RMB, down by 6.592 billion RMB year on year, a drop of 16.8%. In breakdown, the welfare lottery sales were 18.127 billion RMB, down by 1.559 billion RMB year on year, or 7.9%; sports lottery sales were 14.514 billion RMB, down by 5.033 billion RMB, or 25.7%. ∎

CHINA FINANCE 2016

18 China's fiscal revenue and expenditure in January and February

The data released by MOF on March 16 showed that in January and February, revenue under China's general public budget was 2.7385 trillion RMB, up by 6.3% year on year, among which, revenue at the central government level was 1.1765 trillion RMB, up by 1.6%; revenue at the local government level was 1.562 trillion RMB, up by 10%. Expenditure under China's general public budget was 2.117 trillion RMB, up by 12% year on year, among which, expenditure at the central government level was 314.7 billion RMB, down by 2.1%; expenditure at the local government level was 1.8023 trillion RMB, up by 14.9%. Revenue of the national governmental fund was 569.8 billion RMB, basically flat year on year, among which, revenue at the central government level was 61.4 billion RMB, up by 1.3%; revenue at the local government level was 508.4 billion RMB, down by 0.2%. Expenditure under the national governmental fund was 347.7 billion RMB, down by 22.1% year on year, among which, expenditure at the central government level was 13 billion RMB, down by 31.9%; expenditure at the local government level was 334.7 billion RMB, down by 21.6%. ∎

19 China's aggregate financing to the real economy in February

The data released by PBOC on March 16 showed that, as of the end of February, China's aggregate financing to the real economy stood at 142.5 trillion RMB, up by 12.7% year on year. Specifically, the outstanding RMB loans to the real economy was 96.1 trillion RMB, up by 14.3%; the outstanding foreign currency-denominated loans to the real economy was equivalent to 2.81 trillion RMB, down by 19.3%; the outstanding entrusted loans was 11.39 trillion RMB, up by 19.2%; the outstanding trust loans totaled 5.54 trillion RMB, up by 3.4%; the undiscounted bankers' acceptance notes amounted to 5.62 trillion RMB, down by 20.3%; the outstanding corporate bonds stood at 15.24 trillion RMB, up by 26.8%; the domestic outstanding stock of non-financial enterprises was 4.75 trillion RMB, up by 22.7%. ∎

20 China's estimated revenue and expenditure arrangement for 2016

According to the data released on March 18 by MOF, by estimation, the 2016 central government revenue under the general public budget is 7.057 trillion RMB, an increase of 2.2% compared with 2015. The estimated expenditure of the central government is 8.5885 trillion RMB, an increase of 6.3%. Central government deficit is 1.4 trillion RMB, an increase of 280 billion RMB over 2015. The central government fund revenue is 427.165 billion RMB, an increase of 5%. With carried-over revenue of 24.817 billion RMB from last year, the total revenue of the central government funds is 451.982 billion RMB. The expenditure of central government funds is 451.982 billion RMB, an increase of 5.5%. The revenue for provincial government funds is 3.290209 trillion RMB, down by 12.4%. The central state-owned capital operation budget income is 140 billion, down by 13.2%. The central state-owned capital budget expenditure is 155.123 billion RMB, an increase of 37.3%. The provincial state-owned capital operation budget is 89.47 billion RMB, down by 5.5%. Adding the transfer payment of 36 billion RMB from the central level, the income for local state-owned capital operation budget is 125.47 billion RMB. The revenue of National Social Insurance Fund is 4.714419 trillion RMB, an increase of 5.6%, and the expenditure of the Fund is 4.354653 trillion RMB, an increase of 10.6%.∎

The performance of Chinese SOEs from January to February

The data published by MOF on March 25 show that from January to February, the operating income of SOEs totaled 6.24155 trillion RMB, down by 5.8% year on year; the operating costs of SOEs totaled 6.1209 trillion RMB, down by 5.2% year on year, among which, the sales expenses were up by 5.5%, management expenses increased by 4.9% and financial expenses were down by 1.7%; the profits of SOEs totaled 222.61 billion RMB, down by 14.2% year on year; the payable taxes of SOEs totaled 639.74 billion RMB, down by 0.5% year on year; the assets of SOEs totaled 120.32818 trillion RMB, up by 15.6% year on year; the liabilities totaled 79.73067 trillion RMB, up by 17.9% year on year; and the owner's equity totaled 40.59751 trillion RMB, up by 11.2% year on year.∎

China's lottery sales in February

The data released by MOF on March 25 showed that nationwide lottery sales in February totaled 22.454 billion RMB, down by 2.335 billion RMB year on year, or 9.4%, among which, welfare lottery sales were 12.341 billion RMB, down by 672 million RMB, or 5.2%; sports lottery sales were 10.114 billion RMB, down by 1.663 billion RMB, or 14.1%. Cumulative nationwide lottery sales from January to February totaled 55.096 billion RMB, down by 8.927 billion RMB year on year, or 13.9%, among which, welfare lottery sales were 30.468 billion RMB, down by 2.231 billion RMB, or 6.8%; sports lottery sales were 24.628 billion RMB, down by 6.696 billion RMB, or 21.4%.∎

The total profits of industrial enterprises above designated size in China rose by 4.8% year on year from January to February

The data published by NBS on March 27 showed that from January to February, the profits of industrial enterprises above designated size in China totaled 780.71 billion RMB, up by 4.8% year on year, among which, the figure stood at 117.13 billion RMB for state-controlled ones, down by 14.5% year on year; 6.36 billion RMB for collectively owned ones, down by 0.3%; 521.61 billion RMB for joint-stock ones, up by 6.4%; 192.51 billion RMB for foreign and Hong Kong, Macau and Taiwan invested ones, up by 5.6%; and 310.37 billion RMB for private ones, up by 7.5%. From January to February, the operating income of industrial enterprises above designated size totaled 15.2601 trillion RMB, up by 1% year on year; and the operating costs totaled 13.01011 trillion RMB, up by 0.7% year on year. By the end of February, the assets of industrial enterprises above designated size totaled 95.73759 trillion RMB, up by 5.8% year on year; the liabilities totaled 54.38361 trillion RMB, up by 5.5%; and the owner's equity totaled 41.35398 trillion RMB, up by 6.1%.∎

24 China's manufacturing PMI reached 50.2% in March

According to the data released on April 1 by NBS, China's manufacturing PMI in March was 50.2%, up by 1.2 percentage points month on month. In terms of various size of businesses, PMI for large enterprises was 51.5%, 1.6 percentage points higher over the last month; 49.1% for medium-sized enterprises, up by 0.1 percentage point; and 48.1% for small businesses, rising by 3.7 percentage points. In terms of categorized indexes, the production index was 52.3%, increasing by 2.1 percentage points over the last month; new orders index was 51.4%, up by 2.8 percentage points; employees index was 48.1%, up by 0.5 percentage point; and raw materials inventory index was 48.2%, rising by 0.2 percentage point. ■

25 China's land transfer revenue and expenditure in 2015

According to the data released on April 5 by MOF, China's land transfer revenue in 2015 was 3.365773 trillion RMB, down by 21.6% year on year, among which, the auction proceeds and negotiated transactions totaled 2.98202 trillion RMB, down by 22.4%; after-transaction revenue was 145.518 billion RMB, down by 23.0%; the proceeds from allocation of leveled land was 110.357 billion RMB, an increase of 17.8%; and land rental income was 127.878 billion RMB, down by 24.4%. In 2015, funds supporting education and agricultural water conservancy and irrigation withdrawn from land transfer revenue were 43.669 billion RMB and 42.351 billion RMB, down by 33.4% and 35.6% respectively. The national outlays from land transfer totaled 3.372778 trillion RMB, down by 18.5% year on year. ■

Figure4 China's land transfer revenue and expenditure in 2015

unit: billion RMB

Category	2015	2014
National outlays from land transfer	3373	4138
Funding withdrawn to support agriculture	42	66
Funding withdrawn to support education	44	66
Land-rental income	128	169
Proceeds from allocation of leveled land	110	94
After-transaction revenue	146	89
Auction proceeds and negotiated transactions	2982	3843

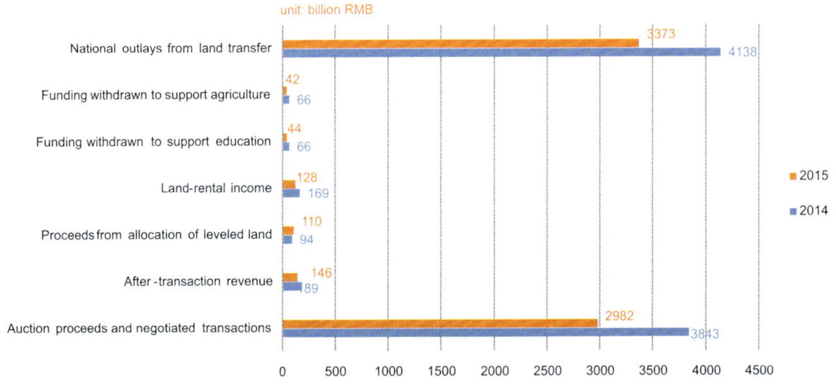

Source: Ministry of Finance of China

26 China's CPI rose by 2.3% year on year in March

The data released by NBS on April 11 showed that China's CPI rose by 2.3% year on year in March, among which, the CPI rose by 2.3% in urban areas and 2.2% in rural areas; 7.6% for food and 1.0% for non-food; 2.5% for consumer goods and 1.9% for services. Average CPI from January to March edged up by 2.1% year on year. In March, CPI went down by 0.4% month on month, among which, the figure dropped by 0.4% in both urban and rural areas; decreased by 1.8% for food and 0.1% for non-food; fell by 0.6% for consumer goods and 0.2% for services. ■

FACTS & FIGURES

27 China's PPI in March fell by 4.3% year on year

The data released by NBS on April 11 showed that China's PPI in March rose by 0.5% month on month, and fell by 4.3% year on year. IPI went up by 0.3% month on month, and down by 5.2% year on year. The average PPI fell by 4.8% year on year and the average IPI decreased by 5.8% year on year from January to March. With respect to PPI, specifically, price of the means of production increased by 0.7% month on month, and down by 5.7% year on year; price of the means of consumption rose by 0.1% month on month, and dropped by 0.2% year on year.■

28 China's imports and exports totaled 1.905574 trillion RMB in March

The data released by General Administration of Customs (GAC) on April 13 showed that in March China's imports and exports totaled 1.905574 trillion RMB, among which, exports amounted to 1.050063 trillion RMB, up by 27.9% month on month, or up by 18.7% year on year; imports reached 855.511 billion RMB, up by 39.8% month on month, and down by 1.7% year on year. Trade surplus was running at 194.552 billion RMB.■

29 Departmental budget of MOF in 2016

The data released by MOF on April 15 showed that MOF's total budgetary receipts and expenditures in 2016 reached 12.223876 billion RMB. All receipts come from the disbursements of the general public budget, which totaled 11.912227 billion RMB, with 311.649 million RMB being carried over from the previous year, and none of the receipts are funded by the disbursements from the governmental fund budget. The expenditures include 1.6602365 billion RMB of general public service expenditure, 10.0263028 billion RMB of foreign affairs expenditure, 272.386 million RMB of education expenditure, 71.591 million RMB of science and technology expenditure, 21.9303 billion RMB of culture, sports and media expenditure, 96.3338 million RMB of social security and employment expenditure, 13.5215 million RMB of agriculture, forestry and water conservancy expenditure, 61.43 million RMB of subsidized housing expenditure. 144,100 RMB of expenditure is carried over to the next year.■

30 China's GDP in Q1 of 2016 rose by 6.7% year on year

The data released by NBS on April 15 showed that China's initially verified GDP in Q1 stood at 15.8526 trillion RMB, up by 6.7% year on year at comparable prices. In breakdown, the value-added for the primary industry was 880.3 billion RMB, up by 2.9% year on year; 5.951 trillion RMB for the secondary industry, up by 5.8% year on year; and 9.0214 trillion RMB for the tertiary industry, up by 7.6% year on year. At the comparable prices of 2015, the increment of GDP in Q1 reached 985.1 billion RMB, up by 22.2 billion RMB year on year.■

"Three public expenses" in 2015 and the budget arrangement in 2016

According to data released on April 19 by MOF, the "three public expenses" in 2015 were 5.373 billion RMB, of which, expense on official overseas trips was 1.743 billion RMB, expense on government vehicle purchasing and maintenance was 3.088 billion (of which, expense on vehicle purchasing was 110 million RMB and expense on maintenance was 2.978 RMB billion), expense on receptions was 542 million RMB. The total expense were reduced by 943 million RMB from the budget figure in the beginning of 2015, among which, expense on official oversea trips went down by 195 million RMB, expense on government vehicle purchasing and maintenance dropped by 371 million RMB, and expense on receptions was cut by 377 million RMB. In 2016, the budget allocation for the "three public expenses" at the central level was 6.31 billion RMB, of which, the expense on official oversea trips was 2.027 billion RMB, expense on government vehicle purchasing and maintenance was 3.441 billion RMB (of which, expense on vehicle purchasing was 149 million RMB and expense on maintenance was 3.292 billion RMB), and expense on receptions is 842 million RMB. The 2016 budget for those expense is down by 0.1% compared with the budget at the beginning of 2015. In breakdown, the expense on official overseas trips is up by 89 million RMB, expense on government vehicle purchasing and maintenance is reduced by 18 million, and expense on receptions is down by 77 million RMB. The expense on official overseas trips is higher mainly due to increased overseas visits and more participation in international competitions in 2016. The 2016 budget increased by 937 million RMB from the actual execution figure of 2015, an increase of 17.4%, of which, expense on official overseas trips increased by 284 million RMB, expense on government vehicle purchasing and maintenance went up by 353 million RMB, and expense on receptions increased by 300 million RMB. ∎

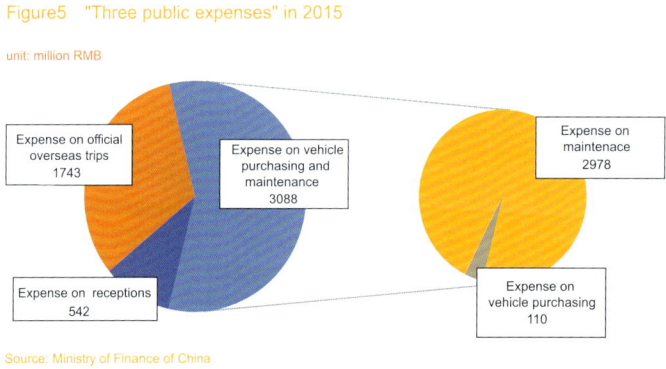

Figure5   "Three public expenses" in 2015
unit: million RMB

Expense on official overseas trips 1743
Expense on vehicle purchasing and maintenance 3088
Expense on receptions 542
Expense on maintenace 2978
Expense on vehicle purchasing 110

Source: Ministry of Finance of China

The performance of Chinese SOEs from January to March

The data published by MOF on April 26 showed that the operating incomes of SOEs totaled 9.94925 trillion RMB from January to March, down by 3% year on year, among which, the figure for central SOEs was 6.14105 trillion RMB, down by 4.6% year on year, and the figure for local SOEs was 3.8082 trillion RMB, down by 0.1% year on year. The operating costs of SOEs totaled 9.69913 trillion RMB, down by 3% year on year, among which, the figure for central SOEs was 5.88302 trillion RMB, down by 4.2% year on year, and the figure for local SOEs was 3.81611 trillion RMB, down by 1.1% year on year. The profits of SOEs totaled 432.3 billion RMB, down by 13.8% year on year, among which, the figure for central SOEs was 339.88 billion RMB, down by 13.2% year on year, and the figure for local SOEs was 92.42 billion RMB, down by 15.8% year on year. The payable taxes of SOEs totaled 941.04 billion RMB, down by 0.4% year on year, among which, the figure for central SOEs was 750.77 billion RMB, down by 0.5% year on year, and the figure for local SOEs was 190.27 billion RMB, up by 0.1% year on year. As of the end of March, the assets of SOEs totaled 122.51551 trillion RMB, up by 15.6% year on year; the liabilities totaled 81.20242 trillion RMB, up by 18.1% year on year; and the owners' equities totaled 41.31309 trillion RMB, up by 10.8% year on year.■

33 China's manufacturing PMI stood at 50.1% in April

According to the data released by NBS on May 1, China's manufacturing PMI was 50.1% in April, a decline of 0.1 percentage point month on month. Compared with the previous month, the PMI for large enterprises was 51.0%, dropping by 0.5 percentage point; for medium-sized business, it was 50.0%, edging up by 0.9 percentage point; and for small businesses, it was 46.9%, a decline of 1.2 percentage points. In categorized indexes, the production index was 52.2%, a decline of 0.1 percentage point; the new orders index was 51.0%, down by 0.4 percentage point; the employee index was 47.8%, a decline of 0.3 percentage point; the raw materials inventory index was 47.4%, decreasing by 0.8 percentage point; and the supplier delivery time index was 50.1%.■

34 China's CPI rose by 2.3% year on year in April

The data released by NBS on May 10 showed that China's CPI rose by 2.3% year on year in April, among which, the CPI rose by 2.3% in urban areas and 2.4% in rural areas; 7.6% for food and 1.1% for non-food; 2.5% for consumer goods and 2.0% for services. Average CPI from January to April edged up by 2.2% year on year. In April, CPI went down by 0.2% month on month, among which, the figure dropped by 0.2% in both urban and rural areas; decreased by 1.4% for food and rose by 0.1% for non-food; fell by 0.4% for consumer goods and went up by 0.2% for services.■

35 China's PPI in April fell by 3.4% year on year

The data released by NBS on May 10 showed that China's PPI in April rose by 0.7% month on month, and fell by 3.4% year on year. IPI went up by 0.6% month on month, and down by 4.4% year on year. The average PPI fell by 4.5% year on year and the average IPI decreased by 5.4% year on year from January to April. With respect to PPI, the price of the means of production dropped by 4.5% year on year, specifically, the figure fell by 13.0% in the extractive industry, 7.7% in the raw material industry, and 2.5% in the processing industry. The price of the means of consumption dropped by 0.2% year on year, specifically, the figure rose by 0.7% for food and apparel, fell by 0.5% for daily necessities, and went down by 1.7% for durable consumer goods.■

36 Housing prices in 70 large and medium-sized Chinese cities in April

According to the data released on May 18 by NBS, compared with March, of the 70 large and medium-sized cities, the price for newly-built commercial housing declined in 5 cities, while increasing in 65 cities. Among the month-on-month price changes, the highest was up by 5.8%, and the lowest was down by 0.5%. In terms of year-on-year comparison, of the 70 cities, the price dropped in 23 cities, increased in 46 cities, and stayed flat in 1 city. In April, the highest year-on-year increase was 63.4%, and the lowest was down by 3.2%. Compared with last month, of the 70 cities, the price of second-hand housing fell in 10 cities, increased in 51 cities, and stayed flat in 9 cities. In terms of month-on-month changes, the highest increase was 6.8%, and the lowest was down by 0.4%. In terms of year-on-year comparison, of the 70 cities, the price dropped in 22 cities, increased in 47 cities, and stayed flat in 1 city. In April, the highest year-on-year price increase was 56.1%, and the lowest was down by 7.2%.∎

37 MOF allocated 27.643 billion RMB of grants for local governments to address overcapacity in steel and coal industries in 2016

According to the data released on May 19 by MOF, MOF allocated 27.643 billion RMB of special restructuring funds for industrial enterprises in 2016. The special fund includes basic incentive grants and progressive grants. Local governments are requested to make co-ordinated use of the fund to resettle laid-off workers.∎

38 The central finance authority has disbursed 134.5 billion RMB of subsidies for compulsory education in urban and rural areas in 2016

The data released by MOF on May 24 showed that the central finance authority has disbursed 134.5 billion RMB of subsidies for compulsory education in urban and rural areas in 2016, an increase of 3% over 2015. In the western region, the subsidy is 600 RMB per primary school student and 800 RMB per middle school student; and in the eastern region, the subsidy is 650 RMB per primary student and 850 RMB per middle school student. The subsidy for urban and rural schools under the compulsory education scheme (including private schools) shall be no lower than the basic standard.∎

39 The central finance authority has earmarked 790 million RMB in 2016 to continue to support the efforts of national modern agricultural demonstration zones to replace subsidies with rewards

The data released by MOF on May 25 showed that the central finance authority has earmarked 790 million RMB in 2016 to continue to support the efforts of national modern agricultural demonstration zones to replace subsidies with rewards. Guided by the principle of "promoting steady output, higher income, better model, and quality, efficient and sustainable production", the funds will be used to strengthen the agricultural industry, improve agricultural production and operation, accelerate the development of demonstration zones and spearhead the agricultural modernization with Chinese characteristics.∎

40 China's lottery sales in March

The data released by MOF on May 25 showed that nationwide lottery sales in March totaled 35.688 billion RMB, up by 4.876 billion RMB year on year, or 15.8%, among which, welfare lottery sales were 19.113 billion RMB, up by 1.29 billion RMB, or 7.2%; sports lottery sales were 16.575 billion RMB, up by 3.586 billion RMB, or 27.6%. Cumulative nationwide lottery sales from January to March totaled 90.784 billion RMB, down by 4.051 billion RMB year on year, or 4.3%, among which, welfare lottery sales were 49.58 billion RMB, down by 941 million RMB, or 1.9%; sports lottery sales were 41.204 billion RMB, down by 3.111 billion RMB, or 7.0%.∎

41 The performance of Chinese SOEs from January to April

The data published by MOF on May 25 showed that the operating incomes of SOEs totaled 13.51706 trillion RMB from January to April, down by 1.7% year on year, among which, the figure for central SOEs was 8.21914 trillion RMB, down by 3.9% year on year, and the figure for local SOEs was 5.29792 trillion RMB, up by 2% year on year. The operating costs of SOEs totaled 13.16728 trillion RMB, down by 1.5% year on year, among which, the figure for central SOEs was 7.87415 trillion RMB, down by 3.4% year on year, and the figure for local SOEs was 5.29313 trillion RMB, up by 1.3% year on year. The profits of SOEs totaled 652.26 billion RMB, down by 8.4% year on year, among which, the figure for central SOEs was 505.41 billion RMB, down by 6.6% year on year, and the figure for local SOEs was 146.85 billion RMB, down by 14.2% year on year. The payable taxes of SOEs totaled 1.22965 trillion RMB, down by 0.8% year on year, among which, the figure for central SOEs was 972.23 billion RMB, down by 1.2% year on year, and the figure for local SOEs was 257.42 billion RMB, up by 0.7% year on year. As of the end of April, the assets of SOEs totaled 123.63323 trillion RMB, up by 15.2% year on year; the liabilities totaled 81.90607 trillion RMB, up by 18% year on year; and the owners' equities totaled 41.72716 trillion RMB, up by 10.1% year on year.∎

42 China's lottery sales in April

The data released by MOF on May 26 showed that nationwide lottery sales in April totaled 34.889 billion RMB, up by 2.277 billion RMB year on year, or 7%, among which, welfare lottery sales were 17.95 billion RMB, down by 138 million RMB, or 0.8%; sports lottery sales were 16.939 billion RMB, up by 2.415 billion RMB, or 16.6%. Cumulative nationwide lottery sales from January to April totaled 125.673 billion RMB, down by 1.775 billion RMB year on year, or 1.4%, among which, welfare lottery sales were 67.53 billion RMB, down by 1.079 billion RMB, or 1.6%; sports lottery sales were 58.143 billion RMB, down by 695 million RMB, or 1.2%.∎

43 Gross profits of industrial enterprises above designated size increased by 6.5% year on year from January to April

According to the data released on May 27 by NBS, from January to April, industrial enterprises above designated size generated a total profit of 1.84422 trillion RMB, an increase of 6.5% year on year, and the pace of growth slowed by 0.9 percentage point compared with that of from January to March. Among the total profits, the state holding enterprises contributed 326.55 billion RMB, down by 7.8%; the collective enterprises contributed 13.73 billion RMB, an increase of 0.4%; the joint-stock enterprises contributed 1.23164 trillion RMB, an increase of 7.4%; foreign and Hong Kong, Macao and Taiwan invested enterprises contributed 476.16 billion RMB, an increase of 7.3%; private enterprises contributed 662.61 billion RMB, an increase of 8.4%. From January to April, mainstay business revenue of industrial enterprises above designated size was 33.56138 trillion RMB, an increase of 2.3%; mainstay business cost was 28.74731 trillion RMB, an increase of 2.1%; profit rate of main business was 5.5%. As of the end of April, the total assets of industrial enterprises above designated size were 98.13082 trillion RMB, an increase of 5.7%; the total liabilities were 55.76814 trillion RMB, an increase of 4.8%; the total equity was 42.36268 trillion RMB, an increase of 6.9%; the assets to liabilities ratio was 56.8%.∎

44 Manufacturing PMI stood at 50.1% in May

According to the data released on June 1 by NBS, China's manufacturing PMI in May was 50.1%, a third consecutive month in expansionary territory. In terms of various sizes of enterprises and compared with last month, the PMI was 50.3% for large enterprises, falling by 0.7 percentage point; 50.5% for medium enterprises, up by 0.5 percentage point; 48.6% for small businesses, up by 1.7 percentage points. In terms of indexes, the production index was 52.3%, edging up by 0.1 percentage point. The new orders index was 50.7%, 0.3 percentage point lower. Employees index was 48.2%, up by 0.4 percentage point. Raw materials inventory index was 47.6%, up by 0.2 percentage point. Supplier delivery time index was 50.4%, increasing by 0.3 percentage point.∎

45 China's CPI rose by 2.0% year on year in May

The data released by NBS on June 9 showed that China's CPI rose by 2.0% year on year in May, among which, the CPI rose by 2.0% in urban areas and 2.1% in rural areas; 5.9% for food and 1.1% for non-food; 2.0% for consumer goods and 2.1% for services. Average CPI from January to May edged up by 2.1% year on year. In May, CPI went down by 0.5% month on month, among which, the figure dropped by 0.5% in urban areas and 0.4% in rural areas; decreased by 2.7% for food and rose by 0.1% for non-food; fell by 0.7% for consumer goods and stayed flat for services.∎

46 China's PPI in May fell by 2.8% year on year

The data released by NBS on June 9 showed that China's PPI in May rose by 0.5% month on month,

FACTS & FIGURES

and fell by 2.8% year on year. IPI went up by 0.6% month on month, and down by 3.8% year on year. The average PPI fell by 4.1% year on year and the average IPI decreased by 5.1% year on year from January to May. With respect to PPI, price of the means of production dropped by 3.7% year on year, specifically, the figure fell by 9.6% in the extractive industry, 7.2% in the raw material industry, and 1.8% in the processing industry. The price of the means of consumption dropped by 0.2% year on year, specifically, the figure rose by 0.6% for food and by 0.7% for apparel, fell by 0.3% for daily necessities, and went down by 1.7% for durable consumer goods. ∎

47 China's fiscal revenue and expenditure in May

According to the data released on June 13 by MOF, in May, the general public budget revenue was 1.5461 trillion RMB, an increase of 7.3% year on year, among which, the central budget revenue was 756.9 billion RMB, down by 2.2%; the local budget revenue was 789.2 billion RMB, an increase of 18.3%. The national tax revenue was 1.3252 trillion RMB, an increase of 8.3%. The national budget expenditure was 1.5461 trillion RMB, an increase of 17.6%, among which, the central budget expenditure was 257.4 billion RMB, down by 4.6%; the local budget expenditure was 1.2887 trillion RMB, an increase of 23.3%. From January to May, the total national budget revenue was 6.988 trillion RMB, an increase of 8.3%, among which, the central budget revenue was 2.9678 trillion RMB, an increase of 0.6%; the local budget revenue was 4.0202 trillion RMB, an increase of 14.9%. The national budget expenditure was 6.6528 trillion RMB, an increase of 13.6%, among which, the central budget expenditure was 1.022 trillion RMB, an increase of 3.8%; the local budget expenditure was 5.6308 trillion RMB, an increase of 15.6%. ∎

48 Private fixed asset investment grew by 3.9% from January to May

According to the data released by NBS on June 13, China's private fixed asset investment was 11.6384 trillion RMB from January to May, an increase of 3.9% in nominal growth rate, down by 1.3 percentage points compared with that of January to April. Private investment accounted for 62.0% of the total national fixed assets investment, down by 3.4 percentage points from the same period of previous year. In terms of various industries, the private fix assets investment in agriculture was 408.6 billion RMB, an increase of 17.9%, down by 0.2 percentage point compared with that of January to April. The investment in manufacturing industry was 5.87 trillion RMB, an increase of 4.6%, down by 1.5 percentage points; and the investment in the service industry was 5.3599 trillion RMB, an increase of 2.2%, down by 1.2 percentage points. ∎

49 MOF is to issue 28 billion RMB of RMB-denominated treasury bonds in Hong Kong

According to the news released by MOF on June 21, with the approval of the State Council, MOF is to issue, in 2 installments, 28 billion RMB of RMB-denominated treasury bonds in Hong Kong in 2016. 14 billion RMB will be issued to the institutional investors on June 29, while the remaining 14 billion

RMB will be issued when appropriate in the second half of this year, and the specific arrangement will be published before its issuance. The RMB-denominated treasury bonds, after their issuance in 2016, will continue to be listed and traded on Hong Kong Exchanges and Clearing Limited. ∎

Economic performance of SOEs from January to May

According to the data released on June 27 by MOF, from January to May, SOEs in China generated a total revenue of 17.15984 trillion RMB, down by 0.6% compared with the same period of last year, among which, the central enterprises contributed 10.3988 trillion RMB, down by 1.7%; local state-owned enterprises contributed 6.76104 trillion RMB, up by 1.2%. The total operating costs of SOEs were 16.70434 trillion RMB, down by 0.3%, of which, the central enterprises accounted for 9.96799 trillion RMB, down by 0.9%; local state-owned enterprises accounted for 6.73635 trillion RMB, increasing by 0.6%. The total profits of SOEs were 837.39 billion RMB, down by 9.6%, among which, the central enterprises generated 624.55 billion RMB, down by 9.6%; local SOEs contributed 212.84 billion RMB, down by 9.6%. Taxes payable of SOEs were 1.51306 trillion RMB, down by 2.3%, among which, there were 1.18896 trillion RMB for the central enterprises, down by 2.7%; and 324.1 billion RMB for local SOEs, down by 1%. As of the end of May, the total assets of SOEs were 124.81337 trillion RMB, an increase of 15.1%; the total liabilities were 82.7573 trillion RMB, an increase of 17.7%; and the total equity was 42.05607 trillion RMB, an increase of 10.2%. ∎

Gross profits of industrial enterprises above designated size increased by 6.4% from January to May

According to the data released on June 27 by NBS, China's industrial enterprises above designated size achieved a total profit of 2.38164 trillion RMB, an increase of 6.4%. Among the total profits, the state holding enterprises contributed 429.02 billion RMB, down by 7.3%; collective enterprises contributed 17.78 billion RMB, down by 2%; joint-stock enterprises contributed 1.59929 trillion RMB, an increase of 7.6%; foreign and Hong Kong, Macao and Taiwan-invested enterprises contributed 608.29 billion RMB, an increase of 6%; private enterprises contributed 848.89 billion RMB, an increase of 9.4%. Main business revenue was 42.62856 trillion RMB, an increase of 2.9%; main business cost occurred was 36.5458 trillion RMB, an increase of 2.7%; the income margin of main business was 5.59%. As of the end of May, the industrial enterprises above designated size registered total assets of 98.56587 trillion RMB, an increase of 5.8%; the total liabilities were 55.95874 trillion RMB, an increase of 4.9%; the total equity was 42.60713 trillion RMB, an increase of 7.1%; the assets to liability ratio was 56.8%. ∎

MOF successfully issued 14 billion RMB treasury bonds in Hong Kong

According to the data released on June 29 by MOF, MOF issued 14 billion RMB of treasury bonds in the HKSAR for institutional investors through bid invitation. The issuance includes 7 billion RMB of 3-year notes, 4.5 billion RMB of 5-year notes, 1 billion RMB of 7-year notes, 1 billion RMB of 10-year notes, and 500 million RMB of 20-year bonds. The bidding rates were 2.90%, 3.25%, 3.30%, 3.38% and 3.90% respectively. ■

53 China's central government final accounts report for 2015

The data released by MOF on July 1 showed that the general public budget revenue at the central government level was 6.926719 trillion RMB in 2015, or 100.1% of the budget, which reached 7.026719 trillion RMB when the 100 billion RMB transferred from the central budget stabilization fund in early 2015 was added. The general public budget expenditure at the central government level was 8.063966 trillion RMB, or 99% of the budget, which reached 8.146719 trillion RMB when the 82.753 billion RMB used to supplement the central budget stabilization fund was added. The revenue could basically cover the expenditure, and the central fiscal deficit stood at 1.112 trillion RMB. The outstanding central government bond was 10.659959 trillion RMB in late 2015, which was within the limit of 11.190835 trillion RMB. In 2015, central governmental fund revenue was 411.819 billion RMB, or 94.4% of the budget, which reached 478.044 billion RMB when the 612 million RMB of transfer from local governments and the 65.613 billion RMB of revenue carried over from 2014 were added. The central governmental fund expenditure was 436.342 billion RMB, or 85.8% of the budget. The central state capital operating income was 161.306 billion RMB, or 104.1% of the budget, which reached 175.704 billion RMB when the 14.398 billion RMB of revenue carried over from 2014 was added. The central state capital operating expenditure was 136.257 billion RMB, completing 80.4% of the budget. ■

54 China's lottery sales in May

The data released by MOF on July 1 showed that nationwide lottery sales in May totaled 34.619 billion RMB, up by 2.512 billion RMB year on year, or 7.8%, among which, welfare lottery sales were 18.374 billion RMB, up by 322 million RMB, or 1.8%; sports lottery sales were 16.245 billion RMB, up by 2.19 billion RMB, or 15.6%. Cumulative nationwide lottery sales from January to May totaled 160.292 billion RMB, up by 738 million RMB year on year, or 0.5%, among which, welfare lottery sales were 85.904 billion RMB, down by 757 million RMB, or 0.9%; sports lottery sales were 74.388 billion RMB, up by 1.495 billion RMB, or 2.1%. ■

55 China's manufacturing PMI in June was 50.0%

The data published by NBS on July 1 showed that China's manufacturing PMI in June was 50.0%, down by 0.1 percentage point month on month. In breakdown, PMI was 51.0% for large-sized enterprises, up by 0.7 percentage point month on month; 49.1% for medium-sized ones, down by 1.4 percentage points month on month; and 47.4% for small-sized ones, down by 1.2 percentage points month on month. In specific terms, the production index was 52.5%, up by 0.2 percentage point month on month; the new order index was 50.5%, down by 0.2 percentage point month on month;

the employee index was 47.9%, down by 0.3 percentage point month on month; the raw material inventory index was 47.0%, down by 0.6 percentage point month on month; and the supplier delivery time index was 50.7%, up by 0.3 percentage point month on month.■

56　China's CPI rose by 1.9% in June

According to the data released on July 10 by NBS, CPI in China rose by 1.9% in June year on year, among which, the prices rose by 1.9% for cities and rural areas; increased by 4.6% for food and 1.2% for non-food products; and went up by 1.7% for consumer goods and 2.2% for services. In the first half of the year, CPI increased by 2.1% year on year. In June, CPI fell by 0.1% month on month, among which, the prices dropped by 0.1% for cities and rural areas, down by 1.4% for food and up by 0.2% for non-food products, while down by 0.4% for consumer goods and up by 0.3% for services.■

57　Industrial producer prices fell by 2.6% in June

According to the data released on July 10 by NBS, China's industrial producer prices decreased by 0.2% in June month on month, or down by 2.6% year on year. Industrial purchase price rose by 0.2% month on month, or down by 3.4% year on year. In the first half of the year, industrial producer prices fell by 3.9% year on year, and the industrial purchase price fell by 4.8%. Industrial producer prices for production materials fell by 3.5%, among which, the mining and quarrying industry fell by 8.2%, industrial raw materials fell by 6.1%, and processing industry fell by 2.0%. Prices of consumer goods fell by 0.1%, among which, the prices rose by 0.6% for food and 1.0% for clothing, remained on par for consumer non-durables, while dropped by 1.7% for consumer durables.■

58　The central government allocated 800 million RMB as emergency disaster relief funds

According to the data released on July 12 by MOF, in order to fight against flooding in southern regions caused by heavy rainfall, MOF and relevant ministries allocated 800 million RMB as emergency disaster relief funds, including 500 million RMB of subsidies for fighting against severe flooding and drought. The special relief went to Jiangsu, Zhejiang, Anhui, Henan, Hubei, Hunan, Guangxi, Sichuan, Chongqing, Guizhou and other provinces (autonomous regions and municipalities) for their efforts in flood control and disaster relief, as well as repairment of damaged water conservancy facilities. The funds also included 300 million RMB relief for agricultural production, which supports replanting and agricultural recovery in Jiangsu, Anhui, Jiangxi Hubei, Hunan, and Sichuan Province, and etc..■

FACTS & FIGURES

MOF arranged 199 million RMB of grants for artificial weather intervention

According to the data released on July 14 by MOF, in consideration of the severity of meteorological disasters, weather and climate forecasting, artificial weather intervention requirements and fiscal resources at the provincial level, 199 million RMB of grants for artificial weather intervention were arranged in 2016. The funds are to be used to support local governments' efforts in fighting drought by introducing more rainfall, and in hailstone disaster reduction. The funds have provided a solid foundation to alleviate economic and social impacts of meteorological disasters, enhance capacity-building against drought and hailstones in major grain producing areas, and improve people's livelihood and working conditions.∎

China's GDP grew by 6.7% in the first half of 2016

According to the data released on July 15 by NBS, China's GDP stood at 34.0637 trillion RMB in the first half of the year. Calculated at comparable prices, it has grown by 6.7% year on year. The first and second quarter growth was 6.7% each. The value-added of primary industry was 2.2097 trillion, an increase of 3.1%; the secondary industry was 13.425 trillion RMB, an increase of 6.1%; the tertiary industry was 18.429 trillion RMB, an increase of 7.5%. The second quarter GDP growth was 1.8% over the first quarter.∎

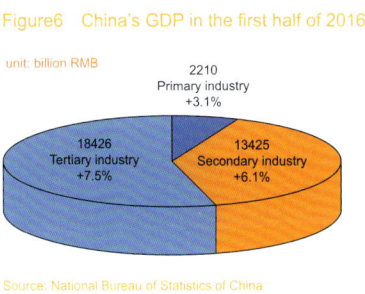

Figure6   China's GDP in the first half of 2016

Source: National Bureau of Statistics of China

China's fiscal revenue and expenditure in June

The data released by MOF on July 15 showed that revenue under China's general public budget was 1.5634 trillion RMB in June, up by 1.7% year on year, among which, revenue at the central government level was 748.6 billion RMB, up by 16%; revenue at the local government level was 814.8 billion RMB, down by 8.6%. Expenditure under China's general public budget was 2.2637 trillion RMB, up by 19.9% year on year, among which, expenditure at the central government level was 274.9 billion RMB, up by 22.1%; expenditure at the local government level was 1.9888 trillion RMB, up by 19.6%. Cumulative revenue under the national governmental fund from January to June was 1.8335 trillion RMB, up by 7.5%; expenditure under the national governmental fund was 1.664 trillion RMB, down by 1.5% year on year.∎

The central finance disbursed 66.095 billion RMB for poverty reduction

The data released by MOF on July 19 showed that the central finance, in accordance with the requirements of targeted poverty reduction, has substantially increased the fiscal resources for poverty reduction in 2016. A total of 66.095 billion RMB was made available in the central government budget for poverty reduction of localities, up by 43.4% over the previous year. Up to now, all these funds have been disbursed to the localities. ■

38.3 billion RMB of transfer payment funds for comprehensive agricultural development in 2016 have been disbursed

The data released by MOF on July 20 showed that the central finance has recently disbursed 12.659 billion RMB of transfer payment for comprehensive agricultural development in addition to the tranche of 25.641 billion RMB disbursed in early 2016. As a result, all the transfer payment funds for comprehensive agricultural development in 2016 have been disbursed, up by 1.8 billion RMB over the previous year, or 4.9%. ■

39.997 billion RMB of funds for farmland water conservancy facilities and water and soil conservation in 2016 have been disbursed

The data released by MOF on July 20 showed that the central finance has made available 39.997 billion RMB for farmland water conservancy facilities and water and soil conservation, and all the funds have been disbursed as of early May. Among the 39.997 billion RMB, 21.962 billion RMB was used to support farmland water conservancy facilities, mainly the large-scale water efficient irrigation; 4.58 billion RMB was used for water diversion and spare wells as required by the national anti-drought plan; 5.3 billion RMB was used to support the rehabilitation of areas in Hebei Province with problems of groundwater over-extraction; 4.855 billion RMB was used for the repair and maintenance of water conservancy facilities and the price reform of water for agricultural purpose; 3.3 billion RMB was used to support the conservation of water and soil and the removal of the hazards of the silt retention dams, with particular attention to poor region and old revolutionary bases. ■

18.5 billion RMB of funds for the comprehensive treatment of the water system involving rivers, lakes and reservoirs have been disbursed

The data released by MOF on July 21 showed that the central finance has arranged 18.5 billion RMB of funds for the comprehensive treatment of the water system involving rivers, lakes and reservoirs. The funds have all been disbursed as of mid-June, among which, 10 billion was used for the treatment of medium and small sized rivers and key counties; 5.361 billion RMB was used for the construction of small sized reservoirs required by the national anti-drought plan; 3 billion RMB was used for the connectivity of rivers, lakes and reservoirs; and 139 million RMB was used for the (second phase) development of national water resource surveillance capacity. ■

FACTS & FIGURES

66 Annual final accounts of MOF in 2015

According to the data released on July 22 by MOF, in 2015, the annual revenue of MOF totaled 15.1326684 billion RMB, and the spending was 15.1326684 billion RMB. Compared with 2014, both the revenue and expenditure increased by 10.637368 billion RMB, or 236.63%. The revenue from the current year was 13.6801306 billion RMB, among which, the fiscal allocation revenue was 12.6877 billion RMB, accounting for 92.75%; revenue from public services was 804.7972 million RMB, accounting for 5.88%; operating income was 31.2467 million RMB, accounting for 0.23%; and other income was 156.3867 million RMB, accounting for 1.14%. The total expenditures of the current year were 1.35960169 billion RMB, among which, the basic expenditure was 1.4900926 billion RMB,

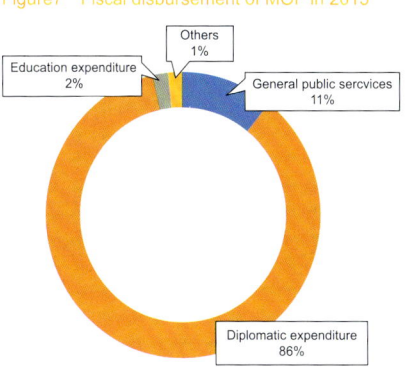

Figure7 Fiscal disbursement of MOF in 2015

Source: Ministry of Finance of China

accounting for 10.96%; project expenditure was 12.0818326 billion RMB, accounting for 88.86%; operating expense was 24.0917 million RMB, accounting for 0.18%. In the fiscal year of 2015, fiscal disbursement was 12.7478759 billion RMB, mainly used in the following areas: expenditure for general public services was 1.3838417 billion RMB, accounting for 10.85%; diplomatic expenditure was 10,932,976,300 RMB, accounting for 85.76%; education expenditure was 228.72 million RMB, accounting for 1.79%; science and technology spending was 134,000 RMB, accounting for 0.01%; culture, sports and media spending was 49.8027 million RMB, accounting for 0.39%; social security and employment expenditure was 92.5762 million RMB, accounting for 0.73%; agriculture, forestry and water expenditure was 9.4269 million RMB, accounting for 0.07%; housing security expenditure was 50.3981 million RMB, accounting for 0.40%.■

67 Economic performance of SOEs from January to June

According to the data released on July 26 by MOF, from January to June, total revenues of state-owned enterprises were 21.38758 trillion RMB, down by 0.1%, among which, the central enterprises contributed 12.952 trillion RMB, down by 1.3%; local SOEs contributed 8.43558 trillion RMB, an increase of 1.8%. Total operating costs were 20.82668 trillion RMB, an increase of 0.2%, among which, the costs for central enterprises were 12.42431 trillion RMB, down by 0.5%; and the costs for local SOEs were 8.40237 trillion RMB, an increase of 1.2%. The total profits were 1.12724 trillion RMB, down by 8.5%, among which, the profits for central enterprises were 798.37 billion RMB, down by 9%; the profits for local SOEs were 328.87 billion RMB, down by 7.1%. Taxes payable were 1.83509 trillion RMB, down by 3%. As of the end of June, total assets of SOEs were 125.95397 trillion RMB, an increase of 15.2%; the total liabilities were 83.54972 trillion RMB, up by 17.8%; and the owner's equity was 42.40425 trillion RMB, an increase of 10.3%.■

68 The gross profits of industrial enterprises above designated size increased by 6.2% from January to June

According to the data released by NBS on July 27, from January to June, the industrial enterprises above designated size realized a total profit of 2.99982 trillion RMB, an increase of 6.2% year on year, though the pace of growth rate went down by 0.2 percentage point from May. The main business revenue of those enterprises was 52.84123 trillion RMB, an increase of 3.1%; the main business cost occurred was 45.33009 trillion RMB, an increase of 3%; the profit margin of main business was 5.68%. At end-June, the total assets of industrial enterprises above designated size were 99.44609 trillion RMB, an increase of 5.7%; the total liabilities were 56.32049 trillion RMB, an increase of 4.6%; and the owner's equity was 43.1256 trillion RMB, an increase of 7%; the asset-to-liability ratio was 56.6%.∎

69 China's manufacturing PMI in July was 49.9%

The data published by NBS on August 1 showed that China's manufacturing PMI in July was 49.9%, down by 0.1 percentage point month on month. In a breakdown of enterprises, PMI was 51.2% for large-sized ones, up by 0.2 percentage point month on month; 48.9% for medium-sized ones, down by 0.2 percentage point month on month; and 46.9% for small-sized ones, down by 0.5 percentage point month on month. In specific terms, the production index was 52.1%, down by 0.4 percentage point month on month; the new order index was 50.4%, down by 0.1 percentage point month on month; the employee index was 48.2%, up by 0.3 percentage point month on month; the raw material inventory index was 47.3%, up by 0.3 percentage point month on month; and the supplier delivery time index was 50.5%, down by 0.2 percentage month on month.∎

70 China's lottery sales in June

The data released by MOF on August 2 showed that nationwide lottery sales in June totaled 33.961 billion RMB, up by 5.837 billion RMB year on year, or 20.8%, among which, welfare lottery sales were 16.381 billion RMB, up by 198 million RMB, or 1.2%; sports lottery sales were 17.58 billion RMB, up by 5.639 billion RMB, or 47.2%. Cumulative nationwide lottery sales from January to June totaled 194.253 billion RMB, up by 6.575 billion RMB year on year, or 3.5%, among which, welfare lottery sales were 102.285 billion RMB, down by 559 million RMB, or 0.5%; sports lottery sales were 91.968 billion RMB, up by 7.134 billion RMB, or 8.4%.∎

71 China's CPI went up by 1.8% in July

According to the data released on August 9 by CPI went up by 1.8% in July year on year. The prices grew by 1.8% in cities and 1.5% in rural areas. The food prices went up by 3.3%, and the non-food prices increased 1.4%. The prices of consumer goods went up by 1.4% and the prices of services grew by 2.3%. On month-on-month terms, the CPI grew by 0.2%. The prices grew by 0.3% in cities and remained stable in rural areas. The food prices dropped by 0.2% and the non-food prices increased 0.3%. The prices of consumer goods dropped by 0.3% and prices of services grew by 0.6%.■

PPI in July declined by 1.7%

According to the data released on August 9 by the NBS, Producer Price Index (PPI) for manufactured goods increased 0.2% month on month in July, and decreased 1.7% year on year. The purchasing price index for manufactured goods increased 0.3% month on month, and decreased 2.6% year on year. On average from January to July, the PPI decreased 3.6% year on year, the purchasing price index for manufactured goods went down by 4.5% year on year.■

China's fiscal revenue and expenditure in July

The data released by MOF on August 12 showed that revenue under China's general public budget was 1.477 trillion RMB in July, up by 3.3% year on year, among which, revenue at the central government level was 775 billion RMB, up by 9.8%; revenue at the local government level was 702 billion RMB, down by 3%. Expenditure under the general public budget was 1.2768 trillion RMB, up by 0.3% year on year, among which, expenditure at the central government level was 218.9 billion RMB, down by 7.4%; expenditure at the local government level was 1.0579 trillion RMB, up by 2%. Cumulative revenue under the national governmental fund from January to July was 2.1968 trillion RMB, up by 9.4%; expenditure under the national governmental fund was 1.9917 trillion RMB, up by 2.7% year on year.■

China's manufacturing PMI in August was 50.4%

The data published by NBS on September 1 showed that China's manufacturing PMI in August was 50.4%, up by 0.5 percentage point month on month. In a breakdown of enterprises, PMI was 51.8% for large-sized ones, up by 0.6 percentage point month on month; 48.9% for medium-sized ones, staying flat month on month; and 47.4% for small-sized ones, up by 0.5 percentage point month on month. In specific terms, the production index was 52.6%, up by 0.5 percentage point month on month; the new order index was 51.3%, up by 0.9 percentage point month on month; the employee index was 48.4%, up by 0.2 percentage point month on month; the raw material inventory index was 47.6%, up by 0.3 percentage point month on month; and the supplier delivery time index was 50.6%, up by 0.1 percentage month on month.■

The growth rate of China's electricity consumption and production gathered pace in July

The data published by NBS on September 1 showed that China's electricity consumption in July increased by 8.2% year on year, up by 5.6 percentage points over the comparable figure in June. From January to July, electricity consumption of the society rose by 3.6%, up by 0.9 percentage point over the comparable figure from January to June. In July, the electricity consumption of industrial firms went up by 6.9% year on year, up by 5.5 percentage points over the comparable figure in June; the electricity consumption of the service industry climbed by 15.3%, up by 7.3 percentage points over the comparable figure in June. In July, the electricity consumption of major industrial firms rose by 7.2%, the biggest increase since February 2014, and up by 5.1 percentage points over the comparable figure in June; from January to July, the electricity consumption of major industrial firms rose by 2%, up by 1 percentage point over the comparable figure from January to June. ∎

The central government allocated 333 million RMB of comprehensive agricultural development funds to support new agricultural business entities to develop high-standard farmland

According to the data released on September 8 by MOF, the central government has disbursed the first batch of comprehensive agricultural development funds, totaling 333 million RMB, which was allocated to 216 new agricultural business entities in 23 provinces, to develop high-standard farmland. The funds have attracted 110 million RMB of self-financing and are expected to be used in developing 350,000 acres of high standard farmland. ∎

China's imports and exports grew by 6% in August month on month

According to the data released on September 8 by GAC, China's imports and exports in August totaled 2.19599 trillion RMB. The month-on-month growth was 6%, and the year-on-year growth was 7.9%. The imports were 1.271008 trillion RMB, the month-on-month growth was 5.9%, on par with the year-on-year growth. The exports were 924.982 billion RMB, the month-on-month growth was 6.1%, and the year-on-year growth was 10.8%. In the first 8 months, the accumulated imports and exports amounted to 15.366027 trillion RMB. ∎

The performance of Chinese SOEs from January to July

The data published by MOF on September 13 showed that the operating incomes of SOEs totaled 24.88355 trillion RMB from January to July, up by 0.2% year on year, among which, the figure for central SOEs was 15.06883 trillion RMB, down by 0.9% year on year, and the figure for local SOEs was 9.81472 trillion RMB, up by 1.8% year on year. The operating costs of SOEs totaled 24.20461 trillion RMB, down by 2.3% year on year, among which, the figure for central SOEs was 14.44905 trillion RMB, down by 0.1% year on year, and the figure for local SOEs was 9.75556 trillion RMB, down by 5.4% year on year. The profits of SOEs totaled 1.3128 trillion RMB, down by 6.5% year on year, among which, the figure for central SOEs was 915.97 billion RMB, down by 9% year on year, and the figure for local SOEs was 396.83 billion RMB, down by 0.3% year on year. The payable taxes

FACTS & FIGURES

of SOEs totaled 2.11344 trillion RMB, down by 2% year on year, among which, the figure for central SOEs was 1.64169 trillion RMB, down by 3.2% year on year, and the figure for local SOEs was 471.75 billion RMB, up by 2.2% year on year. As of the end of July, the assets of SOEs totaled 126.51074 trillion RMB, up by 15.2% year on year; the liabilities totaled 83.74178 trillion RMB, up by 17.6% year on year; and the owners' equities totaled 42.76896 trillion RMB, up by 10.7% year on year. ∎

79 China's fiscal revenue and expenditure in August

The data released by MOF on September 13 showed that revenue under China's general public budget was 989.4 billion RMB in August, up by 1.7% year on year, among which, revenue at the central government level was 479.7 billion RMB, up by 2.5%; revenue at the local government level was 509.7 billion RMB, up by 1%; tax revenue was 768 billion RMB, up by 1.9% year on year. Expenditure under China's general public budget was 1.4187 trillion RMB in August, up by 10.3% year on year, among which, expenditure at the central government level was 216.5 billion RMB, up by 3.2%; expenditure at the local government level was 1.2022 trillion RMB, up by 11.7%. ∎

80 China's lottery sales in July

The data released by MOF on September 21 showed that nationwide lottery sales in July totaled 32.403 billion RMB, up by 5.356 billion RMB year on year, or 19.8%, among which, welfare lottery sales were 16.622 billion RMB, up by 1.045 billion RMB year on year, or 6.7%; sports lottery sales were 15.781 billion RMB, up by 4.31 billion RMB, or 37.6%. Cumulative nationwide lottery sales from January to July totaled 226.656 billion RMB, up by 11.931 billion RMB year on year, or 5.6%, among which, welfare lottery sales were 118.907 billion RMB, up by 486 million RMB, or 0.4%; sports lottery sales were 107.749 billion RMB, up by 11.445 billion RMB, or 11.9%. ∎

81 China's electricity consumption and production continued to maintain rapid growth in August

The data published by NBS on September 19 showed that China's electricity consumption in August increased by 8.3% year on year, up by 0.1 percentage point over July. From January to August, nationwide electricity consumption rose by 4.2% year on year, up by 0.6 percentage point over the comparable figure from January to July. In August, the electricity consumption of industrial firms went up by 4.8% year on year; the figure for urban and rural households increased by 19.9%; and the figure for the service industry climbed by 15.5%. The electricity consumption of major industrial firms rose by 7.8% year on year, up by 0.6 percentage point over July; from January to August, the electricity consumption of major industrial firms rose by 3%, up by 1 percentage point over the comparable figure from January to July. ∎

82. MOF and the Ministry of Civil Affairs disbursed 220 million RMB from central budget for disaster relief

According to the news released on September 27 by MOF, MOF and the MOCA disbursed 220 million RMB from the central budget for natural disaster relief in Fujian and Zhejiang Province, mainly for emergency resettlement, living allowance, rehabilitation and condolences for the victims.

83. China's lottery sales in August

According to the data released on September 23 by MOF, the lottery sales in August totaled 31.012 billion RMB, an increase of 29.15 billion RMB or 10.4%. Among the total sales, welfare lottery sales were 158.89 billion RMB, an increase of 866 million RMB or 5.8%; sports lottery sales were 15.123 billion RMB, an increase of 2.049 billion yuan or 15.7%. From January to August, the total lottery sales were 257.667 billion RMB, an increase of 14.846 billion RMB or 6.1%. The welfare lottery sales contributed 134.796 billion RMB, an increase of 1.352 billion RMB or 1.0%; sports lottery sales were 122.871 billion RMB, an increase of 13.494 billion RMB or 12.3%.

84. The performance of Chinese SOEs from January to August

The data published by MOF on September 29 showed that the operating revenue of SOEs totaled 28.66525 trillion RMB from January to August, up by 0.2% year on year. The operating costs of SOEs totaled 27.88092 trillion RMB, up by 0.3% year on year, among which, the sales expenses and the management expenses increased by 5.4% and 6.3% respectively and the financial expenses fell by 6.8%. The profits of SOEs totaled 1.54182 trillion RMB, down by 1.3% year on year. The payable taxes of SOEs totaled 2.42283 trillion RMB, down by 1.9% year on year. As of the end of August, the assets of SOEs totaled 127.89417 trillion RMB, up by 15.1% year on year; the liabilities totaled 84.64538 trillion RMB, up by 17.5% year on year; and the owners' equities totaled 43.24879 trillion RMB, up by 10.6% year on year.

85. China's manufacturing PMI in September was 50.4%

The data published by NBS on October 1 showed that China's manufacturing PMI in September was 50.4%, staying flat month on month. In a breakdown of enterprises, PMI was 52.6% for large-sized ones, up by 0.8 percentage point month on month; 48.2% for medium-sized ones, down by 0.7 percentage point month on month; and 46.1% for small-sized ones, down by 1.3 percentage points month on month. In specific terms, the production index was 52.8%, up by 0.2 percentage point month on month; the new order index was 50.9%, down by 0.4 percentage point month on month; the employee index was 48.6%, up by 0.2 percentage point month on month; the raw material inventory index was 47.4%, down by 0.2 percentage point month on month; and the supplier delivery time index was 49.9%, down by 0.7 percentage point month on month.

FACTS & FIGURES

86 ▶ 1.298 billion RMB was disbursed by MOF to raise the standard of benefits and allowances for the disabled veterans and other people entitled to special care by the government

The data published by MOF on October 10 showed that 1.298 billion RMB was disbursed by MOF to raise the standard of benefits and allowances for the disabled veterans, old Red Army soldiers and family members of the deceased servicemen. Until now, 38.371 billion RMB was spent on the allowances and benefits for 8.8 million people in 2016. ∎

87 ▶ China's total imports and exports fell by 1.2% month on month in September

The data released by GAC on October 13 showed that in September China's imports totaled 944.785 billion RMB, up by 2.2% month on month and 2.2% year on year; exports amounted to 1.223139 trillion RMB, down by 3.6% month on month and 5.6% year on year; total imports and exports reached 2.167924 trillion RMB, down by 1.2% month on month and 2.4% year on year. ∎

88 ▶ China's CPI rose by 1.9% year on year in September

The data released by NBS on October 14 showed that China's CPI rose by 1.9% year on year in September, among which, the CPI rose by 2.0% in urban areas and 1.6% in rural areas; 3.2% for food and 1.6% for non-food; 1.7% for consumer goods and 2.4% for services. In September, CPI edged up by 0.7% month on month, among which, the figure rose by 0.7% in urban areas and 0.7% in rural areas; increased by 1.7% for food and 0.4% for non-food; went up by 0.8% for consumer goods and 0.5% for services. ∎

89 ▶ China's fiscal revenue and expenditure in September

According to the data released on October 19 by MOF, China's public revenue in September was 1.1222 trillion RMB, an increase of 4.9%. Among the total revenue, the central government revenue was 491.7 billion RMB, an increase of 6.2%; the local government income was 630.5 billion RMB, an increase of 3.8%. The national tax revenue was 824.3 billion RMB, down by 0.75% year on year, which was mainly due to the tax-cutting effects of rolling-out of VAT reform. In September, the national public expenditure was 1.9836 trillion RMB, an increase of 11.3%. Among the total expenditure, the central government expenditure was 213.9 billion RMB, an increase of 12.4%; the local government expenditure was 1769.7 billion RMB, growing by 11.1%. From January to September, the national income from government funds was 2977.7 billion RMB, an increase of 11.3%. The national expenditure from government funds was 2.8121 trillion RMB, an increase of 7%. ∎

CHINA FINANCE 2016

90 Preliminary accounting results of GDP for the third Quarter of 2016

According to the data released on October 20 by the NBS, the third-quarter GDP grew by 6.7%. The output of primary industry was 1.8569 trillion RMB, an increase of 4%; the secondary industry was 7.5165 trillion RMB, an increase of 6.1%; and the tertiary industry was 9.5601 trillion RMB, an increase of 7.6%. GDP in the first three quarters of 2016 was 5.299710 trillion RMB, an increase of 6.7%. ∎

91 China's lottery sales in September

The data released by MOF on October 26 showed that nationwide lottery sales in September totaled 32.071 billion RMB, up by 2.993 billion RMB year on year, or 10.3%, among which, welfare lottery sales were 16.544 billion RMB, up by 1.044 billion RMB year on year, or 6.7%; sports lottery sales were 15.527 billion RMB, up by 1.95 billion RMB, or 14.4%. Cumulative nationwide lottery sales from January to September totaled 289.738 billion RMB, up by 17.839 billion RMB year on year, or 6.6%, among which, welfare lottery sales were 151.34 billion RMB, up by 2.396 billion RMB, or 1.6%; sports lottery sales were 138.399 billion RMB, up by 15.443 billion RMB, or 12.6%. ∎

92 The performance of Chinese SOEs from January to September

The data published by MOF on October 26 showed that the operating incomes of SOEs totaled 32.70158 trillion RMB from January to September, up by 0.8% year on year, among which, the figure for central SOEs was 19.78746 trillion RMB, down by 0.4% year on year, and the figure for local SOEs was 12.91412 trillion RMB, up by 2.7% year on year. The operating costs of SOEs totaled 31.81796 trillion RMB, up by 0.8% year on year, among which, the figure for central SOEs was 18.99292 trillion RMB, staying flat year on year, and the figure for local SOEs was 12.82504 trillion RMB, down by 2% year on year. The profits of SOEs totaled 1.72068 trillion RMB, down by 1.6% year on year, among which, the figure for central SOEs was 1.19156 trillion RMB, down by 5.4% year on year, and the figure for local SOEs was 529.12 billion RMB, up by 8.1% year on year. The payable taxes of SOEs totaled 2.75519 trillion RMB, down by 1.7% year on year, among which, the figure for central SOEs was 2.13433 trillion RMB, down by 3% year on year, and the figure for local SOEs was 620.86 billion RMB, up by 3.3% year on year. As of the end of September, the assets of SOEs totaled 128.76779 trillion RMB, up by 9.7% year on year; the liabilities totaled 85.34485 trillion RMB, up by 9.9% year on year; and the owners' equities totaled 43.42294 trillion RMB, up by 9.3% year on year. ∎

93 China's manufacturing PMI in October stood at 51.2%

According to the data released by NBS on November 1, in October, China's manufacturing PMI was 51.2%, an increase of 0.8 percentage point month on month. In breakdown of the sizes of enterprises,

FACTS & FIGURES

the PMI of large-sized enterprises was 52.5%, decreasing 0.1 percentage point month on month; that of medium-sized and small-sized enterprises were 49.9% and 48.3%, increasing 1.7 percentage and 2.2 percentage points respectively. In breakdown of the sub-indices, production index was 53.3%, an increase of 0.5 percentage point month on month. New orders index was 52.8%, increasing 1.9 percentage points month on month. Employee index was 48.8%, increasing 0.2 percentage point month on month. Raw materials inventory index was 48.1%, an increase of 0.7 percentage point over the last month. Supplier delivery time index was 50.2%, an increase of 0.3 percentage point over the last month. ∎

94 The final accounts of China's Social Security Fund in 2015

The data released by MOF on November 9 showed that national social insurance revenue totaled 4.6354 trillion RMB in 2015, up by 14.6% year on year; expenditure totaled 3.9118 trillion RMB, up by 16.1% year on year; the balance between revenue and expenditure stood at 723.6 billion RMB in 2015, and the cumulative balance in 2015-end reached 5.8893 trillion RMB. The revenue of the basic pension fund for enterprise employees was 2.6554 trillion RMB, up by 328.1 billion RMB year on year, or an increase of 14.1%, completing 109.2% of the budget. The revenue of the basic pension fund for urban and rural residents was 287.9 billion RMB, up by 53.6 billion RMB year on year, or an increase of 22.9%, completing 104.6% of the budget. The revenue of the basic health insurance fund for urban employees was 892.6 billion RMB, up by 107.2 billion RMB year on year, or an increase of 13.6%, completing 107.6% of the budget. The revenue of the basic health insurance fund for residents was 540.5 billion RMB, up by 92.8 billion RMB year on year, or an increase of 20.7%, completing 104.6% of the budget. The revenue of the work-related injury insurance fund was 72.9 billion RMB, up by 5.8 billion RMB over the previous year, or an increase of 8.6%, completing 102.7% of the budget. The revenue of the unemployment insurance fund was 136.5 billion RMB, down by 1.5 billion RMB over the previous year, or a decrease of 1.1%, completing 97.4% of the budget. The revenue of the maternity insurance fund was 49.6 billion RMB, up by 5.7 billion RMB over the previous year, or an increase of 13.0%, completing 108.5% of the budget. ∎

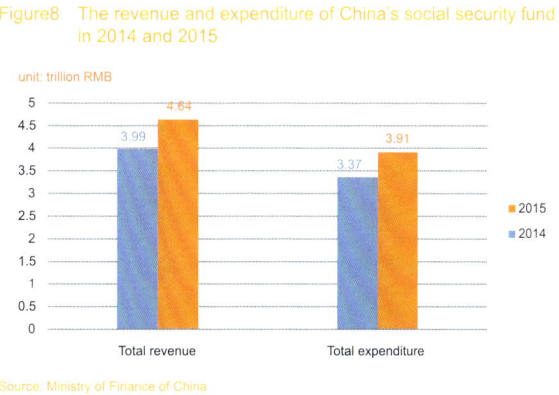

Figure8 The revenue and expenditure of China's social security fund in 2014 and 2015

Source: Ministry of Finance of China

95 China's CPI rose by 2.1% year on year in October

The data released by NBS on November 9 showed that China's CPI rose by 2.1% year on year in

October, among which, the CPI rose by 2.2% in urban areas and 1.8% in rural areas; 3.7% for food and 1.7% for non-food; 1.9% for consumer goods and 2.5% for services. The average CPI from January to October was 2.0% higher than the same period of last year. In October, CPI edged down by 0.1% month on month, among which, the figure dipped by 0.1% in both urban and rural areas; decreased by 1.0% for food and rose by 0.1% for non-food; went down by 0.2% for consumer goods and stayed flat for services.■

China's PPI in October rose by 1.2% year on year

The data released by NBS on November 9 showed that China's PPI in October rose by 0.7% month on month, and went up by 1.2% year on year. IPI went up by 0.9% month on month, and up by 0.9% year on year. The average PPI fell by 2.5% year on year and the average IPI decreased by 3.3% year on year from January to October. The price of the means of production rose by 1.6% year on year, and the price of the means of consumption increased by 0.1% year on year.■

China's fiscal revenue and expenditure in October

According to the data released on November 14 by MOF, China's public revenue was 1,535.9 billion RMB, an increase of 5.9% year on year. Among the total revenue, the central government revenue was 796.3 billion RMB, an increase of 9.9%; local government revenue was 739.6 billion RMB, an increase of 1.9%. The public expenditure was 1181.9 billion RMB, down by 12.5%. Among the total expenditure, the central government expenditure was 199 billion RMB, an increase of 5.6%; and the local government expenditure was 982.9 billion RMB, down by 15.5%. In the first ten months, revenue from national governmental funds was 3,368.5 billion RMB, growing by 12.3%; the expenditure from national governmental funds was 3,120.7 billion RMB, up by 8.5%.■

China's private investment in fixed assets increased by 2.9% during the first ten months of 2016

According to the data released on November 14 by NBS, in the first ten months of 2016, the private investment in fixed assets reached 29,772.5 billion RMB, an increase of 2.9% year on year in nominal terms, and the growth rate was 0.4 percentage point higher than that in the first nine months. The proportion of private investment in fixed assets to the total investment in fixed assets was 61.5%, an increase of 0.1 percentage point over the first nine months, and 3.2 percentage points lower year on year. In term of different areas, the private investment in fixed assets in eastern region amounted to 13,372.1 billion RMB, rising by 7.1% year on year; that of central region was 8,606.8 billion RMB, increasing 6.2%; that of western region was 5,874.9 billion RMB, increasing 2.5%; that of northeastern region was 1,918.8 billion RMB, decreasing 26.8%. In term of different industries, the private investment in fixed assets in primary industry reached 1,218.5 billion RMB, a year on year increase of 19.0%; that in the secondary industry amounted to 14,904.1 billion RMB, increasing 2.4%; that in the tertiary industry was 13,650.0 billion RMB, going up by 2.1%.■

FACTS & FIGURES

The added value of the industrial enterprises above designated size was up by 6.1% in October

According to the data released on November 14 by NBS, in October 2016, the total value added of the industrial enterprises above designated size was up by 6.1% year on year in real terms, remaining at the same level over September. In October 2016, the total value added of the industrial enterprises above designated size went up by 0.5% month on month. In the first ten months of 2016, the total value added of the industrial enterprises above designated size was up by 6.0% year on year. In breakdown of sectors, the value added of mining and quarrying decreased 2.2% in October, that of manufacturing increased 6.7%, and that of production and distribution of electricity, heating power, gas and water was up by 7.9% year on year. In breakdown of different types of enterprises, in October, the value added of the state holding enterprises increased 3.2% year on year, that of collective enterprises decreased 3.8%, that of joint-stock enterprises increased 6.8%, that of enterprises funded by foreign investors or investors from Hong Kong, Macao and Taiwan increased 4.8%.∎

China's lottery sales in October

The data released by MOF on November 22 showed that nationwide lottery sales in October totaled 33.827 billion RMB, up by 2.593 billion RMB year on year, or 8.3%, among which, welfare lottery sales were 17.307 billion RMB, up by 975 million RMB year on year, or 6%; sports lottery sales were 16.52 billion RMB, up by 1.618 billion RMB, or 10.9%. Cumulative nationwide lottery sales from January to October totaled 323.565 billion RMB, up by 20.432 billion RMB year on year, or 6.7%, among which, welfare lottery sales were 168.647 billion RMB, up by 3.371 billion RMB, or 2%; sports lottery sales were 154.919 billion RMB, up by 17.061 billion RMB, or 12.4%.∎

Industrial profits of enterprises above designated size increased by 8.6% in the first ten months of 2016

According to the data released on November 27 by NBS, in the first 10 months, the profits made by industrial enterprises above the designated size reached 5,256.77 billion RMB, an increase of 8.6% year on year, and the growth rate was up by 0.2 percentage point over the first nine months. Among the enterprises, the profits of state-holding industrial enterprises gained 957.7 billion RMB, increasing by 4.8% year on year; that of collective-owned enterprises reached 37.57 billion RMB, a decrease of 2.7%; that of joint-stock enterprises stood at 3,601.07 billion RMB, up by 8.9%; that of foreign-funded enterprises, and enterprises funded by Hong Kong, Macao and Taiwan totalled 1,303.33 billion RMB, increasing by 9.6%; and that of private enterprises gained 1,854.55 billion RMB, an increase of 6.6%. In October, the profits made by industrial enterprises above the designated size reached 616.1 billion RMB, an increase of 9.8% year on year, and the growth rate increased by 2.1 percentage points over September.∎

102 Manufacturing PMI stood at 51.7% in November

According to the data released on December 1 by NBS, in November 2016, China's manufacturing PMI was 51.7%, an increase of 0.5 percentage point month on month, continuing an upward trend. In breakdown of the sizes of enterprises, the PMI of large-sized and medium-sized enterprises were 53.4% and 50.1%, increasing 0.9 and 0.2 percentage point respectively, and were both higher than the threshold; that of small-sized enterprises was 47.4%, decreasing 0.9 percentage point, continuing to stay in the contraction range, and the pace of decline extended. ∎

103 The non-manufacturing PMI for November was 54.7%

According to the data released on December 1 by NBS, in November 2016, China's non-manufacturing PMI was 54.7%, an increase of 0.7 percentage point month on month, rose for the third consecutive month, and hit the highest since July 2014. Non-manufacturing continued a steady and rapid growth momentum, and the growth rate went up further. In view of different industries, non-manufacturing PMI of service industry was 53.7%, an increase of 1.1 percentage points month on month, hit this year's high, showing that the service industry realized a moderate but stable and sound growth. ∎

104 MOF issued 12 billion RMB of RMB-denominated treasury bonds in Hong Kong

According to the news released by MOF on December 8, MOF has issued 10 billion RMB of RMB-denominated treasury bonds to institutional investors in Hong Kong, including 5 billion RMB of 3-year bonds, 3 billion RMB of 5-year bonds, 1 billion RMB of 10-year bonds, 500 million RMB of 15-year bonds and 500 million RMB of 30-year bonds, with interest rates at 3.4%, 3.55%, 3.85%, 4.15% and 4.4% respectively. 2 billion RMB of 3-year bonds were also sold to foreign central banks and regional monetary authorities, with an interest rate on par with that of the treasury bonds of the same maturity. ∎

105 China's CPI rose by 2.3% year on year in November

The data released by NBS on December 9 showed that China's CPI rose by 2.3% year on year in November, among which, the CPI rose by 2.3% in urban areas and 2.0% in rural areas; 4.0% for food and 1.8% for non-food; 2.1% for consumer goods and 2.4% for services. The average CPI from January to November was up by 2.0% year on year. In November, CPI edged up by 0.1% month on month, among which, the figure rose by 0.1% in urban areas and 0.2% in rural areas; increased by 0.2% for food and 0.1% for non-food; went up by 0.3% for consumer goods and dipped by 0.1% for services. ∎

FACTS & FIGURES

106 China's fiscal revenue and expenditure in November

According to the data released by MOF on December 13, China's general public budget revenue in November was 1149.1 billion RMB, an increase of 3.1% year on year. Among the total revenue, the central revenue was 567.2 billion RMB, an increase of 8.2%; the local revenue was 581.9 billion RMB, down by 1.4%. The total tax revenue was 855.4 billion RMB, down by 2.5%, however, if noncomparable tax rebate is excluded, the tax revenue grew by 3.3%. The national general public budget expenditure was 1806.4 billion RMB, an increase of 12.2%. Among the total expenditure, the central expenditure was 219.2 billion RMB, an increase of 12.4%; the local expenditure was 1587.2 billion RMB, an increase of 12.1%. From January to November, the revenue from national government funds was 3885 billion RMB, an increase of 15.4%; the expenditure from government funds was 3599.4 billion RMB, up by 10.2% year on year. ∎

107 Total retail sales of consumer goods in November grew by 10.8%

According to the data released by NBS on December 13, in first eleven months of 2016, the total retail sales of consumer goods reached 3,095.9 billion RMB, up by 10.8% year on year on nominal terms. Of the total, the retail sales of consumer goods of units above designated size were 1,479.2 billion RMB, increasing 9.5%. From January to November, the total retail sales of consumer goods reached 30,056.0 billion RMB, up by 10.4% year on year. Of the total, the retail sales of consumer goods of units above designated size were 13,720.3 billion RMB, increasing 7.9%. In terms of different consumption patterns, the catering services in November gained 334.2 billion RMB, up by 10.1% year on year. The retail sales of goods gained 2,761.7 billion RMB, up by 10.9%. From January to November, the catering services gained 3,244.7 billion RMB, up by 10.8% year on year. The retail sales of goods gained 26,811.3 billion RMB, up by 10.3%. From January to November, the national online retail sales of goods and services were 4,599.0 billion RMB, increasing 26.2% year on year. ∎

108 Investment in fixed assets grew by 8.3% in the first 11 months

According to the data released by NBS on December 13, in the first eleven months of 2016, the investment in fixed assets reached 53,854.8 billion RMB, up by 8.3% year on year in nominal terms, and the growth rate remained at the same level compared with that in the first ten months. In term of different industries, the investment in the primary industry was 1,709.9 billion RMB, up by 21.9% year on year; that in the secondary industry was 21,006.2 billion RMB, up by 3.3 %; that in the tertiary industry was 31,138.7 billion RMB, up by 11.3%. In terms of jurisdiction of project management, the central investment reached 2,151.5 billion RMB, increasing 0.7% year on year; the local investment was 51,703.3 billion RMB, up by 8.8%. ∎

109 The electricity use of industrial sector increased by 5.9% year on year in China in November

The data released by NBS on December 15 showed that the electricity use of industrial sector increased by 5.9% year on year in November, up by 1.0 percentage point month on month, contributing 62.9% to the increase of overall electricity use in China. Specifically, the electricity use rose by 3.8% for the mining sector, up by 2.4 percentage points; 6.9% for the manufacturing sector, up by 1.2 percentage points; 3.2% for the production and supply sector of power, gas and water, up by 0.4 percentage point. The electricity use went up by 11.8% for the tertiary industry year on year in November, down by 1.7 percentage points over the last month; rose by 9.0% for urban and rural residents, down by 3.2 percentage points. The combined electricity use of tertiary industry and residents contributed 35.1% to the increase of overall electricity use in China. ∎

110 Lottery sales in November 2016

According to the data released on December 23 by MOF, the national sales of lottery in November totaled 34.482 billion RMB, increasing by 3.852 billion RMB year on year, or 12.6%. Among the total sales, welfare lottery sales were 17.861 billion RMB, an increase of 839 million RMB, up by 4.9%. Sports lottery sales were 16.621 billion RMB, growing by 3.013 billion RMB, an increase of 22.1%. From January to November, the nationwide lottery sales were 358.048 billion RMB, an increase of 24.284 billion RMB, or 7.3%. Among the total sales, welfare lottery sales were 186.508 billion RMB, an increase of 4.21 billion RMB, up by 2.3%; sports lottery sales were 171.54 billion RMB, an increase of 20.074 billion RMB, or 13.3%. ∎

111 Economic performance of SOEs from January to November

According to the data released on December 27 by MOF, from January to November, the total revenue of SOEs was 40788.94 billion RMB, up by 2.4% year on year; the total operating costs were 39750.04 billion RMB, an increase of 2.2%, of which sales expenses, management spending and financial costs were up by 6.6%, 7.1% and down by 4.2% respectively. The total profit was 2110.1 billion RMB, up by 2.8% year on year; the tax payable was 3387.26 billion RMB, down by 0.8% year

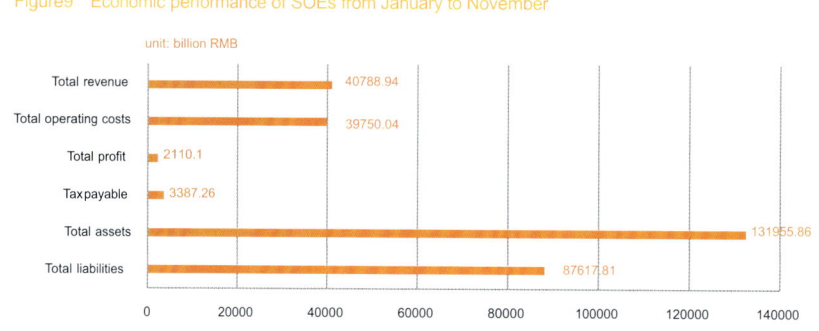

Figure9 Economic performance of SOEs from January to November

Source: Ministry of finance of China

on year. As of the end of November, the total assets of SOEs were 131.95586 trillion RMB, an increase of 10.6%; the liabilities totaled 87.61781 trillion RMB, an increase of 10.9%; the owner's equity was 44.33805 trillion RMB, an increase of 10.1%. ∎

112 Total profits of industrial enterprises above designated size increased by 9.4% in the first eleven months of 2016

According to data released on December 27 by NBS, the profits made by industrial enterprises above the designated size achieved 6,033.41 billion RMB in the first eleven months of 2016, up by 9.4% year on year, and the growth rate was up by 0.8 percentage point over the first ten months. In the first eleven months, the profits of state-holding industrial enterprises above the designated size gained 10,97.49 billion RMB, increased by 8.2% year on year; those of collective-owned enterprises reached 42.06 billion RMB, a decrease of 3.7%; those of joint-stock enterprises stood at 4,134.24 billion RMB, up by 9.9%; that of foreign-funded enterprises, and enterprises funded by Hong Kong, Macao and Taiwan achieved 1,507.36 billion RMB, increasing by 10.8%; and those of private enterprises gained 2,116.9 billion RMB, an increase of 5.9%. In the first eleven months, the profits of mining and quarrying reached 154.98 billion RMB, a decrease of 36.2% year on year; those of manufacturing were 5,430.68 billion RMB, an increase of 13.7%; those of production and distribution of electricity, heat, gas and water reached 447.75 billion RMB, down by 10.1%. ∎

Figure 10 Total profits of industrial enterprises above designated size in the first eleven months of 2016

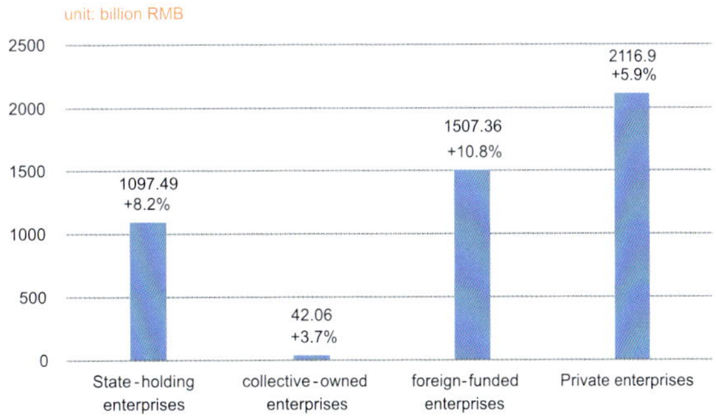

Source: Ministry of Finance of China

MOF EVENTS

 On December 24-25, 2015, **Assistant Finance Minister Zou Jiayi** visited the BRICS Bank in Shanghai and met with President Kamath of the Bank and other senior management members. They exchanged views on the host country agreement, personnel arrangement, first projects and funding costs, member expansion, and institutional building. ∎

 On January 8, **Vice Finance Minister Shi Yaobin** met with Mr. Gupta, Vice President of the Asian Development Bank (ADB), and exchanged views on China-ADB cooperation and the issuance of RMB bonds by the ADB in China. ∎

 On January 12, **Vice Finance Minister Zhu Guangyao** met with the visiting IMF delegation for the IMF Article IV middle session consultation. The two sides exchanged views on strengthening bilateral cooperation under the framework of the G20, China's macroeconomic situation and the current fiscal policy. ∎

 On January 13, **Vice Finance Minister Shi Yaobin** met with Peter Ong, Permanent Secretary of Singaporean Prime Minister's Office and the Ministry of Finance. The two sides exchanged views on China's economic situation, G20 and ASEAN+3 Macroeconomic Research Office (AMRO) related issues. ∎

 On January 14, **Assistant Finance Minister Dai Bohua** met with Ms. Bai Rong, the visiting CEO of the Association of Chartered Certified Accountants (ACCA). ∎

 During the opening ceremonies of the Asian Infrastructure Investment Bank (AIIB) on January 15-16, **Vice Finance Minister Shi Yaobin** met with the visiting British Deputy Secretary of the Treasury Mark Bowman, the Swedish Minister for Consumer Affairs and Deputy Minister of Finance in financial markets Pell Bu Longde, the New Zealand's Deputy Secretary of the Treasury Gabriel Makhlouf, and Michael Sarel, the Chief Economist of the Israeli Ministry of Finance. ∎

Photo1 Chinese Finance Minister Low Jiwei at the opening ceremonies of AIIB

Source: Ministry of Finance of China

 During the opening ceremonies of the AIIB on January 16-17, **Finance Minister Lou Jiwei** met with

CHINA FINANCE 2016

UNIDO's Director-General Li Yong, Korean Deputy Prime Minister and Minister of Strategy and Finance Yoo Il-ho, Singaporean Finance Minister Heng Swee Keat, Indonesian Finance Minister Bambang Brodjonegoro, Pakistan Finance Minister Ishaq Dar, Nepal Finance Minister Bishnu Prasad Broder and Luxembourg Finance Minister Graham Menia. ∎

The AIIB successfully held the inaugural meeting of the Council in Beijing on January 16-17. **Finance Minister Lou Jiwei** presided over the meeting as the chairman of the Board of Governors. **Vice Minister Shi Yaobin** delivered a speech as the Chinese alternate governor. ∎

On January 16, **Vice Finance Minister Liu Kun** attended the Seminar on the Structural Reform Supported by Fiscal and Financial Policies, which was jointly hosted by the Finance Society and Finance Association of China, and delivered a keynote speech. **Assistant Finance Minister Dai Bohua** also delivered a speech. ∎

On January 19-22, **Vice Finance Minister Shi Yaobin** visited Brunei and the Philippines, and had meetings with Mr. Abd Rahman Ibrahim, Minister at Prime Minister's Office and Finance Minister II of Brunei, Mr. Nazmi, Permanent Secretary of the Finance Ministry of Brunei, Mr. Yusof Abd Rahman, Managing Director of the Monetary Authority of Brunei, Mr. Adi Marhain Leman, Deputy Managing Director of the Monetary Authority of Brunei, Mr. Roberto B. Tan, Deputy Finance Secretary and Treasurer of the Philippines, Ms. Edita Z. Tan, Assistant Finance Secretary of the Philippines, and Mr. Diwa C. Guinigundo, Deputy Governor of the Central Bank of the Philippines, to exchange views over the issues related to financial cooperation in East Asia, particularly the enhancement of the AMRO's capacity building. ∎

On January 28, **Vice Finance Minister Zhu Guangyao** met with Mr. Timothy Geithner, the visiting former U.S. Treasury Secretary in Beijing. The two sides exchanged views on the state of world economy. ∎

On January 29, **Vice Finance Minister Liu Kun** attended the inaugural meeting of the first National SME Development Fund and delivered a speech. ∎

On February 2, **Vice Finance Minister Zhu Guangyao** met with the visiting US Trade Representative Froman in Beijing. The two sides exchanged views on China-U.S. economic relations. ∎

MOF EVENTS

On February 19, **Vice Finance Minister Shi Yaobin** attended the opening ceremony of AMRO as an international organization in Singapore and delivered a speech. During his visit, Shi chaired the Finance Deputies' Meeting between China, Japan and South Korea, and held bilateral talks with counterparts from Laos, Singapore and Japan to exchange views on AMRO development and financial cooperation in East Asia.■

On February 23, **Assistant Finance Minister Xu Hongcai** attended and delivered a speech on the video conference held by MOF and MOA on providing further incentives and awards for grassland ecological protection.■

On February 25, **Vice Finance Minister Zhu Guangyao** was invited to attend the G20 seminar sponsored by the Institute of International Finance (IIF) in Shanghai, and participated in the discussion of global economic outlook.■

On February 26, the G20 High-level Seminar on Structural Reform was held in Shanghai. The seminar was jointly sponsored by the Ministry of Finance of the People's Republic of China, International Monetary Fund (IMF) and Organization for Economic Co-operation and Development (OECD), and was hosted by China MOF Think Tank on International Economics. **Lou Jiwei, Finance Minister of China**, Christine Lagarde, Managing Director of the IMF, Angel Gurria, Secretary-General of the OECD, and Yang Xiong, Mayor of Shanghai Municipal Government attended the opening ceremony and delivered speeches. A total of more than 200 people attended the seminar, including representatives of G20 member countries, relevant international organizations, and renowned experts from home and abroad.■

On February 24, **Finance Minister Lou Jiwei** met with Mr. Jim Yong Kim, President of the World Bank Group, who was visiting China for the G20 Finance Ministers and Central Bank Governors Meeting. The two sides exchanged views on the joint research on healthcare reform, the design of the loans for healthcare reform, the research on fostering new drivers of economic growth and other issues related to bilateral practical cooperation, multilateral coordination of policies and global common development.■

On February 25, **Vice Finance Minister Shi Yaobin** met with Mr. Axel Trotsenburg, Vice President of the World Bank, and exchanged views on IDA18, the World Bank's support to the economic transition of low-income countries, and the countering of the refugee crisis from the perspective of long-term development.■

CHINA FINANCE 2016

On February 27, **Finance Minister Lou Jiwei** attended the press conference of the G20 Finance Ministers and Central Bank Governors Meeting, briefed on the discussion and outcomes of the meeting, and answered questions from the press. ∎

Photo2 Chinese Finance Minister Lou Jiwei at the press conference of G20 Finance Ministers and Central Bank Governors Meeting

Source: Ministry of Finance of China

On February 27, on the sidelines of the G20 Finance Ministers and Central Bank Governors Meeting in Shanghai, **Finance Minister Lou Jiwei** attended the signing ceremony of the Agreement and the Memorandum of Understanding Regarding the Headquarter of the New Development Bank (NDB) in Shanghai, the People's Republic of China. ∎

On February 27-28, **Vice Finance Minister Hu Jinglin** visited Xinjiang Uygur Autonomous Region to study the issues facing the reform and development of the Xinjiang Production and Construction Corps. ∎

On February 29, **Vice Finance Minister Zhang Shaochun** chaired a ministerial working meeting to deliberate the National Fiscal Planning Outlines for the 13th Five-Year Plan Period. Available ministerial officials at MOF attended the meeting. Officials from 14 departments of MOF participated in the meeting. ∎

On March 7, **Finance Minister Lou Jiwei** and Assistant Finance Minister Xu Hongcai attended the press conference of the fourth session of the 12th NPC, which was held in the Media Center in Beijing. They took questions on fiscal and taxation reforms from domestic and foreign reporters. ∎

On March 15, **Vice Finance Minister Zhu Guangyao** met with Mr. Szubin, the acting under secretary for terrorism and financial intelligence of the U.S. Treasury Department, and exchanged views over international cooperation on combating terrorist financing. ∎

On March 20, **Finance Minister Lou Jiwei** met with OECD Secretary-General Angel Gurria, the Asian Development Bank President Takehiko Nakao, Inter-American Development Bank President Luis Alberto Moreno, and UBS CEO Sergio Ermotti, who were attending the 2016 China Development Forum. ∎

MOF EVENTS

27 On March 21, **Vice Finance Minister Yu Weiping** met with the PwC Global Chairman Mr. Dennis Nally. The two sides exchanged views on values and trust building of the CPA profession, as well as accounting reform and progress.■

28 On March 23, **Vice Finance Minister Zhu Guangyao** met with the Director of the Asia and Pacific Department of IMF Changyong Rhee. The two sides exchanged views on the situation of Chinese and global economy.■

29 On March 24, **Vice Finance Minister Zhu Guangyao** met with Kurt Campbell, the former Assistant Secretary of State of the U.S., and exchanged views over China-U.S. economic relations.■

30 On March 24, **Vice Finance Minister Shi Yaobin** met with Jonathan Taylor, the Vice President of the EIB, and exchanged views over the enhanced cooperation between China and the EIB.■

31 On March 28, **Finance Minister Lou Jiwei** met with Timothy Geithner, the former Secretary of Treasury of the U.S. and the President of Warburg Pincus, and exchanged views over global economy and Chinese economy.■

32 On March 30, **Finance Minister Lou Jiwei** attended and addressed the video Conference for the Roll-out of the Pilot VAT Reform held by MOF and SAT in Beijing. The meeting was tasked to implement the decision of the Executive Meeting of the State Council on March 18, gear up the fiscal and tax authorities for the reform, and ensure the smooth implementation of the reform on May 1.■

33 On March 29, **Vice Finance Minister Shi Yaobin** met with Jamal Sager, senior adviser to the vice president in charge of African regions in the World Bank, who was leading a delegation of African national bureau directors to China. The two sides exchanged views on further strengthening tripartite cooperation in Africa and the preparation for the second African Investment Forum.■

34 On April 12, Vice **Finance Minister Shi Yaobin** attended the Press Briefing organized by the News Office of the State Council, made a presentation on the roll-out of the pilot VAT reform, and took questions from the media.■

CHINA FINANCE 2016

 On April 14-15, **Finance Minister Lou Jiwei** and Governor Zhou Xiaochuan co-chaired the G20 Finance Ministers and Central Bank Governors Meeting in Washington, D.C.. The meeting discussed the current state of global economy, growth framework, the international financial architecture, investment and infrastructure, financial sector reform, international tax cooperation, anti-terrorism financing, green financing and climate financing, and issued a joint communique. ■

Photo3 Group photo of G20 Finance Ministers and Central Bank Governors Meeting in Washington, D.C.

Source: Ministry of Finance of China

 On April 14, Finance Minister Lou Jiwei and Vice Finance Minister Shi Yaobin attended the Special Council meeting of NDB in Washington, D.C.. The meeting reviewed a report on the first batch of projects approved by the Board of Directors, and discussed the first strategy paper and the expansion of members. ■

 On April 14, **Finance Minister Lou Jiwei** visited Washington, D.C. and co-chaired the second G20 Finance Ministers and Central Bank Governors Meeting in 2016, during which he held bilateral meetings with U.S. Treasury Secretary Jacob Lew, Federal Reserve Chair Janet Yellen, French Finance Minister Saban, Indian Finance Minister Jaitley, South African Finance Minister Gordhan, respectively, and had in-depth exchange of views. Vice Finance Minister Shi Yaobin also attended the meetings. ■

 On April 16, **Finance Minister Lou Jiwei** attended the 93rd session of the Ministerial Meeting of the Development Committee in Washington, D.C., which was sponsored by the World Bank and IMF. UN Secretary-General Ban Ki-moon attended the meeting as a special guest. ■

 On April 16, **Finance Minister Lou Jiwei**, as the representative of the Presidency of the G20 Finance Track in 2016, attended the Global Infrastructure Forum in Washington D.C., and delivered opening remarks along with UN Secretary-General Ban Ki-moon and the World Bank President Jim Yong Kim. ■

MOF EVENTS

 On April 21, **Assistant Finance Minister Xu Hongcai** met with Said, Deputy Head of the Parliamentary Budget Committee of Indonesia, and exchanged views over the macroeconomic situation of China and China's fiscal and tax system. ■

 On April 25, **Vice Finance Minister Shi Yaobin** met with Sim Ann, Senior State Minister for the Ministry of Finance and the Ministry of Culture, Community and Youth of Singapore, and exchanged views over the macroeconomic situation of China and China-Singapore economic and financial cooperation. ■

 On April 26, **Finance Minister Lou Jiwei** met with Kimmitt, former U.S. Deputy Treasury Secretary, and Cantor, former U.S. House Majority Leader, and exchanged views over the political and economic situation of the U.S. ■

 On April 28, **Vice Finance Minister Hu Jinglin** led a delegation of the National Command Office for Flood and Drought Control in an inspection tour to the Huai River region to give guidance on flood and drought control. ■

 On May 2-4, **Finance Minister Lou Jiwei** led a Chinese government delegation to attend the ADB's 49th Annual Meeting of Board of Governors in Frankfurt, Germany. During the meeting, Minister Lou attended the Board Meeting and Board Seminar, and met with Taro Aso, Deputy Prime Minister and Finance Minister of Japan, Finance Minister of Pakistan Dar, and ADB President Takehiko Nakao. Minister Lou also visited the exhibition of the China Poverty Reduction and Regional Cooperation Fund. ■

 On May 2, **Vice Finance Minister Shi Yaobin** attended and chaired the ASEAN+3 Finance and Central Bank Deputies' Meeting in Frankfurt, Germany. ■

Photo4 Chinese Vice Finance Minister Shi Yaobin chaired the ASEAN+3 Finance and Central Bank Deputies' Meeting

Source: Ministry of Finance of China

CHINA FINANCE 2016

Source: Ministry of Finance of China

On May 3, **Finance Minister Lou Jiwei** attended and chaired the 16th China, Japan and South Korea Finance Ministers and Central Bank Governors' Meeting in Frankfurt, Germany.∎

Photo5 Chinese Finance Minister Low Jiwei at the 16th China, Japan and South Korea Finance Ministers and Central Bank Governors' Meeting

On May 3, **Finance Minister Lou Jiwei** attended and chaired the 19th ASEAN+3 Finance Ministers and Central Bank Governors' Meeting in Frankfurt, Germany. After the meeting, Minister Lou attended the press conference.∎

On May 17, **Finance Minister Lou Jiwei** met with Mr. Lim Chow Kiat, the visiting Chief Investment Officer of Singapore's Government Investment Corporation (GIC) in Beijing. The two sides exchanged views on China's economic situation and structural reforms.∎

On May 20, **Assistant Finance Minister Dai Bohua** met with Andre Berghegger, the head of the delegation of the Budget Committee of the German Bundestag, and exchanged views over the macroeconomic situation of China, government budget and fiscal and tax system.∎

On May 23, Assistant Finance Minister Zhao Mingji met with Olivia Kirtley, President of the International Federation of Accountants (IFAC), and exchanged views over the future development of China's accountancy profession and the role of China's accountancy profession in IFAC and other international accountancy organizations.∎

On May 31, witnessed by **Finance Minister Lou Jiwei** and the European Investment Bank (EIB) President Werner Hoyle, Vice Finance Minister Shi Yaobin and Vice President of the EIB Jonathan Taylor signed the Memorandum of Understanding on the Cooperation between the People's Republic of China and the European Investment Bank.∎

On May 31, **Finance Minister Lou Jiwei** met with Werner Hoyer, President of EIB, and exchanged views on the enhanced cooperation between China and the EIB and the future cooperation between AIIB and EIB.∎

MOF EVENTS

On June 2, **Vice Finance Minister Zhu Guangyao** attended the 16th Lanting Forum, and briefed domestic and foreign media on the Economic track of the 8th round of China-U.S. Strategic and Economic Dialogue. ∎

On June 4, **Vice Finance Minister Shi Yaobin** attended the SSC Roundtable between China and three UN food and agriculture agencies, which was held in Xi'an, Shaanxi Province. On behalf of MOF, Vice Finance Minister Shi Yaobin signed the Memorandum of Understanding on the Establishment of Partnership between the Ministry of Finance, the Ministry of Agriculture of the People's Republic of China and IFAD with the Ministry of Agriculture and IFAD. ∎

On June 6, **Finance Minister Lou Jiwei** attended the 8th China-U.S. Strategic and Economic Dialogue. ∎

Photo6   Finance Minister Lou Jiwei at the 8th China-U.S. Strategic and Economic Dialogue

Source: Ministry of Finance of China

On June 6, **Finance Minister Lou Jiwei** had a press briefing on the First Session of "Macroeconomic Situation and Policy" of the Economic Track of the 8th China-U.S. Strategic and Economic Dialogue. ∎

On June 6, **Assistant Finance Minister Zhao Mingji** met with Charles Tilley, Chief Executive of the Chartered Institute of Management Accountants (CIMA) and exchanged views on the development trend, application and international cooperation of management accounting. ∎

On June 12, **Finance Minister Lou Jiwei** met with Wolfgang Schaeuble, the visiting German Finance Minister, who was attending the 4th round of the China-Germany government consultations in Beijing. The two sides exchanged views on the macroeconomic situation, G20, and China-Germany financial and economic cooperation. ∎

On June 13, **Finance Minister Lou Jiwei** met with David Lipton, the visiting IMF First Deputy Managing Director in Beijing. The two sides exchanged views on China's macroeconomic situation, fiscal and tax systems reform and debt-related issues. ∎

CHINA FINANCE 2016

60 On June 15, **Vice Finance Minister Zhu Guangyao** met with the US delegation who was attending the China-U.S. economic dialogue sponsored by the Peking University in Beijing. The two sides exchanged views on the 8th round of China-U.S. Strategic and Economic Dialogue, China's economic reforms, G20 and other topics of common interest.■

61 On June 16-17, **Vice Finance Minister Liu Kun** attended and addressed the National Conference on IT Application in Public Finance in Beijing.■

62 On June 22, **Assistant Finance Minister Zhao Mingji** attended and addressed the Symposium on the 3rd National Top CFO Executive Development Program in Beijing.■

63 On June 22-23, **Vice Finance Minister Zhu Guangyao** and Yi Gang, Deputy Governor of PBoC, co-chaired the G20 Finance and Central Bank Deputies' Meeting in Xiamen, Fujian Province.■

64 On June 25, **Finance Minister Lou Jiwei** chaired the first Annual Meeting of the Board of Governors of the AIIB in Beijing. Vice Minister Shi Yaobin delivered a speech at the meeting as the deputy governor from China. Board members and representatives of AIIB member countries, prospective member countries and international organizations attended the meeting.■

65 On June 25, **Vice Finance Minister Shi Yaobin** met with Vice President of the World Bank kwakwa and New Zealand Treasury Secretary Makhlouf respectively, who were visiting China for the first Annual Meeting of the Board of Governors of AIIB.■

66 On June 26, **Finance Minister Lou Jiwei** attended the Seminar on Infrastructure and Global Economic Growth during the first Annual Meeting of AIIB.■

67 On June 28, **Vice Finance Minister Hu Jinglin** attended and addressed the Work Conference on the Pilot Program of Consolidating Agriculture-related Funds for Poor Counties in Dawu County, Hubei Province. The officials of the State Council Leading Group Office of Poverty Alleviation and Development as well as the officials from some provincial finance departments and poverty alleviation offices also attended the conference.■

MOF EVENTS

On June 28, at the 2016 Summer Davos Forum in Tianjin, **Vice Finance Minister Zhu Guangyao** attended the session themed "Global Economic Outlook: Asian Perspective" and took questions from the audience. ■

On June 29, **Assistant Finance Minister Zhao Mingji** met with visiting President of KPMG John Veihmeyer. The two sides exchanged views on Chinese CPA profession development, training of accounting professionals, and KPMG development in China. ■

On June 29, Vice Finance Minister Shi Yaobin met with Chang Junhong, Director of ASEAN+3 AMRO and signed the Agreement on the Establishment of P.R.C Technical Assistance Trust Fund. ■

On June 29, the 21st Meeting of the 12th Standing Committee of NPC held the 2nd Plenary Meeting. Entrusted by the State Council, **Finance Minister Lou Jiwei** delivered the report on the central government final accounts for 2015. ■

On July 11, **Vice Finance Minister Shi Yaobin** met with Ms. Naoko Ishii, CEO and Chairman of the Global Environment Facility (GEF). The two sides exchanged views on cooperation between China and GEF, among other issues. After the meeting, the two sides jointly attended the opening ceremony of the 5th China GEF Project Management Conference and gave remarks. ■

On July 20, **Finance Minister Lou Jiwei**, as the Governor for China, attended and chaired the first Meeting of the Board of Governors of the NDB in Shanghai. The Governors or representatives of the members of NDB attended the meeting. ■

Photo7   Chinese Finance Minister Lou Jiwei chaired the first Meeting of the Board of Governors of the NDB in Shanghai

Source: Ministry of Finance of China

On July 21, **Finance Minister Lou Jiwei** attended and delivered a speech at the High-level Roundtable on Opportunities and Challenges Facing NDB during the first NDB Annual Meeting. ■

CHINA FINANCE 2016

Photo8   Chinese Finance Minister Lou Jiwei at the G20 Finance Ministers and Central Bank Governors Meeting

Source: Ministry of Finance of China

On July 23-24, **Finance Minister Lou Jiwei** and Governor Zhou Xiaochuan co-chaired the G20 Finance Ministers and Central Bank Governors Meeting in Chengdu. The meeting was the last gathering for G20 finance ministers and central bank governors before the Hangzhou Summit. The meeting mainly discussed the current global economic situation, the strong, sustainable and balanced growth framework, the international financial architecture, investment and infrastructure, the financial sector reform, international tax cooperation, green finance, climate finance, anti-terrorism financing, among other topics. The meeting endorsed the major outcomes and issued a communique, which delivered economic and financial outcomes for the Hangzhou Summit.■

On July 23-24, **Finance Minister Lou Jiwei** met with guests attending the G20 Finance Ministers and Central Bank Governors Meeting in Chengdu, including the newly appointed British Chancellor of the Exchequer Philip Hammond, French Finance Minister Michel Sapin, Canadian Finance Minister William Morneau, South Korea Deputy Prime Minister and Finance Minister Yoo Il-ho, Slovak Finance Minister Peter Kazimir, and Argentine Finance Minister Alfonso Prat-Gay.■

On July 23, **Vice Finance Minister Shi Yaobin** met with Ms. Odile Renaud-Basso, the head of the French Treasury, who was attending the G20 Finance Ministers and Central Bank Governors Meeting in Chengdu. The two sides exchanged views on China-France bilateral economic and financial cooperation.■

On July 24, **Finance Minister Lou Jiwei**, the OECD Secretary-General Gurria, the World Bank President Jim Yong Kim, and Mr. Lipton, IMF First Deputy Managing Director attended and gave remarks on the opening ceremony of the High-Level International Symposium on New Approaches to Economic Challenges, which was jointly organized by MOF and OECD in Chengdu. Vice Finance Minister Shi Yaobin presided over the meeting.■

Photo9   Finance Minister Lou Jiwei at the opening ceremony of the High-Level International Symposium on New Approaches to Economic Challenges

Source: Ministry of Finance of China

MOF EVENTS

79 On August 2, **Vice Finance Minister Shi Yaobin** met with Mr. Zhang Wencai, Vice President of ADB. The two sides exchanged views on cooperation between China and the ADB, the ADB 2030 Strategy, PPP and regional cooperation, among other issues.■

80 On August 15, **Vice Finance Minister Zhu Guangyao** met with Max Baucus, U.S. Ambassador to China.■

81 On August 18, **Finance Minister Lou Jiwei** met with Indian Deputy Finance Minister Shaktikanta Das in Beijing, who was attending the 8th China-India Financial Dialogue. Vice Finance Minister Shi Yaobin and Indian Ambassador Vijay Gokhale attended the meeting.■

82 On August 19, **Vice Finance Minister Shi Yaobin** and Indian Deputy Finance Minister Shaktikanta Das co-chaired the 8th China-India Financial Dialogue in Beijing.■

83 On August 24-25, **Vice Finance Minister Shi Yaobin**, who is also the head of MOF's Leading Group on PPP Work, visited Hunan Province where he heard report on the local PPP work and made field trip to some PPP projects, such as the underground pipes, maglev train and international convention center in Changsha City as well as the new Chenglingji port in Yueyang City.■

84 On August 31, **Finance Minister Lou Jiwei** made the report on the state of budget execution since 2016 at the 2nd Plenary Meeting of the 22nd Meeting of the Standing Committee of the 12th NPC.■

85 On September 2, **Vice Finance Minister Shi Yaobin** attended the opening ceremony of the 8th Senior Seminar on Development Experience Sharing between China and Africa and the 7th China-IFAD South-South Cooperation Workshop, which were co-sponsored by MOF, the Ministry of Commerce, the Ministry of Agriculture, the State Council Poverty Alleviation Office, the World Bank, and IFAD. Vice Finance Minister Shi Yaobin addressed the event.■

86 On September 2, on the occasion of the Press Conference of the G20 Hangzhou Summit, Vice **Finance Minister Zhu Guangyao** took questions from the domestic and foreign journalists on issues of China's hosting of the Hangzhou Summit, the global economic situation and the state of the Chinese economy.■

On September 7, **Vice Finance Minister Shi Yaobin** attended the 2nd Investing in Africa Forum in Guangzhou and delivered a keynote speech. The Forum was co-organized by the provincial government of Guangdong, the China Development Bank and the World Bank. Around 300 domestic and foreign guests, including Vice Premier Ma Kai, South African President Zuma, Beninese President Talon, and the World Bank President Jim Yong Kim, attended the Forum.■

On September 12-13, **Vice Finance Minister Hu Jinglin** made a field trip to Ji'an City, Jiangxi Province to investigate the consolidation of agriculture-related funds in poverty-stricken counties.■

From September 11-14, the Delegation of Chinese Economic Experts, which was headed by **Zhou Qiangwu, Director General of the International Economics and Finance Institute (IEFE) of MOF**, and comprised of Zhao Jinping, Director General of the Research Department of Foreign Economic Relations of the Development Research Center of the State Council, Zhang Yuyan, Director General of the Institute of World Economics and Politics of Chinese Academy of Social Sciences(CASS), Bi Jiyao, Director General of the Institute for International Economic Research of NDRC, and Liu Shangxi, Director General of Chinese Academy of Fiscal Sciences(CAFS), visited Tokyo, Japan and met with the officials of Japanese House of Representatives, the Ministry of Foreign Affairs, the Ministry of Finance as well as representatives of the Japanese think tanks, media and industries. The delegation exchanged views over the macroeconomic situation and policy of China, the Belt and Road Initiative, China's monetary policy and fiscal and tax reform, and the outcomes of the G20 Hangzhou Summit.■

On September 19, **Vice Finance Minister Shi Yaobin** attended the event that celebrated the 20th Anniversary of China-Israel Government Loans Cooperation and held talk with Michal Abadi-Boiangiu, the Accountant General of Israeli Finance Ministry, over issues such as strengthening bilateral financial cooperation and promoting PPP projects.■

On September 20, **Vice Finance Minister Zhu Guangyao** met with the delegation of American journalists in Beijing.■

On September 23, **Mr. Lou Jiwei, Finance Minister**, Mr. Wang Anshun, Mayor of Beijing and Mr. Jin Liqun, President of AIIB attended the ceremony of laying the foundation stone for AIIB headquarters at the center of Olympic Park in Beijing.■

MOF EVENTS

On September 29, **Mr. Shi Yaobin, Vice Finance Minister** and Ms. Zhang Xiaohui, Assistant Governor of PBOC led the Chinese delegation to attend the 3th Finance Ministers and Central Bank Governors Meeting of the Shanghai Cooperation Organization (SCO) in Bishkek, the capital of Kyrgyzstan.■

Photo10　Chinese Vice Finance Minister Shi Yaobin at the 3th Finance Ministers and Central Bank Governors Meeting of the Shanghai Cooperation Organization (SCO)

Source: Ministry of Finance of China

From September 25-28, **Vice Finance Minister Shi Yaobin** visited ADB in Manila, the Philippines, met with the ADB President Takehiko Nakao, and attended the meeting of the Advisory Council of the ADB Institute (ADBI) and the policy dialogue on hotspot economic issues organized by the ADBI .■

On October 6, Finance Minister Lou Jiwei and PBoC Governor Zhou Xiaochuan co-chaired the G20 Finance Ministers and Central Bank Governors Meeting in Washington D.C.. The meeting, the final Finance Ministers and Central Bank Governors Meeting under China's G20 Presidency, discussed issues including the global economic situation, tax, beneficial ownership and anti-money laundering, and heard presentations from Germany, the host of G20 in 2017, on the agenda for next year's G20 Finance Track.■

Photo11　Chinese Finance Minister Lou Jiwei and at the G20 Finance Ministers and Central Bank Governors Meeting in Washington, D.C.

Source: Ministry of Finance of China

On October 9-10, **Assistant Finance Minister Zhao Mingji** visited the Xiamen National Accounting Institute, inspected the damage caused by typhoon, express his sympathy to the affected staff and held discussion on improving the management system of the national accounting institute.■

On October 10, **Assistant Finance Minister Dai Bohua** attended the press briefing of the Press Office of the State Council on reducing the corporate leverage and took questions regarding the fiscal and tax policies to support market-based deleveraging.■

On October 6-8, **Finance Minister Lou Jiwei** chaired the G20 Finance Ministers and Central Bank Governors Meeting in Washington D.C.. Minister Lou met with Mr. Jacob Lew, the U.S. Treasury

Secretary, Mr. Philip Hammond, British Chancellor of the Exchequer, Mr. Arun Jaitley, the Indian Finance Minister, Mr. Henrique Meirelles, the Brazilian Finance Minister, Mr. Petteri Orpo, the Finnish Finance Minister, and Mr. Ali Tayebnia, the Iranian Finance Minister, respectively. The two sides had in-depth exchange of views on the issues of mutual interest. Vice Finance Minister Zhu Guangyao and Vice Finance Minister Shi Yaobin attended the meetings. ■

On October 11, Vice Finance Minister Shi Yaobin met with Mr. Fuchtel, Parliamentary State Secretary to the Federal Minister for Economic Cooperation and Development of the Federal Republic of Germany. The two sides exchanged views on bilateral cooperation in ADB and AIIB, as well as on bilateral loans. ■

On October 13, **Vice Finance Minister Zhu Guangyao** met with Mike Daniels, Moody's President and CEO. ■

On October 14-15, **Assistant Finance Minister Dai Bohua** led a delegation of MOF to attend the 23rd APEC Finance Ministers' Meeting in Lima, Peru. They held in-depth discussions with APEC economies and relevant international organizations on the global and regional economic and financial situation, implementation of the Cebu Action Plan, ways to improve the APEC Finance Ministers' Meeting, infrastructure finance and development, PPP knowledge portal, inclusive finance, and response to tax base erosion and profit transfer (BEPS). ■

On October 21, the International Seminar on Deepening Asian Financial Cooperation and Promoting Regional Integration was successfully held in Beijing by IEFI, MOF. **Vice Finance Minister Shi Yaobin** attended the opening ceremony and delivered a speech. Luky Eko Wuryanto, Vice President of the AIIB, and Huang Xilian, Deputy Director General of the Asian Department of the Ministry of Foreign Affairs, made keynote speeches respectively. Participants also included representatives from international institutions including the World Bank, IMF, AIIB, AMRO, and experts and scholars from Australia, Japan and South Korea. Officials from the Ministry of Foreign Affairs, MOF, the National Development and Reform Commission, the Ministry of Commerce and scholars from the China Academy of Social Sciences, the Development Research Center of the State Council, China Development Bank, Shanghai Institute of International Studies, China Finance 40 Forum, Chongyang Institute of Finance of Renmin University, Ali Cross-border E-commerce Research Center were also present. Zhou Qiangwu, the Director General of IEFI presided over the opening ceremony and made concluding remarks at the closing session. ■

On October 19, **Assistant Finance Minister Xu Hongcai** attended and addressed the Asia-Pacific Summit on Low Carbon Technology co-sponsored by the Provincial government of Hunan and ADB, in Changsha, Hunan Province. ■

MOF EVENTS

On October 20, **Finance Minister Lou Jiwei** met with Henry Paulson, the former U.S. Treasury Secretary and the Chairman of Paulson Institute, and exchanged views on the U.S.-China economic relationship and other issues of common interests. ∎

On October 24, **Assistant Finance Minister Zhao Mingji** attended and addressed the First Plenary Meeting of the Members of the Advisory Committee of ASBE (Accounting Standards for Business Enterprises) and the Members of the Committee of Government Accounting Standards. ∎

On October 25-27, **Vice Finance Minister Hu Jinglin** carried out studies in Lvliang, Shanxi Province, on fiscal support of poverty alleviation. ∎

On October 26, **Vice Finance Minister Liu Kun** attended the 15th Ministerial Meeting of Central Asia Regional Economic Cooperation(CAREC) and delivered a speech. ∎

On November 2, **Vice Finance Minister Shi Yaobin** and Mr. Keith Hansen, Vice President of the World Bank, attended the 4th Global Delivery Initiative (GDI) and the 8th China-ADB Knowledge Sharing Platform, which was jointly sponsored by MOF, the World Bank, the ADB, the German Agency for International Cooperation and the United States Agency for International Development. ∎

On November 4-5, the Seminar on the 60 Years of Public Finance and National Governance and Financial Think-tanks co-sponsored by the Chinese Academy of Fiscal Sciences and the Society of Public Finance of China was held in Beijing. **Assistant Finance Minister Dai Bohua** attended and addressed the seminar. ∎

On November 14, **Vice Finance Minister Shi Yaobin** attended the 4th China-France High-level Economic and Financial Dialogue in Paris, and answered questions from Chinese and foreign media after the meeting. ∎

Photo12　Chinese Vice Finance Minister Shi Yaobin attended the 4th China-France High-level Economic and Financial Dialogue

Source: Ministry of Finance of China

CHINA FINANCE 2016

 On November 29, **Finance Minister Xiao Jie** met with Mr. John Tsang, Financial Secretary of the Hong Kong Special Administrative Region.■

Photo13   Chinese Finance Minister Xiao Jie and the Financial Secretary of the Hong Kong Special Administrative Region Mr. John Tsang

Source: Ministry of Finance of China

 On December 1, **Assistant Finance Minister Dai Bohua** attended the 21st Ministerial Meeting of the Greater Mekong Sub-regional Economic Cooperation.■

 On November 30, MOF held a seminar in Beijing to study the use of asset income for poverty reduction. **Vice Finance Minister Hu Jinglin** attended and addressed the seminar.■

 On December 1, **Vice Finance Minister Zhu Guangyao** attended the G20 Finance and Central Bank Deputies Meeting in Berlin. On the sidelines, he also attended the Launching Ceremony of Germany's G20 Presidency, "Troika" Finance and Central Bank Deputies Meeting, G20 High-level Seminar on Strengthening Global Economic Resilience, and the First Meeting of the G20 Advisory Panel on the Promotion of African Investment.■

Photo14   Group photo of G20 Finance and Central Bank Deputies Meeting in Berlin

Source: Ministry of Finance of China

MOF EVENTS

 On December 5, **Vice Finance Minister Zhu Guangyao** and Under Secretary Nathan Sheets of the U.S. Treasury co-chaired the 11th China-US Joint Economic Committee (JEC) in Beijing. ∎

 On December 10-11, the ASEAN 10+3 Finance and Central Bank Deputies Meeting was held in Guiyang. **Vice Finance Minister Shi Yaobin** and Assistant Governor Yin Yong of PBOC, together with Vice Finance Minister Thipphakone Chanthavongsa and Central Bank Vice President Vathana Dalaloy of Laos, co-chaired the meeting. At the margin of the meeting, Vice Minister Shi Yaobin attended the ASEAN+3 Financial Forum sponsored by AMRO and delivered a keynote speech. ∎

Photo15 Group photo of ASEAN 10+3 Finance and Central Bank Deputies Meeting

Source: Ministry of Finance of China

 On December 12, during his trip to the ASEAN+3 deputies meeting of finance ministers and central bank governors, **Vice Finance Minister Shi Yaobin** made a special trip to Guizhou Inspector's Office to conduct research and give guidance. ∎

 On December 21, **Vice Finance Minister Shi Yaobin** and the NDB President Kamath signed the Loan Agreement for the Shanghai Lingang Distributed Solar Power Project at the Headquarters of the NDB. ∎

 On December 23, the 3rd plenary meeting of the 25th session of the 12th NPC Standing Committee was held. **Finance Minister Xiao Jie** reported on the progress of deepening the reform of the fiscal transfer payment system. ∎

CHINA FINANCE 2016

 On December 27, MOF and SAT jointly held a media briefing on the VAT reform. **Vice Finance Minister Zhang Shaochun** and Mr. Wang Jianfan, Director General of Tax Policy Department, briefed on the full roll-out of VAT reform, and answered questions from the media. ∎

 On December 29, **Finance Minister Xiao Jie** chaired a national finance work conference in Beijing and delivered a speech. ∎

Source: Ministry of Finance of China

Photo16　Chinese Finance Minister Xiao Jie chaired the national finance work conference

LOCAL FINANCE

Guangdong Province steadily promoted the reform of zero-based budgeting

According to the news released on January 5 by the Finance Department of Guangdong Province, the *Implementation Rules for 2016 Provincial Zero-based Budgeting Reform* is issued to expand the piloting scope and improve the zero-based budgeting process. The implementation rules provides the following. First, 14 agencies are added to the piloting program, expanding the scope of zero-based budgeting reform to 20 budget agencies. Second, efforts are made to improve the financial expenditure standards for the payroll of government employees. Third, budget control for the agencies in the 2016 zero-based budgeting pilot program is to be verified. Fourth, the performance target mechanism is applied for all project application and verification. All the expenditure items in the 2016 zero-based budgeting program are to undergo the performance targets identification and verification process before entering the project pool. Fifth, applicant projects are to undergo a rigorous feasibility study and examination process, and the budget is to be allocated based on local financial conditions and arranged in a priority order. Sixth, the zero-based budgeting reform is to be coordinated with the medium-term financial planning and the project pool reform. All project expenditures are to be included in the project pool management.■

The Finance Department of Yunnan Province took five measures to improve budget management of the social security fund

According to the news released on January 7 by the Finance Department of Yunnan Province, the provincial finance authority has taken five measures to improve budget management of the social security fund. First, the Health and Family Planning Commission of Yunnan Province issued a *Circular on the Pilot Scheme of Three-year Rolling Budget for the Social Insurance Fund*, which specified the guidelines, basic principles, objectives, scope and requirements of the three-year rolling budget. Second, the budget preparation and reporting mechanism for the social security fund is to be led by the finance authority and joined by relevant agencies, which are to maintain communication and consultation. Third, a set of comprehensive, detailed and standardized evaluation guidelines is established for the budget management of the social security fund. Fourth, monthly analysis on the balance of the social security fund is to be carried out, and the implementation progress of the fund budget is to be reported. Fifth, the evaluation measures for budget management of the social security fund are designed and published, which are to link the assessment results with the allocation of supplementary fund for the budget management of the fund.■

Gansu Province focused great efforts on consolidating the use of fiscal funds for poverty reduction

According to the news released by the Finance Department of Gansu Province on January 11, Gansu Province, in 2015, focused great efforts on building a long-term mechanism to consolidate the use of fiscal funds for poverty reduction. (1) The relevant provincial departments drafted plans for fund consolidation, made guidelines for project application, and set requirements for the direction and management of fund use; the county-level governments submitted their annual demand of project funds to the municipal governments for approval. (2) The relevant provincial departments guided the county-level governments in selecting project for application in accordance with sector plans and in using the funds according to specified purpose; the county-level governments used, in a consolidated way, all sorts of poverty reduction funds arranged by the provincial, municipal and county-level governments. (3) The provincial finance department would supervise the disbursement and reporting of funds; and the municipal governments would ask relevant agencies to enhance day-to-day oversight. ■

Qinghai Province has established a mechanism that covers the whole process from budgeting to implementation so as to revitalize the stock of fiscal funds

According to the news released by the Finance Department of Qinghai Province on January 12, Qinghai, in 2015, has established a mechanism that covers the whole process from budgeting to implementation so as to revitalize the stock of fiscal funds. (1) Accelerating the fiscal expenditure. A series of effective measures, e.g. improving the spending responsibility mechanism, qualifying and breaking down the monthly spending task, and making advance disbursement, have been adopted to ensure the balanced and steady growth of fiscal expenditure. (2) Stepping up the recoup of the stock of fiscal funds. On the basis of the statistics of the stock of fiscal funds, all localities and government departments in Qinghai were urged to sort out and recoup the surplus and carryover funds. (3) Cleaning up the bank accounts of budget units. The Finance Department of Qinghai Province worked with the Xining Branch of the PBOC in comprehensively cleaning up the bank accounts of provincial departments. (4) Strengthening the performance evaluation and accountability. The areas and departments that open bank accounts in violation of regulations or fake the stock of fiscal funds would be held accountable. (5) Formulating budget in a scientific way. More efforts were put on improving the project pipeline, enhancing budget management, making budgeting more detailed and ensuring budget is in place at the beginning of the year. ■

Luoyang City of Henan Province implemented six mechanisms to enhance accreditation management of fiscal investment

According to the news released on January 18 by the Finance Department of Henan Province, Luoyang city implemented innovative fiscal management to enhance investment accreditation through early warning, auditing, pricing and information mechanisms. First, in order to raise assessment efficiency, pre-warning mechanism is introduced for overdue projects, so as to ensure early intervention and on-time completion. Second, the assessment procedure is rigorously practiced, which ensures four stage of auditing, i.e. trial assessment, review, inspection by deputy head, and final accreditation. Third, the price information section is established to collect monthly updated data, so as to meet the requirement of economic management. Fourth, special accreditation office is set up for projects under 500,000 RMB of investment, which is to simplify procedures with designated personnel. Fifth, information platform is built on special website to improve assessment efficiency and exchange. Sixth, both the fiscal budget accreditation and auditing are put under the oversight mechanism. ■

LOCAL FINANCE

Xiamen City promoted supply-side fiscal reform from four aspects

According to the news released on January 21 by the Finance Bureau of Xiamen City, the city implemented four measures to promote supply-side reform. First, industrial supporting funds were restructured to speed up commercialization of scientific and technological achievements, and encourage the use of robots in enterprises. Second, the VAT for business tax reform was actively implemented, innovative financial tools were used to lower financial costs for enterprises, and institutional mechanisms of FTA were improved. Third, innovative industrial supporting policies were adopted, including PPP models, municipal development funds, state-owned assets operation platforms, and government purchase of services. Fourth, measures were taken to improve the budget management system, including optimizing the municipal finance system, clarifying property rights and obligations, fiscal consolidation and revitalizing the stock of capital, strictly controlling administrative expenses, and streamlining and decentralizing the administrative power.■

Finance authorities of Xinjiang Uygur Autonomous Region poised to adjust policies to better support the development of industries

According to the news released by the Finance Department of Xinjiang Uygur Autonomous Region on January 26, the finance authorities of Xinjiang will adjust policies to better support industry development. (1) Improving fiscal policies to better support industry development. Efforts will be put on fostering the environment for the development of industries, and fiscal policies will be deployed to make financial capital and private capital more accessible for enterprises. (2) Studying the creation of a fund by governments to guide industry development. In three years, the direct fiscal support to enterprises will all be converted into the fund to attract more private capital so as to spur the growth of enterprises. (3) Continuing to support the development of emerging industries of strategic importance. Private capital will be guided to support the development of emerging industries of strategic importance in Xinjiang, including the manufacturing of advanced equipments, new energy and new material. (4) Supporting the transformation and upgrading of conventional industries. The excess capacity will be digested while enterprises will be called on to cut energy consumption and enhance product quality.■

Finance authorities of Shandong Province eased the access of SMEs to finance by promoting financing based on government procurement contract

According to the news released by the Finance Department of Shandong Province on January 28, the *Interim Measures for the Administration of Government Procurement Contract Financing in Shandong* was issued, which provided the following. (1) Finance authorities will create a platform of symmetric information that connects businesses and banks, but will not involve in the selection of financing institutions, nor will they provide third party guarantee to financing projects. (2) Collateral requirements will be scrapped and financing is readily accessible upon the obtainment of government procurement contract. (3) Preferential interest rate will be provided with the rate based on government procurement contract falling by over 10%. (4) Green lane will be established by financial institutions to approve government procurement contract financing, special staff will be manned to provide tailored services and the approval procedures will be simplified. (5) E-operation and disclosure of information will be implemented throughout the procurement process to ensure that the contract is authentic and the contract number is unique.∎

Finance authorities in Shenyang City achieved remarkable results in promoting comprehensive rural reform

According to the news released on February 3 by the Finance Department of Liaoning Province, the Shenyang municipal finance authorities actively promoted comprehensive rural reform and achieved remarkable results. First, progress was made in providing fiscal subsidies for public services in villages based on case-by-case consultation. Throughout 2015, Shenyang municipal authorities have invested 14.7351 million RMB of fiscal funds at various levels, which completed 505.6 km of village roads, covering 74 towns and 159 villages, benefiting nearly 0.3 million farmers. Second, the village fund for constitutional building of the CPC grassroots organization was increased from 12,500 RMB to 25,000 RMB per village, an increase of 100%. Stronger financial status has effectively promoted grassroots organizational building and enhanced their vitality. Third, the mechanism for maintenance of rural public service was launched with 100 million RMB of fiscal input. The maintenance was focused on services relating to village sanitation, public facilities and venues. Fourth, the new agricultural social service system was actively promoted. 11 new projects in Shenyang were approved by provincial authorities as demonstrative services for agricultural modernization, an increase of 10 projects over the previous year.∎

Guangdong Province initiated five measures in preparing the 2016 budget

According to the news released on February 4 by the Finance Department of Guangdong Province, the province has taken the lead in designing and disclosing the project pool for earmarked funds and policy funds, and achieved remarkable results. Efforts were taken in the following aspects: first, developing the general working plan and project pool for the earmarked funds. The auditing focus was shifted from "how much money was spent" to "what difference has been made". Second, designing the fact-sheet for policy funds, which was to disclose the overview status of policy funds. Third, taking into account the social insurance billing rates, so as to enable more detailed budget planning for the Social Insurance Fund. Fourth, initiating early intervention in the projects relating to budget planning, so as to integrate the guidelines of provincial People's Congress in the budget preparation. Fifth, taking the lead in designing animated Reader's Guide to improve the readability of the budget report.∎

Finance authorities of Guizhou Province have made headway in fiscal supervision and inspection

According to the news published by the Finance Department of Guizhou Province on February 15, finance authorities in Guizhou have been making headway in fiscal supervision and inspection.

(1) Following the principle of "treating both symptoms and root causes", they combined the tackling of the misrepresentation of accounting information with the combating of corruption to hold accountable the people that misrepresent accounting information. (2) They put forth many constructive advices and suggestions by integrating accounting inspection with fiscal regulation, fiscal reform and improvement of economic system. (3) They further enhanced the efficiency of using funds by punishing the failure of compiling complete departmental and city-level budgets or incorporating carryovers and surplus into budget. (4) Through the inspection of the accounting information, they helped correct the negligence over the importance of financial management on the part of the heads of some inspected institutions.■

Financial authorities of Yunnan Province have been working on four areas to support the establishment of a new system for the grass-root health service network

According to the news released by the Finance Department of Yunnan Province on February 17, it has been working on four areas to support the establishment of a new system for the grass-root health service network. (1) It disbursed 103.74 million RMB of funds to standardize 244 township clinics and 2627 village clinics. (2) It arranged 100 million RMB to support the integrated management over 395 township clinics and county hospitals, and invested 6.1054641 billion RMB to fund the free-of-charge training of medical students and recruitment of practicing doctors at grass-root health institutions. (3) It implemented the policy of providing rewards and subsidies for the grass-root health institutions engaging in comprehensive reforms, and helped improve the basic drug system and the new system for the functioning of grass-root health institutions. (4) From 2014 onwards, the number of village doctors that receive subsidies from it increased from 33241 to 37390, and the level of subsidy rose from 200 RMB to 300 RMB per person per month.■

Finance authorities in Qinghai Province have duly performed their tasks of 2015 to support the sustainable and healthy development of economy and society

According to the news published by the Finance Department of Qinghai Province on February 18, finance authorities in Qinghai have duly performed their role to support the sustainable and healthy development of economy and society. (1) 26.71 billion RMB of budget revenue was collected in Qinghai, up by 6.1%, and 150.55 billion RMB of budget expenditure was made, up by 11.7%. (2) 100 billion RMB of central-level subsidies were disbursed, up by 7.5%. (3) The policy of structural tax cut and across-the-board fee reduction was implemented, with 101 central and provincial administrative charges scrapped, suspended and exempted, and 9.44 billion RMB of taxes slashed in 2015. (4) 75% of fiscal expenditure continued to be used on areas related to people's livelihood. (5) The tasks of fiscal and tax reform were earnestly implemented and the *Master Plan of Deepening Fiscal and Tax Reform in Qinghai Province* was introduced.■

The 2016 centralized government procurement catalog and standards of Yunnan Province featured new content, accurate description and detailed requirements

According to the news released on February 24 by the Finance Department of Yunnan Province, the 2016 centralized government procurement catalog and standards of Yunnan Province, which was issued by the General Office of the provincial government, featured new content, accurate description and detailed requirements. First, for the new content, the threshold for centralized and decentralized procurement was raised from 100,000 to 200,000 RMB, and "government procurement of services" and "PPP project procurement" were added to the service category of the catalog. Second, for accurate description, seldom-used items were removed from the centralized government procurement catalog; professional computer software, photography and some other items that used to be in the centralized governmental procurement catalog were adjusted to the centralized departmental procurement catalog; the tax invoices and other financial instruments were included in government procurement. Third, for detailed requirements, the purchaser is required to provide policy support to small and micro enterprises when preparing procurement budget; the purchaser or procurement agency is required to disclose purchased item and related documents of the procurement. ∎

Huainan City of Anhui Province identified six objectives for public welfare projects

According to the news released on February 25 by the Finance Department of Anhui Province, the public welfare projects in Huainan City met people's expectation and delivered tangible benefits. First, four measures were taken to tackle poverty, i.e. industrial development, land swap and relocation, social security and employment medical assistance. With those measures, 50,000 people were lifted out of poverty throughout the year, including 31,000 from Shou County. Second, policies were adopted to support start-up businesses and employment, with stronger efforts in providing jobs for the disadvantaged groups. Third, public inputs in urban and rural compulsory public schools were increased across the board, and poor high school students were exempt from tuition fees. Fourth, efforts were made to implement universal coverage of social security, as well as to improve medical insurance for critical illness and the pension insurance system. Fifth, strategic adjustment was made in the campaign of building the beautiful countryside by focusing on broader areas. Sixth, efforts were made to improve urban functions. ∎

Zhoukou City, Henan Province took measures to promote agricultural insurance reform

According to the news released by the Finance Department of Henan Province on March 1, Zhoukou City has been advancing rural financial reform and promoting agricultural insurance. (1) Establishing a leading group headed by the deputy mayor and with members from fiscal and financial authorities. (2) Creating an agricultural insurance operating mechanism fit for rural circumstances and with both policy and commercial nature, and raising the capacity to deliver covered services.

(3) Requiring the Zhongyuan Agricultural Insurance Corporation to move faster to improve the grass-root service network of agricultural insurance. (4) With guidance from the government and by following a market-determined, voluntary and coordinated approach, introducing new insurance products to support the development of agricultural products with specialties and to offer greater variety of insurance products. (5) Guiding the Zhongyuan Agricultural Insurance Corporation to prioritize its investment in rural infrastructure, major public-welfare projects and new agri-business entities. (6) Conducting performance evaluation and enhancing oversight and accountability. ■

The Finance Bureau of Changsha City, Hunan Province has created a comprehensive and multi-layered cyber security system to ensure the security of fiscal funds and information

According to the news released by the Finance Department of Hunan Province on March 3, in recent years, the Finance Bureau of Changsha City has created a comprehensive and multi-layered cyber security system to ensure the security of fiscal funds and information. (1) Establishing a long-term mechanism for cyber security and regulating the procedures for exclusive network access, terminal management and network troubleshooting to ensure the security of network and data. (2) Further applying the authentication and authorization management system across the city. (3) In accordance with the requirements set out in documents published by MOF and the Finance Department of Hunan Province, conducting the grade III protection evaluation of the information system, and upgrading the security management equipments on the basis of the evaluation results. (4) Using the database security audit system to track all access and operation to the database. (5) Creating a local backup system for fiscal data as well as an off-site disaster-tolerant backup system in Shaoyang City. ■

Guangzhou City, Guangdong Province strengthened local government debt management

According to the news released on March 9 by the Finance Department of Guangdong Province, the municipal government of Guangzhou City steadily promoted reforms on government debt management in recent years, which effectively prevented and defused debt risks. (1) Issuing a series of management documents to cover the government debt under fiscal supervision and standardize the financial management of the debt. (2) Submitting the annual plan of government debt to the standing committee of the Municipal People's Congress for its review and simultaneously webcasting it to the public. (3) Conducting bond swap to reduce the cost of debt from 5.5% to around 3.5%, equivalent to 2 billion RMB of interest saved annually. (4) Conducting a comprehensive stock-taking of existing debt, and reducing government debt by coordinating existing fiscal funds and tapping idle land resources. Efforts were made in rationally differentiating non-operational and operational debt; accelerating the development of idle land of municipal SOEs; and strengthening the monitoring and guidance over district government debt. ■

Finance authorities in Sichuan Province increased financial support to pre-school education

According to the news released on March 10 by the Finance Department of Sichuan Province, fiscal input to pre-school education will be increased in 2016. The annual planned input was 830 million RMB, growing by 270 million RMB over last year, an increase of 48.2%. (1) In 2016, children of ethnic autonomous regions and profiled low-income families of the province will be exempt from nursing fees at kindergartens on a verified basis. The nursing fees in poverty counties at four main areas are to be reduced by 20%, up from the previous 10% deduction. (2) Enhancing support to urban kindergartens and private kindergartens. An additional 50 million RMB is to be mainly used for the expansion and renovation of urban kindergartens. (3) Advancing institutional innovation in providing fiscal support to pre-school education. Private investors are encouraged to participate in piloting public welfare kindergartens through procurement of pre-school services and public support for private organizations.■

The Finance Department of Jilin Province adopted four measures to tackle poverty

According to the news released on March 11 by the Finance Department of Jilin Province, the provincial finance authorities adopted measures to tackle poverty. (1) Increasing provincial fiscal transfer payments to poverty-stricken areas and old revolutionary bases, and prioritizing investment in infrastructure construction and public services in poor areas. (2) Raising 500 million RMB every year to foster economic and social development in poor areas by supporting infrastructure construction and production. (3) Urging municipal and county level authorities to make coordinated arrangement for provincial earmarked funds based on specified targets for poverty reduction, and emphasizing the use of market-oriented approach. (4)Disclosing the annual plan of earmarked funds for poverty reduction, the supporting target and capital amount, for the review and supervision of the general public.■

Finance authorities of Shanxi Province have been making full use of public finance to support people's livelihood

According to the news released by the Finance Department of Shanxi Province on March 15, it has been making full use of public finance to support people's livelihood and to promote stable social and economic development. (1) It made advance allocation of fiscal funds and transfer payment to cities and counties, expedited the approval of budget, sorted out the surplus and carryover funds, made more efficient use of funds, and aggressively cut back on the general expenditures. (2) It created a special fund to guide PPP investment to improve the urban living environment in Shanxi. (3) It decided on the credit rating agencies for government bonds in 2016 and moved faster for the bond issuance. (4) It raised 4.39 billion RMB of registered capital through bond issuance and set up the Shanxi Poverty Reduction and Development Company. (5) It stepped up efforts to implement policies that can bring benefits to the people.■

LOCAL FINANCE

Chongqing Municipality has introduced preferential policies to support rural migrant workers to return home to start business

According to the news released by the Finance Bureau of Chongqing Municipality on March 16, to better guide rural migrant workers to return home to start their business, Chongqing Municipal Government has published the *Implementing Plan for Encouraging Rural Migrant Workers and Other People to Return Home to Start Business*. (1) If the start-ups in the business incubation center stay in business for over a year and create certain number of jobs, the incubation center will receive special funds as subsidies. (2) The start-ups or new agri-business entities created by those returnees will receive up to 150,000 RMB of secured start-up business loans and interest subsidies, and a special fund will be set up to compensate for the risks associated with those loans. (3) Different sorts of funds that are used to support start-ups will be consolidated, and a special fund will be created to give subsidies to the logistics, premise renting, water, electricity and internet expenses of start-ups and finance the training and learning of those that start their business. (4) Starting from the date of their registration, the micro enterprises and the encouraged SMEs created by the returnees will receive, for two years, tax credits for their corporate income tax, business tax and the locally retained VAT.∎

Finance authorities in Shandong Province adopted 45 initiatives to eliminate poverty in the province

According to the news released on March 21 by the Finance Department of Shandong Province, the Department has issued the *Implementation Opinions on Promoting the Leading Role of Government Investment in Eliminating Poverty in the Province*, to provide solid financial and policy foundation to rid the province of poverty by the end of 2018. (1) The expenditure structure is to be optimized. Earmarked funds for poverty reduction should be increased substantially to ensure the annual growth of the funds to be significantly higher than the growth of fiscal revenue. (2) The earmarked poverty alleviation funds are allocated to specific counties mainly based on the population under poverty line and per capita financial resources, and to be used by county level authorities at their own discretion. (3) Various funds to fight poverty such as earmarked funds, industrial supporting funds and development funds should be coordinated based on root causes of poverty at various localities and local conditions. (4) The provincial finance department is to establish a joint meeting system on poverty reduction and development to coordinate and give guidance to the initiatives supported by fiscal resources, and supervise the implementation of various policy measures.∎

The Finance Department of Yunnan Province provided new guidance to the municipal finance authorities in their work to support auditing

On March 22, according to the news released by the Finance Department of Yunnan Province, four requirements were given to municipal finance bureaus of the province. (1) The finance authorities should better understand the importance of and enhance support to related auditing work, so as to improve fiscal administration of the province. (2) Efforts should be made to win over auditing authorities' understanding and support in major fiscal policies and initiatives, so as to promote synergy. (3) When irregularities are uncovered by auditing, serious corrective measures should be adopted. (4) Laws and regulations such as the *Budget Law* and *Rules on Strengthening Administration of Fiscal Funds by the People's Government of Yunnan Province* should be rigorously implemented to heighten financial discipline and supervision.■

Chongqing Municipality established the platform for the transaction of public resources featuring Internet +

According to the news released by the Finance Bureau of Chongqing Municipality on March 29, Chongqing has introduced the *Plan for Establishing an Integrated Platform for the Transaction of Public Resources* to make the transaction more regulated and transparent and and further enhance the efficiency and effectiveness of the allocation of public resources. (1) Consolidate the existing transaction platforms through "Internet +" to create an integrated electronic transaction information system. (2) Basically complete the consolidation before the end of June 2016, and put in place a standardized, open, transparent, efficient, well-regulated and supervised system for the transaction of public resources. (3) The platform is organized along municipal and district (county) levels on account of local administrative circumstances. (4) Transaction service function and transaction oversight function shall be separated and one shall not be subordinated to the other. (5) Build a tiered supervision system, have a defined line of responsibility, and enhance oversight accountability of government agencies.■

The Finance Bureau of Hohhot, Inner Mongolia Autonomous Region took five measures to ensure the sustained and stable development of economy and society

According to the news released by the Finance Department of Inner Mongolia Autonomous Region on March 30, to adapt to the new normal of economic growth, the finance authorities of Hohhot have taken multiple measures to boost the social and economic development of localities by leveraging the role of fiscal funds. (1) Step up supports to priority areas and set up special funds to guide the development of industrial and service sectors. (2) Create a platform for communication and cooperation among finance authorities, banks and businesses, support key businesses to expand production, and boost tertiary industry such as cloud computing, tourism and logistics. (3) Implement supportive fiscal and tax policies and encourage businesses to phase out outdated production capacity, digest excess capacity and advance merger and reorganization. (4) Actively support counties and districts to operationalize new key projects, accelerate the timetable of development zones and industrial parks, and boost the headquarters economy. (5) Assess the trend of fiscal revenue, regulate the collection of non-tax revenue, improve the incentive-disincentive mechanism, and ensure fiscal revenue is collected to the fullest extent possible.■

LOCAL FINANCE

The Finance Department of Yunnan Province adopted six initiatives to enhance fiscal performance supervision in 2016

According to the news released on April 6 by the Finance Department of Yunnan Province, six initiatives were adopted to enhance fiscal performance supervision. (1) Establish and improve a performance mechanism covering performance objectives, progress tracking, evaluation and results utilization. (2) Strengthen the leading role of performance objectives, and conduct audit and appraisal there of to build a solid foundation for performance supervision. (3) Guide all levels of departments in Yunnan to gradually build a multi-level performance evaluation index system, and actively explore piloting programs for interim performance evaluation. (4) Various levels of departments in Yunnan should effectively enforce supervision over budget performance throughout the whole process of budget management. (5) Establish a regular reporting mechanism for performance supervision and publish the progress reports on government portals for public oversight. (6) Establish a performance information disclosure platform to publish management progress, institutional building status and other updates.∎

Finance authorities in Shandong Province strengthened supervision to ensure safe and efficient use of poverty alleviation funds

According to the news released on April 7 by the Finance Department of Shandong Province, four measures were adopted to improve the management and supervision of poverty alleviation funds. (1) The Finance Department of Shandong Province is to establish a joint-meeting system to coordinate and guide poverty alleviation and development efforts supported by fiscal funds. (2) Clarify power and responsibilities for finance authorities at various levels based on respective features, supporting areas and management requirements of the earmarked fiscal funds and industry-specific funds for poverty alleviation. (3) Improve the management system for poverty alleviation funds and projects by specifying responsibilities and clarifying detailed operational process, so as to cover the funds under holistic and institutional supervision. (4) Enhance tracking management of the funds, expand "one-pass" for agriculture subsidies, and roll out the grassroot digital management system for fiscal funds. Establish a regular statistical reporting mechanism for the funds, launch a performance oversight system, and heighten supervision and inspection efforts.∎

The Finance Bureau of Hengyang City, Hunan Province has created the interview mechanism in its fiscal inspection and supervision to ensure well-regulated law enforcement

According to the news released by the Finance Department of Hunan Province on April 11, the Finance Bureau of Hengyang City has created the interview mechanism in its fiscal inspection and supervision to ensure that finance authorities exercise their authority in accordance with laws and laws are enforced in a well-regulated way. (1) It called meetings and conducted interviews through various ways to enhance awareness about the importance and necessity of the interview mechanism. (2) It introduced the *Interview Mechanism of Fiscal Supervision and Inspection*, and specified that the misconducts and illegal behaviors of the supervised entities would be subject to the interview. (3) The interview would be focused on analyzing the severity and harm of the illegal behavior to help the supervised entities realize their problems so that they would understand and support the law enforcement of finance authorities.■

Yangzhou City, Jiangsu Province used innovative fiscal measures to support mass innovation and entrepreneurship

According to the news released by the Finance Department of Jiangsu Province on April 14, Yangzhou City used innovative fiscal measures to support the public to start businesses and make innovations, which has yielded good effects. (1) In light of the information asymmetry and weak capacity for risk mitigation in financing for start-ups and innovative firms, it introduced fiscal incentives and policy guidance to make finance more accessible and affordable for those firms. (2) It improved the public service to medium, small and micro firms, and delivered financial, tax, legal and business start-up assistance services to spur innovation and entrepreneurship. (3) Starting from 2010, the finance authorities of Yangzhou have made available 100 million RMB of earmarked funds in each year to attract top-notch talents from home and abroad to start up businesses in Yangzhou. (4) The finance authorities of Yangzhou also earmarked 80 million RMB to set up the Yangzhou Property Rights Service Market and disbursed 10 million RMB to create the Yangzhou Equity Trust Center to support businesses to have better access to the capital market.■

Baoji City, Shaanxi Province advocated innovative mechanisms to address financing bottlenecks

According to the news released on April 19 by the Finance Department of Shaanxi Province, the Finance Bureau of Baoji City fully leveraged fiscal resources to attract capital from financial institutions and private sector in priority areas. (1) Establish the Baoji Municipal Venture Capital Investment Guidance Fund. The fund was structured as limited partners with a parent fund and subsidiary funds. The parent fund was established by the municipal finance authority with capital of 1 billion RMB. The capital pool for the first subsidiary funds was up to 5-10 billion. (2) The municipal finance authority is to, through tender procurement, reach contract with a number of professional PPP service providers as soon as possible, and to specify the required services, payment process and standards. (3)The government debt is to be incorporated under budget management, and the borrowing ceiling is to be strictly observed. (4) Advance supply-side structural reforms. Measures should be adopted to make the agricultural industry stronger and more competitive, support the technological innovation of the manufacturing industry, and encourage the upgrading of the service industry.■

LOCAL FINANCE

The Finance Department of Shanxi Province identified seven priorities on improving performance and efficiency of financial asset management

According to the news released on April 20 by the Finance Department of Shanxi Province, the Department would focus on seven aspects on improving performance and efficiency of financial asset management. (1) Design and release guidelines on standardizing and further strengthening supervision over the management of state-owned assets under administrative institutions. Provincial administrative institutions should standardize asset management and asset liquidation, optimize asset management processes and mechanism, and align asset management with budget management. (2) Comprehensively deepen SOE reforms, and participate in the pilot program of restructuring state-owned capital investment and operation companies. (3) Improve the supervision over state-owned capital operation budget and financial information of SOEs. (4) Make innovative use of the special fund for the supply-side reform on the power sector. The Shanxi Investment Group is fully authorized in the whole management process of project selection, fund allocation and investment recovery. (5) Internal control requirements of the provincial finance department should be observed strictly to rigorously guard against and resolve potential risks. ∎

Finance authorities of Sanmenxia City, Henan Province took four measures to strengthen the supervision of government procurement

According to the news published by the Finance Department of Henan Province on April 26, in recent years, the finance authorities of Sanmenxia City have been constantly expanding the channels of procurement and regulating the conduct of procurement. (1) On the basis of the pre-warning mechanism for major projects, it made great efforts to foster a fair, open and equitable competition regime and market environment, and strengthened the awareness for service and integrity. (2) It gradually put into place relatively comprehensive rules for the transaction as well as supervision and operation of public resources. (3) It developed various supervision approaches, used online portals and comments-seeking platforms to improve the public supervision of government procurement, and further enhanced its institutional capacity building. (4) It assessed whether procurers complied with procurement rules, made unauthorized procurement, colluded with suppliers, had discriminatory conduct, and followed the statutory integrity requirements. ∎

Suzhou City, Anhui Province took six measures to further enhance the supervision of government procurement

According to the news published by the Finance Department of Anhui Province on April 28, the Finance Bureau of Suzhou City has strengthened the supervision of government procurement to make it more scientific, meticulous and institutionalized. (1) It further emphasized the use of fiscal funds for procurement and conducted procurement for the items on the catalogue of centralized government procurement. (2) It strengthened the organization and management of procurement, and required procurement to be law-based, accountable and well-regulated. (3) It made a point of compiling procurement budget at the beginning of a year. (4) It made budget more binding, and banned the unbudgeted and unfunded procurement, the unauthorized procurement as well as the intentional circumvention of government procurement. (5) It developed a flow chart for E-procurement to enhance procurers' understanding of procurement process. (6) It raised the procurers' awareness of strictly abiding by the procurement laws and regulations and enhanced the decision-making management over procurement.■

Finance authorities in Guangdong Province promoted reform and innovation to improve budget performance

According to the news released on May 3 by the Finance Department of Guangdong Province, in recent years, finance authorities in Guangdong promoted reforms and innovation to improve budget performance, which has effectively enhanced the performance of fiscal funds. (1) Over 150 management measures were designed for budget performance, which formed a structured, coordinated and comprehensive management system. (2) specialized index system was developed to include general purpose indicators and specific evaluation indicators for agriculture, forest, science and technology, as well as for trade and investment. A management information system was established to cover professional assessment, departmental budget, standards and project pool. Efforts were made to train high-quality human resources for performance evaluation. (3) Establish mechanisms for managing performance objective, enhance interconnection between departmental budgets and performance management, and develop evaluation system based on diversified perimeters to improve the credibility of the evaluation. A special evaluation is designed for priority projects.■

Finance authorities in Shandong Province actively built cooperation platform to accelerate in-depth cooperation between Hong Kong and Shandong in PPP projects

According to the news released on May 5 by the Finance Department of Shandong Province, the Department had in-depth exchange of views with the visiting Hong Kong Trade Development Council (HKTDC) delegation on PPP projects in the province. (1) Sharing successful experiences. Hong Kong has advanced experience in PPP projects and extensively participated in the construction and operations of PPP projects globally. It formulated sophisticated and standardized PPP models and boasted the world-famous "Hong Kong experience". (2) Expanding cooperation platform. Through in-depth exchanges, the two sides built up platforms for mutual understanding, communication and cooperation, which may lead to more successful PPP projects. (3) Promoting showcase projects. Through case briefings on Ningyang City, Jiaxiang City and Yucheng City, Hong Kong delegates established a deeper understanding on the PPP projects in Shandong.■

LOCAL FINANCE

Chongqing Municipality regulated payout of the minimum living standard guarantee

According to the news released by the Finance Bureau of Chongqing Municipality on May 10, to prevent the ineligible people from defrauding the minimum living standard guarantee, Chongqing has revised the *Regulations on the Minimum Living Standard Guarantee of Urban and Rural Residents.* (1) Make more detailed definition of the recipients of the minimum living standard guarantee, which further includes their spouses, underage children, adult children unable to live independently, adult children in schools, and other people to whom they have duties of providing for, supporting and rearing and with whom they have lived together for a long time. (2) Allow the application for the minimum living standard guarantee to be processed at townships (streets) rather than at village (neighborhood) committees, exercise close monitoring and make more detailed requirements on the application materials and processing time. (3) The minimum living standard guarantee will be linked to the changes related to the social and economic development, the living and consumption standards of residents and the price index of basic daily necessities. (4) Carry out regular and dynamic surveillance over the minimum living standard guarantee recipients to remove the ineligible ones. (5) Impose more stringent and specific penalties to deter and curb frauds of the minimum living standard guarantee. ■

Dali City, Yunnan Province took innovative measures to promote fiscal reforms

According to the news released by the Finance Department of Yunnan Province on May 11, the finance authorities of Dali City will take more solid measures to promote sustained and healthy development of economy in Dali. (1) Enhance the monitoring and analysis of key industries and enterprises, make scientific judgment of development trend and ensure the stable growth of fiscal revenue. (2) Identify the promotion of people's wellbeing and social harmony as government objectives, stick to the principle of letting government play the major role while encouraging the private sector participation, continue to advance the government procurement of services, and increase people's income through multiple channels. (3) Make fiscal management more scientific, regulated and IT-based, promote internal control system to prevent and contain all sorts of risks in public finance management and to enhance the efficiency of work, make departmental budget and final accounts as well as the "three public expenses"[1] more transparent and open to the public, require more stringent execution of budget and strengthen budget discipline. ■

Finance authorities in Shandong Province adopted measures to help the poor in employment and starting-up businesses

On May 18, the Finance Department of Shandong Province adopted innovative supporting measures to help the rural poor in getting jobs and starting businesses, so as to raise their income. (1) Initiate

---

[1] "Three public expenses" refer to expenses on official overseas trips, expenses on government vehicle purchasing and maintenance, and expenses on receptions.

supporting programs for junior high graduates from poor families to get vocational education. (2) Tap the employment and venture fund to provide vocational skills training for the rural poor so they may transfer to other sectors. (3) Support loan guarantees and interest discounts for start-ups and poverty alleviation efforts. Registered poor residents who are engaged in planting, breeding, agricultural processing and logistics may apply for up to 30,000 RMB of loans without collaterals or counter-guarantees. (4) Based on training programs for farmers, carry out technology-featured poverty alleviation efforts in several poor villages, and provide training for science and technology front runners, showcase households and management staff in rural cooperatives. (5) Promote tourism to create more jobs and encourage new start-ups. (6) Prioritize the improvement of postal outlets in rural poor areas by adding regular letters, newspaper subscriptions, mail delivery and other basic postal services. ∎

Shanxi Province introduced a number of policy measures to accelerate the development of PPP projects

On May 19, the Finance Department of Shanxi Province announced that in order to promote PPP development in the province, eight supporting policy measures have been introduced. (1) Establish joint review mechanism for PPP implementation to improve government services and optimize procedures. (2) For PPP projects listed as provincial showcase projects, the provincial finance authority is to provide a lump-sum grant based on the total investment. (3) Encourage debt conversion and PPP projects at various levels. (4) Make coordinated use of existing special funds to give priority to PPP projects. (5) Integrate fiscal subsidies into mid to long term budget arrangement to ensure financing, and gradually shift the focus from construction subsidies to operational subsidies. (6) Completed PPP projects can be used as collaterals based on legal approval process. The land-use rights should remain unchanged and be returned to the government after the expiration of the contract. (7) Establish financial supporting funds for PPP projects, and coordinate with the supporting fund established by MOF. (8) Provide policy supports to innovative financial services, encourage franchises pledge, asset securitization and other innovative financial products. ∎

Finance authorities of Jilin Province achieved breakthroughs in using agriculture-related fiscal resources to increase financial support for agriculture

According to the news released by the Finance Department of Jilin Province on May 23, it has taken the opportunities offered by reforms and innovation to make a meaningful attempt of using agriculture-related fiscal resources to increase financial support for agriculture. (1) It consolidated all sorts of agriculture-related fiscal funds, properly increased the size of such funds, and used the funds more effectively. (2) It studied and introduced all sorts of supportive policies to increase financial support for agriculture and make more science-based decisions on supporting agriculture. (3) It created the performance evaluation mechanism for the agriculture-related services of financial institutions, encouraged and guided financial institutions to increase credit supply to key agriculture-related infrastructure projects, agri-businesses, and rural households. (4) It made available 1.23 billion RMB to set up the provincial agricultural credit guarantee agency, which will gradually establish branches in major and non-major grain-producing counties. (5) It enhanced the integration between fiscal funds and financial and private capital.■

The Finance Department of Gansu Province took five measures to comprehensively regulate the payment of provincial budget units

According to the news released by the Finance Department of Gansu Province on May 25, it has taken five measures to comprehensively regulate the payment of provincial budget units. (1) The threshold for the single direct fiscal payment is raised from 50,000 RMB to 100,000 RMB; the threshold for the single payment of expenditures on basic construction, other capital and debt principal and interests is raised from 500,000 RMB to 1 million RMB.(2) The budget unit shall follow relevant regulations and use fiscally authorized payment for the expenditures on wage and benefits, goods and services and subsidies to individuals and households that are below the threshold for the single direct fiscal payment. (3) The *Measures for the Use and Administration of the Government Credit Card of the Budget Units in Gansu Province* shall be strictly enforced. (4) The scope for the permitted use of cash and the amount of cash withdrawal shall be strictly controlled, and the use and withdrawal of cash shall be governed by the *Circular on Further Strengthening the Cash Management of Provincial Budget Units*. (5) The accountability of government departments (units) shall be enhanced.■

Guangxi Zhuang Autonomous Region adopted multiple measures to boost the development of elderly care services

According to the news released on May 30 by the Finance Department of Guangxi Zhuang Autonomous Region, the provincial finance authority has increased input and adopted multiple measures to support the development of elderly care services. (1) Local governments are to forcefully implement the requirement of investing over 60% of the welfare lottery proceeds to elderly care services, and actively adjust and optimize the expenditure structure to ensure effective fiscal input. (2) Take initiative to consult with relevant departments to support priority regions and feature projects based on distribution of resources and local conditions. (3) While the government takes the responsibility as the main investor, the private sector is encouraged to participate in the reform and pilot program of elderly care services. (4) Allocate funds to support the construction of 100 nursery homes in rural areas. Support grass-roots senior group association to purchase mutual care service to meet the demands of in-house care for the elderly.■

The Finance Bureau of Lianyungang City, Jiangsu Province, has adopted five priority measures to promote supply-side structural reforms

According to the news released on June 1 by the Finance Department of Jiangsu Province, in 2016, the Finance Bureau of Lianyungang City has adopted five priority measures to promote supply-side structural reforms. (1) Make good use of fiscal and tax incentives to promote structural transition from extensive industries to high-tech, advanced, featured and new industries. (2) Curb arbitrary charges, and take measures to establish a long-term mechanism to reduce costs for businesses. Actively explore risk compensation for loans extended to micro businesses, support the development of small and medium-sized business entities, and further reduce corporate financing costs. (3) Strengthen social security net, make good use of unemployment insurance to prevent unemployment, and support employment. Provide employment subsidies to settle and re-allocate laid-off workers from industries with overcapacity. (4) Actively advance the renovation of shantytowns. Take targeted measures in poverty alleviation and development, especially for poor villages. (5) Strengthen the coordination of fiscal, industrial and financial policies to form reform synergy, and jointly promote the supply-side structural reforms.■

Finance authorities of Guangzhou City stepped up efforts to support the development of new business models

According to the news released by the Finance Department of Guangdong Province on June 6, finance authorities of Guangzhou City have arranged fiscal funds in a holistic way, optimized the composition of expenditure, increased fiscal supports to industrial upgrading and emerging industries, and sought to give new impetus to economic growth through the development of new industries and new business models. (1) Scale up fiscal support and implement supportive fiscal policies. From 2015 to 2017, a total of 3 billion RMB of fiscal funds are earmarked to support industrial upgrading, meanwhile, 4.74 billion RMB of funds are arranged by Guangzhou for investment into science and technology. (2) Magnify the effects of fiscal funds and create an enabling environment for development. Of the 3 billion RMB funds for industrial transformation and upgrading, 1.5 billion RMB will be used as guiding funds, in addition to which, the Guangzhou Industrial Investment Fund Management Company will raise 4.5 billion RMB of private capital to create a 6 billion RMB Industrial Transformation and Upgrading Fund. (3) Develop measures for the management of the funds and regulate the use of the fiscal funds. The support direction, targets, subsidy standards, scope of use and the application procedures of the funds need to be clarified to ensure the safety and effectiveness of the fund use.■

Finance authorities of Huai'an City, Jiangsu Province supported local specialty industries to advance healthy economic growth

According to the news released by the Finance Department of Jiangsu Province on June 8, in recent years, finance authorities of Huai'an City have made great efforts to promote the clustering of specialty industries to advance the transformation of economic development pattern and enhance the quality of economic growth. (1) Formulate supportive industrial policies that promote the development of industries, private SMEs, industrial parks and commerce circulation, and further step up supportive fiscal policies to boost the development of the real economy. (2) Further strengthen the consolidation of agriculture-related fiscal funds, focus on the key links of agricultural modernization, and raise the efficiency of using the funds. (3) Actively implement all the pro-business policies, make every effort to raise funds, and intensify fiscal inputs to support the development of specialty industries. (4) Further advance the development of cultural industries, develop innovative investment and financing mechanisms for cultural industry, enhance the cooperation between cultural industry and financial industry, and encourage financial institutions to increase financial support to science and technology enterprises. (5) Improve the services to enterprises and grass-root communities, strengthen the inspection of funds, simplify the approval procedures, and conduct supervision and performance evaluation.∎

Finance authorities of Guangxi Zhuang Autonomous Region enhanced efforts to attract more investment

According to the news released on June 14 by the Finance Department of Guangxi Zhuang Autonomous Region, in recent years, the Finance Department has made active efforts to attract investment. (1) Improve government guidance and service. The Finance Department constantly strengthened and improved financial safeguarding mechanisms to attract investors. At the same time, finance authorities in cities and counties have ensured administrative inputs at various levels. (2) Adjust the expenditure structure and increase funding. The Finance Department actively raised funds through spending adjustment and other channels, and arranged departmental budget of 16.64 million RMB for investment promotion. Private investors are also encouraged to participate in investment promotion. (3) Enhance coordination and cooperation while making in-depth policy research. The Finance Department continues to enhance service awareness, and further ensures funding for investment through better management and institutional arrangement. Cross-agency researches were conducted to propose amendment to relevant policy documents and provide policy advice to decision-makers.∎

Finance authorities in Chuzhou City actively supported comprehensive reform in the health system

According to the news released on June 15 by the Finance Department of Anhui Province, Chuzhou City has invested 7.34 billion RMB in medical reform during the 12th Five-Year Plan period. The specific measures included: (1) further consolidated and improved the grass-roots healthcare system and deepened reform of public hospitals at the county level, and initiated urban public hospital reform on April 1 according to the provincial government's overall plan. (2) Arranged 133.48 million RMB in 2016 budget for public hospitals, an increase of 35.98 million over 2015. (3) Prioritized municipal finance resources on key research disciplines and infrastructure development, which helped to shorten the discipline development cycle and HR growth cycle for public hospitals in Chuzhou City, and improved medical technology and service capabilities. (4) Verified the debts of municipal public hospitals and incorporated the debts into government debt system. At the same time, asset management in municipal public hospitals was standardized to establish a modern hospital system.∎

Finance authorities of Shandong Province worked on five fronts to tackle poverty in a targeted way

According to the news released by the Finance Department of Shandong Province on June 20, the finance authorities of Shandong have been working on five fronts to tackle poverty in a targeted way. (1) By optimizing expenditure structure, cutting recurrent spending and tapping unused fiscal funds, the department made available 1.7 billion RMB of funds dedicated for poverty reduction. (2) The pilot program was introduced, on the basis of local conditions and through joint efforts with other government agencies, for the selected poor counties (cities and districts). (3) Funds for the development of special industries were set up to mobilize financial and private capital, and the guarantee fund for the micro finance aimed at poverty reduction was also created to provide loan guarantee for poor people and local special agri-businesses. (4) Innovative industrial policies were designed to help tackle poverty in a more targeted way. (5) The mechanism of monthly financial reporting was established and ten oversight groups were created to guide and supervise the disbursement of poverty reduction funds by the county and city finance authorities. ∎

Finance authorities of Nanchang City, Jiangxi Province took four measures to enhance the wellbeing of citizens

According to the news released by the Finance Department of Jiangxi Province, the finance authorities of Nanchang City have taken four measures to enhance the wellbeing of citizens. (1) They scaled up fiscal resources and raised 38.5 billion RMB in 2016 for people-oriented programs. (2) They strictly contained administrative expenditure and departmental program spending, cut the costs of administrative functioning, tapped the unused fiscal funds, and spent more fiscal resources on areas related to people's livelihood. (3) They pushed forward PPP, improved the government investment platform, and mobilized private capital into people-oriented programs. They also provided rewards and subsidies to incentivize the entities engaging in programs that make people's life better and more convenient. (4) They used the opportunities offered by the fiscal reform to remove institutional barriers, improve service delivery and develop innovative models with a view to improving people's wellbeing and livelihood. ∎

The Finance Department of Yunnan Province adopted all-round measures to promote comprehensive reforms of county-level public hospitals

On June 27, the Finance Department of Yunnan Province announced that measures has been taken to jointly promote the development of a diversified medical service system, strengthen the supervision and performance management of fiscal inputs, and strongly support and safeguard comprehensive reform and development of the public county-level hospitals. (1) Develop the *Interim Measures on Fiscal Compensation for Comprehensive Reforms of the County-level Public Hospitals in Yunnan Province*, in order to strengthen the role of county-level governments in supporting medical institutions, and encourage innovative approaches in providing subsidies by local authorities. (2) Raise a fund of 1.124 billion RMB for county-level public hospitals comprehensive reform, and allocate 286.935 million RMB for capacity building projects in county public hospitals. Provincial authorities have provided special transfer payments of 395.530 million RMB for public health in 2016. (3) Enhance training efforts for healthcare personnel at the county level, encourage and guide the provincial hospitals to strengthen support for county-level public hospitals, and strengthen key clinical specialist development at the provincial level. Strengthen capacity building for weak medical departments, actively promote medical services integration between counties and villages, and support capacity building of traditional Chinese medicine hospitals at the county level. (4) Arrange grants of 100 million RMB to support the development of 135 private hospitals. (5) Improve the hospital budgets and financial management systems, and explore approaches to carry out financial audit on public hospitals. ∎

52. Finance authorities of Shanxi Province focus the issuance of government debt on four priority areas

On June 28, the Finance Department of Shanxi Province announced that issuance of government debts should focus on four priority areas to stabilize growth, facilitate structural adjustment, and promote reforms. (1) Focus on government priorities. Arrange 2.2 billion RMB for poverty alleviation and development; arrange 2.5 billion RMB to repay the deposit of coal enterprises; arrange 1.5 billion RMB for provincial key projects, including railways linking Taiyuan-Jiaozuo, Datong-Zhangjiakou, and Yangquan-Datong, and gasification projects in Shanxi, to ensure project progress. (2) Focus on debt risk indicators. Municipal debt risks are measured through additional debt capacity in 2016, and debt-repaying capacity in 2016-2020. Debt quota allocation will be linked with the risk indicators. (3) Focus on construction investment demand. A total of 22.9 billion RMB bonds was allocated, an increase of 8.8 billion RMB over 2015, an increase of 62.4%. (4) Focus on the management of government debt. The new issuance is linked with the management of existing government bonds. ∎

53. The first provincial-level, whole-process and e-procurement project in Anhui Province has been successfully completed

According to the news released by the Finance Department of Anhui Province on July 4, the first provincial-level, whole-process and e-procurement project in Anhui has been successfully completed. To advance the innovative procurement supervision and better serve the provincial budget units, the procurement supervision office has taken a series of measures. (1) Draw up the flow charts for centralized procurement, local procurement, and wholesale emergency procurement respectively to put in place standardized and unified operational procedures; create a tripartite communication and coordination mechanism to facilitate the communication among the three parties in the process of undertaking procurement. (2) Conduct IT-based procurement supervision and task the procurement supervision office to revamp the entire process of procurement involving budgeting, planning, procedures and results. (3) Use online instant messaging tools and arrange for inspectors to take turns in making online oversight. (4) Make visits to budget units, change the work style, and improve the delivery of service. ∎

The Finance Bureau of Kunming City has implemented 5 measures to ensure steady and fairly fast growth of the city's economy

According to the news released by the Finance Department of Yunnan Province on July 6, the Finance Bureau of Kunming City has implemented 5 measures to ensure steady and fairly fast growth of the city's economy. (1) Compile the 3-year rolling investment plan of Kunming, improve the project pipeline of the 13th Five-Year Plan, accelerate the disbursement of fiscal funds, and advance PPP. (2) Cut fees and taxes, reduce the logistical costs of businesses, steadily address the overcapacity, and alleviate the social insurance contribution burden of businesses. (3) Reduce the financial burden of businesses, adjust and standardize the policy on the use of land for real estate development, introduce fiscal subsidies, and enhance land supply, for example, except for the use of lands for commercial and residential construction purpose, the use of lands for all other purposes will be exempted from the plain area farmland quality compensation fees. (4) Step up rewards for the increase of output and efficiency by industrial enterprises, support the technological retrofitting of industrial enterprises, accelerate the development of service sector, nurture and foster large-scaled enterprises, and promote innovation and entrepreneurship. (5) Develop new areas of high consumer demand, support the regulated development of domestic services sector, intensify efforts to attract investment, and support the international trade of businesses.∎

Tianjin Municipality accelerated the PPP development

According to the news released on July 13 by the Finance Bureau of Tianjin Municipality, Tianjin is to accelerate financing innovation for PPP projects, so as to encourage and guide social capital to invest in public utilities and infrastructure. (1) Establish a municipal facilitation mechanism to promote investment and financing reforms for PPP, to strengthen coordination and form synergy. A series of documents were formulated to create a standardized management system. A PPP information management platform was established to connect with the PPP Center at MOF. Special funds were arranged for the initial funding. (2) PPP projects were accelerated in rail transportation, highway and other municipal public transportation facilities. (3) Project implementation plans were optimized. Priority was given to the supervision of government capitals, guidance funds and operating subsidies in the PPP projects. (4) Establish a standardized process, which includes standardized framework and contract management for PPP projects.∎

Jiangsu Province adopted the *Interim Administration Measures on the Information Disclosure of the Budget and Final Accounts of Jiangsu Province*

According to the news released on July 14 by the Finance Department of Jiangsu Province, the *Interim Administration Measures on the Information Disclosure of the Budget and Final Accounts of Jiangsu Province* was adopted. (1) The finance authorities at various levels of Jiangsu Province are responsible for information disclosure of the budget and final accounts at each corresponding level of government. (2) The finance authorities are to disclose six major government budget and final accounts, including the "three official expenses" and at each corresponding level of governments.

(3) For sub-categories of budget and final accounts required to be published with functional details, their economic ledger should be disclosed as well. (4) Government portals or official departmental websites should be main platforms for information disclosure. (5) The government budget and final accounts should be disclosed within 20 days after approval by the NPC at the same level, and departmental budget and final accounts should be disclosed within 20 days after approval by the finance department at the same level. (6) The Party Committees and governments at all levels of Jiangsu should strengthen the organization and guidance on the information disclosure of budget and final accounts. A sound mechanism of regular assessment should be established with clear guidelines, controllable procedure, accessible findings and easy monitoring.∎

Henan Province has been earnestly performing the duties of fiscal supervision and enhancing the oversight of the state-owned assets of enterprises

According to the news released by the Finance Department of Henan Province on July 19, Henan has been earnestly performing the duties of fiscal supervision and enhancing the oversight of the state-owned assets of enterprises. (1) It actively participates in the reform of SOEs. It carefully studies the policies of SOE reform and actively involves in the formulation of policies and SOE reform in the industrial sector. (2) It strengthens the management of state-owned asset operating budget at the provincial level, which has formed a relatively sound budget system and is covering all the provincial SOEs. (3) It enhances the supervision of the state-owned assets of the enterprises affiliated to public institutions, which are "owned by the state, overseen by the government, and used by the institutions". (4) It strengthens the supervision of the assets and financial accounts of the local financial enterprises. It exercises oversight on the asset valuation of financial enterprises, further controls the executive remuneration, and strictly regulates the benefits and expenses of executives in provincial financial enterprises.∎

The Finance Department of Yunnan Province has recently regulated the compilation of the guiding catalogue for government procurement of services

According to the news released by the Finance Department of Yunnan Province on July 21, it has recently regulated the compilation of the guiding catalogue for government procurement of services. (1) To provide better guidance for the procurers and prevent the purchase of mistaken items, the catalogue of items banned from purchase is specifically drafted this year. (2) The guiding catalogue of this year consists of 6 categories, 58 sections and 300 sub-sections, a notable increase over the 5 categories, 53 sections and 289 sub-sections in 2015. (3) The services procured by the government shall place greater emphasis on the public nature and the public-welfare nature, and give priority to the public services closely connected with people's livelihood. (4) New approaches and models that are conducive to the development of social organizations, effective allocation of public service resources and the improvement of science-based social management should be actively explored. (5) The opinions of different government agencies are adopted to make the compilation more science-based and reasonable.∎

Shandong Province implemented the second batch of 35 demonstrative PPP projects

According to the news released on July 26 by the Finance Department of Shandong Province, the second batch of demonstrative PPP projects were implemented, which presented the following seven characteristics. (1) The projects covered public facilities and education, with investment scale over 100 million RMB for each project, and investment for some projects was billions. (2) The implementation and overall progress were in a fast pace. (3) The transaction structure covered various aspects, including project procedures, services, income, lands, equity and financing, with scientific and reasonable risk-sharing mechanisms and effective risk prevention measures. (4) The demand for services and goods provided by the projects was steady, the charging mechanism was well structured and the pricing adjustment mechanism was relatively flexible. (5) The contract system was sound with clearly defined rights and responsibilities. (6) The operational process was clear, project review was strengthened, process management was specified and strictly abided by standard operating procedures. (7) The target of supports was well-calibrated to deliver clear demonstrative effect.■

Anhui Province standardized the management system for fiscal funds

According to the news released on July 28 by the Finance Department of Anhui Province, the Anhui Provincial Government Office issued the Guiding Opinions on Further Strengthening the Institutional Building of Fiscal Fund Management. (1) The funds should be used for targeted and verified objectives with supporting data. Establish an information cross-check mechanism by using information technology tools to verify the business, tax and international trade information of the recipients of the funds. (2) Fiscal funds allocated to villages should entail relevant public notice at the county, town and village levels. The public notice should be posted at a fixed place and online at the same time. (3) Improve the budget performance management by establishing and improving the financial performance evaluation index system on the projects receiving fiscal support, and strictly apply the results of the performance evaluation.■

Chongqing Municipality took multiple measures to cut over capacity

According to the news released by the Finance Bureau of Chongqing municipality on August 2, the finance authorities of Chongqing have been using fiscal and tax policies to push forward the reduction of excess capacity. (1) Cut overcapacity. For this purpose, Chongqing not only increased fiscal resources by seeking funds from the central government, adjusting its resources at the municipal level and arranging the rolling budget, but also introduced preferential tax policies. (2) Stabilize employment. Chongqing offered laid-off workers options such as retirement, termination of labor contract and self-employment. (3) Advance the transformation and upgrading. Chongqing prioritized the optimal reallocation of resources and factors of production, accelerate the exit of industries with excess capacity, and direct limited fiscal resources towards new drivers of growth, including new industries, new businesses, new models, and new products and services.■

LOCAL FINANCE

Guangzhou City worked on five fronts to establish a third-party fiscal funds performance evaluation mechanism with Guangzhou characteristics

According to the news released by the Finance Department of Guangdong Province on August 3, Guangzhou City has been promoting the third-party performance evaluation over fiscal funds. (1) After the preliminary screening of projects, the Finance Bureau of Guangzhou will seek the comments of the Budget Work Committee of the People's Congress of Guangzhou and the Audit Office of Guangzhou, and undertake third-party evaluation over the projects with major social and economic impact. (2) By following the government procurement procedures, every two years 20 service providers that undertake fiscal performance management will be invited to participate in bidding, and performance management training will be conducted for the bid-winning providers. (3) After the launch of the third-party evaluation, the Finance Bureau of Guangzhou will assign specialists to track the whole process of evaluation to ensure the orderly exercise of the evaluation. (4) The Finance Bureau of Guangzhou will select the well-performing cases for the reference of the third-party institutions and require the evaluation report to be problem-oriented, objectively and truthfully reflect the performance, make evidence-based disclosure, and put forth targeted recommendations. (5) Guangzhou City will make better use of the evaluation results through rectification, disclosure of results, and inspection. ∎

Zhejiang Province accelerated the development of medical institutions with private investment

According to the news released on August 7 by the Finance Department of Zhejiang Province, the Zhejiang Province has recently issued the *Opinions on Promoting the Development of Medical Institutions with Private Investment*, which actively encourages and supports private investment in medical institutions. (1) Increase fiscal supports. The provincial government of Zhejiang will provide fiscal subsidies to private and non-profit medical institutions which offer basic health services. Through government procurement of services, qualified medical institutions can become local providers of public health and basic medical services. (2) Diversify financing channels. Government industry funds should guide the development of the health industry, and form investment funds with participation of private capital and venture capital, so as to speed up the development of medical institutions with private investment. (3) Reduce relevant taxes and fees while providing incentives. According to state regulations, tax incentives for medical institutions with private investment should be actively implemented, while unreasonable and illegal fees should be further cleaned up. (4) Establish incentive mechanisms. After ensuring stable development of the medical institutions, certain proportion of financial incentives can be awarded to the private investors to encourage further participation. ∎

Shandong Province adopted five measures in government procurement of services

According to the news recently announced by the Finance Department of Shandong Province, the provincial finance authority has made evident progress in the reform of government procurement of services, which helped to promote transformation of government functions, explore innovative approaches for government spending, push for the reform of public institutions, and foster the development of social organizations. (1) Push forward the institutional development. The provincial authority has adopted *the Implementation Measures on the Management of Government Procurement of Services*, designed basic procedures of government procurement of services, and published government procurement plans of services. Such measures have provided sound institutional foundation for the government procurement of services. (2) Actively promote innovative measures. Reforms on the government procurement of services include pursuing the reform along the sectoral line, raising procurement standards for services, developing incentives and disciplinary measures for departmental budgeting, and gradually expanding the scope of government procurement of services. (3) Promote procurement of services in cities and counties. The provincial government has held a provincial work conference, issued the *Circular on Further Promoting the Government Procurement of Services*, guided the development of implementation measures and relevant working mechanisms in cities and counties, and established a provincial information reporting system. (4) Actively coordinate with the reform of public institutions, which was taken as a priority in the reform of government procurement of services. (5) Foster the development of social organizations. Relevant policies were adopted to foster the development of social organizations, including better procurement terms for government agencies to acquire services from them, and stronger fiscal supports. ∎

Shandong Province has achieved "three shifts" in the management of agriculture-related fiscal funds

According to the news released by the Finance Department of Shandong Province on August 15, Shandong has achieved "three shifts" in the management of agriculture-related fiscal funds. (1) The shift from "scattered" to "centralized" use. The management of agriculture-related fiscal funds was revamped, the silos among the funds were taken down, and the counties were given the maximum autonomy in the disposal of the funds. (2) The shift from "review and approval" to "deregulation and improved services". A series of policy measures were introduced and more efforts were put on management and services in accordance with the requirements of streamlining administration, delegating power, improving regulation and offering better services. (3) The shift from asking for money to spending money well. County governments adopted the target-oriented and problem-oriented approach, drafted local poverty alleviation plans, compiled the annual plans for the consolidation of agriculture-related funds in light of the poverty alleviation plans, annual development tasks and the disbursement of funds from higher level government, improved project investment, and established the green channel to facilitate investment. ∎

Gansu Province has introduced implementation plans and operational procedures to push forward budget disclosure

According to the news released by the Finance Department of Gansu Province on August 16, Gansu has pushed forward budget disclosure. (1) The budget and final account of all levels of government, the budget and final account of all government departments (units), the budget and final account of all the "three public expenses", the use of funds related to grass-root-level people's wellbeing, and all sorts of information on fiscal and tax management shall be disclosed to the general public. (2) It

LOCAL FINANCE

is made clear that finance authorities shall be responsible for disclosing the government budget and final account, government departments (units) for departmental budget and final account, agencies and units at the county and township level for information related to grass-root-level people's wellbeing. (3) The government budget and final account shall be made public within 20 days after the approval by the people's congress and its standing committee. (4) The government budget and final account shall be made public on the websites of the government or finance authorities and made available for an extended period of time. ■

The finance authority of Hebei Province made breakthroughs in improving the budget performance management

According to the news released on August 23 by the Finance Department of Hebei Province, the Province has established a new mechanism overseeing the whole process of budget performance management, which has incorporated budget objectives, budget implementation oversight, evaluation and application of evaluation results. The measures include: (1) establishing a complete institutional framework for budget performance management, so as to lock-down the reform progress; (2) establishing of a properly structured budget performance management system, by designing an index system of performance targets and developing an integrated budget management information system; (3) preparing performance-based budget on the provincial, municipal and county level respectively, so as to establish a new performance evaluation system and an application mechanism for the evaluation results; and (4) establishing a well-functioning budget management mechanism featuring clearly defined responsibility boundaries and active coordination. ■

Jilin Province promoted coordinated use of agriculture-related funds to support poverty-reduction in poor counties

According to the news released on August 25 by the Finance Department of Jilin Province, the provincial finance authority has optimized the agricultural investment mechanism and enhanced coordination, so as to ensure fiscal resources for poor counties. Measures included: (1) incorporating the 8 national poverty-stricken counties under the pilot program of pooling agricultural-related fiscal funds; (2) pooling all qualified funds of the province; (3) giving prioritized allocation of the pooled funds to the pilot counties, and fully delegating the project approval authority to the county level; and (4) encouraging pilot counties to explore institutional innovation in poverty alleviation through industrial development and capital gains, and giving full play to the guiding and leveraging role of fiscal funds. ■

Zhejiang Province stepped up fiscal investment and introduced policies to shore up the weak links of science and technology innovation

On August 30, according to the news released by the Finance Department of Zhejiang Province, Zhejiang has stepped up fiscal investment to shore up the weak links of science and technology innovation. (1) Zhejiang enterprises that led the construction of national engineering laboratories and national key laboratories will be entitled to up to 30 million RMB of support. (2) The enterprises whose R&D expenditures are eligible for extra deduction of income taxes will be entitled to subsidies from the local city and county government. (3) The establishment of provincial-level major innovation projects will be eligible for priority supports on a case-by-case basis. (4) A fund worth 2 billion RMB will be created to facilitate the commercialization of science and technology findings. (5) The proportion of indirect expenses in science research will be raised. (6) The services provided by the research staff of universities and institutes for the enterprises with respect to technology development and commercialization of research findings will be subject to contract management. ∎

Gansu Province adopted the problem-oriented approach to comprehensively improve the quality of fiscal information disclosure

According to the news release by the Finance Department of Gansu Province on September 1, Gansu has enhanced the quality and efficiency of the disclosure of budget and final account. (1) Make disclosure a regular practice and improve the rules and procedures that deal with the problems identified in inspection. (2) Compile the budget for the year 2016 in a detailed and granular fashion and make sure all the budget items are presented under the functional categorization and all the sub-items are presented under the economic categorization. (3) Disclose all government budgets within 20 days of approval by the local people's congress, and require rectification and re-disclosure within a time limit if the disclosure fails to meet requirement and is untruthful. (4) Create a re-examination and long-term verification mechanism to check and verify the content of disclosure on a regular or irregular basis. ∎

LOCAL FINANCE

Dali City of Yunnan Province tapped the "Finance + X" model in poverty alleviation

According to the news released on September 5 by the Finance Department of Yunnan Province, finance authorities at various levels of Dali made use of the "Financial + X" model to expand financing channels for poverty alleviation and development. (1) In 2016, the municipal authority allocated 180 million RMB of poverty alleviation funds; the county authority consolidated various funds for agriculture-related projects, and the general administrative spending was cut by 5%. (2) The financial channels for poverty alleviation were diversified, with financial institutions playing a major role, the private sector as supplement, and the public finance as the backstop. (3) The PPP model was promoted in the public service sector in the poor areas, so as to give full play to market forces and engage the private sector. (4) A variety of specialized farmers' cooperatives were established to combine the operation of individual rural households. (5) The management of project funds for poverty alleviation was strengthened to ensure the safety and efficiency of the funds.■

Changde City of Hunan Province promoted open government and "sunshine public finance"

According to the news released on September 8 by the Finance Department of Hunan Province, the finance authority of Changde made full efforts in making innovation in the forms and contents of information disclosure, including measures to: (1) prioritize financial information disclosure and online services, provide the online "menu" with more details, speed up administrative procedures and improve public services; (2) provide policy interpretation letters to respond to public concerns and guide public opinions, so as to enhance relevance, authority and timeliness of the policies; and (3) build a consolidated service platform for inquiries for wages, housing funds and disclosure requests.■

Yan'an City of Shaanxi Province transitioned from input-based budget to performance-based budget

According to the news released by the Finance Department of Shaanxi Province on September 9, Yan'an City of Shaanxi has been pushing forward the budget management reform in recent years. (1) The performance-based budget management mechanism was established in 2013, and the scope of performance evaluation was expanded in 2014. (2) The notion of "promoting performance-oriented expenditure and holding underperformance accountable" was introduced, and great efforts were made to establish a new mechanism for performance-based budget management in 2 years. (3) The Finance Bureau of Yan'an City enhanced the review of the budget items proposed by the project agencies. (4) The budget review was firstly focused on the alignment between the performance targets and the tasks and mandates of agencies, secondly on the soundness of performance targets and indicators, thirdly on the relevance and necessity of budget items, and finally on the determination of the budget amount. (5) The priority of fiscal supervision was shifted from compliance to performance. (6) Several workshops were organized by the Finance Bureau of Yan'an City to improve professional skills.■

CHINA FINANCE 2016

Finance authorities of Guangxi Zhuang Autonomous Region built a long-term mechanism for ecological and environmental protection

According to the news released by the Finance Department of Guangxi Zhuang Autonomous Region on September 12, the finance authorities of Guangxi have developed innovative polices to support ecological and environmental protection, which strongly boosted energy efficiency, environmental protection, and new energy development. (1) Fully consider the impact of cities' ecological and environmental protection on fiscal expenditure when disbursing the equalization payment, and step up support for ecological and environmental protection when making institutional design. (2) Make transfer payment to key ecological functional zones since 2009. (3) Establish and improve the ecological compensatory mechanism based on the principle of "beneficiaries pay and polluters pay". (4) Innovate investment and financing approaches and use PPP model to attract private capital for environmentally friendly projects. (5) Innovate approaches for allocating funds and introduce competition mechanism. (6) Improve relevant institutional arrangement to support new energy transportation. ∎

Guangxi Zhuang Autonomous Region issued the *Guidelines on the Trial Program of Supporting Poor Counties to Make Consolidated Use of the Fiscal Funds Related to Agriculture*

According to the news released by the Finance Department of Guangxi Zhuang Autonomous Region on September 19, it has recently issued the *Guidelines on the Trial Program of Supporting Poor Counties to Make Consolidated Use of the Fiscal Funds Related to Agriculture*. (1) The 33 counties (cities and districts) covered in the program in Guangxi and the central and local funds to be consolidated are specified so that each trial county can proceed with their work in a focused and targeted way. (2) The complex consolidation work is broken down to 7 major links, including the formulation of poverty reduction plan and the establishment of project pipelines. (3) The procedures and process of consolidation, which are key to the entire consolidation work, are further regulated and improved. (4) The role of each government agency in the consolidation of those funds is well-defined and the leading agency is designated if there is overlapping mandates among agencies. (5) The oversight and accountability mechanisms are strengthened to ensure the safety of the funds to be consolidated. ∎

Wuhan City, Hubei Province unveiled the plan on reforming the earmarked fiscal funds

According to the news released by the Finance Department of Hubei Province on September 20, the CPC committee and government of Wuhan City, Hubei Province have recently unveiled the *Plan on Reforming the City-level Earmarked Fiscal Funds for Supporting the Development of Industries and the Plan on Reforming the City-level Earmarked Fiscal Funds for Supporting Agricultural and Rural Development*. (1) Instead of the sole model of free and direct investment, a variety of models will be employed to use the earmarked funds, including using the funds to set up special fund and to provide rewards. (2) Different oversight approaches will be used in view of the different models of fund input. (3) The funds will be consolidated and a variety of operating models will be used to boost

LOCAL FINANCE

the development of industries, rural areas and agricultural sector and to upgrade the economy. (4) Better mechanisms for decision-making, coordination and division of labor will be put into place, the budget management will be strengthened, and the assessment and oversight will be enhanced.∎

Anhui Province established an information disclosure mechanism for agriculture-related funds

According to the news released on September 27 by the Finance Department of Anhui Province, the Department established an information disclosure mechanism for agriculture-related funds, which facilitated the implementation of pro-agricultural policies. (1) For subsidies, public notice is to be given at county, village and township levels for the name, use, and policy guidance of the subsidy funds. For construction-related funds, public notice is to be given at county, village and township levels for the project name, policy guideline and approval documents. (2) Public notice at the county level is to be made through official portals, the service hall and the media. In towns, the notice is to be made through the service hall and billboard. At villages, the notice is to be made through billboard and broadcast. (3) Designated phones and email are published to ensure whistle-blowers have channel to voice their concerns to relevant authorities.∎

Yibin City in Sichuan Province adopted five innovative measures in agricultural development to facilitate poverty reduction

According to the news released on September 28 by the Finance Department of Sichuan Province, the City of Yibin adopted five innovative measures in providing fiscal support for agricultural development. (1) Instead of traditional direct fiscal input, the fiscal resource is injected in the form of market investment. By expanding agriculture-related financing, the efficiency of fiscal fund can be improved. (2) Instead of direct subsidy, industrial development fund and contingency bridging fund are established to facilitate local industries. (3) For construction projects supported by fiscal resources, the model of "building - leasing - purchase - transfer" is implemented. (4) By establishing the registered financing platforms and venture funds, fiscal resources can be directly injected into government-supported guarantee platforms. (5) Subsidies for discount loans provided to new types of agricultural businesses are enhanced, in order to reduce social financing costs.∎

The Finance Department of Hunan Province has actively developed innovative mechanisms for the governmental investment funds

According to the news released by the Finance Department of Hunan Province on October 8, Hunan has actively developed innovative mechanisms for the investment of public funds, as evidenced by a number of provincial government investment funds. (1) With respect to the infrastructure investment fund, the Hunan Railway Construction Fund and the Hunan Water Development Fund were established, and through partnership with the China Development Bank, private capital started to participate in the funds through equity investment. (2) In terms of investment fund for the development of industries, Hunan Investment Fund for Health and Elderly Care Industries as well as the Hunan Investment Fund for Commercialization of High Technology were created. (3) The *Interim Measures for the Administration of Hunan provincial Investment Funds* was introduced and the boundary between earmarked fiscal funds and the governmental investment funds was clearly defined.■

The Finance Committee of Shenzhen Municipality has moved faster in supply-side structural reforms by cutting costs and fees and improving the business climate

According to the news released by Finance Department of Guangdong Province on October 9, the Finance Committee of Shenzhen Municipality has moved faster in supply-side structural reforms by cutting costs and fees and improving the business climate. (1) It took lead in drafting the *Action Plan of Shenzhen for Promoting Supply-side Structural Reforms by Reducing Costs and Improving Business Climate (2016-2018)*. (2) It intensified efforts to slash fees and ensured free charge of administrative fees. It also took targeted and systemic measures to cut costs across the board, improve business environment, help enterprises upgrade themselves, and further enhance industrial competitiveness to strengthen the momentum for sustained and steady growth. (3) It constantly improved policy measures and took the lead in implementing the specific tasks of cutting costs and improving business climate.■

The Finance Department of Shanxi Province took multiple measures to promote the application of PPP

According to the news released by the Finance Department of Shanxi Province on October 13, it has actively promoted the application of PPP and took multiple measures to amplify the catalytic effects of public funds. (1) It identified 3 requirements and 8 policy measures to provide policy guidance on

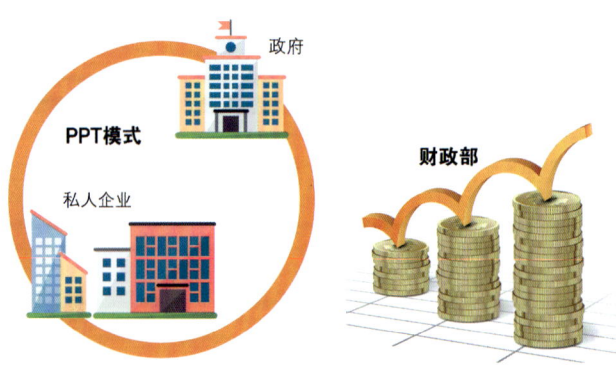

LOCAL FINANCE

the PPP work in Shanxi. (2) It earmarked 50 million RMB in its budget as rewards and incentives for covering the initial expenses of demonstration projects. (3) By following the requirements of MOF and the practice of other provinces, it drafted the *Plan of Shanxi Province for Establishing a Fund for Supporting the Financing of PPP*. (4) Shanxi developed the criteria for assessing the performance of cities in meeting their PPP targets and prodded them to accelerate PPP work by carrying out the assessment. (5) It strengthened the capacity building of PPP. (6) It created platforms for publicizing and implementing policies, enhancing the discipline, publishing project information and providing advisor services.■

Finance authorities in Ningxia Hui Autonomous Region pursued four measures in promoting sound urban and rural development

According to the news released on October 20 by the Finance Department of Ningxia Hui Autonomous Region, finance authorities in Ningxia enhanced public services and goods, improved basic public service system in both urban and rural areas, and facilitated coordinated development of urbanization, industrialization, modernization of agriculture, and harmonious social progress. (1) By pursuing integrated planning for urban and rural development, industrial development, infrastructure construction and social service provision, the finance authority made full efforts to ensure the implementation of the *Spatial Development Strategy of Ningxia* and the national piloting program of integrating various regulations. (2) Efforts were made in coordinating urban and rural areas, and supporting the regional central cities and large counties in the south of Ningxia. (3) Fiscal guarantee mechanisms for cities and counties were established and improved by gradually increasing the size of transfer payments. (4) The earmarked funds for renewable energies were fully tapped to foster growth in the renewable sector.■

Yibin City of Sichuan Province adopted multiple measures to ensure the efficient performance of poverty-alleviation funds

According to the news released on October 21 by the Finance Department of Sichuan Province, the Finance Bureau of Yibin City took proactive and innovative measures to ensure efficient and secured operation of fiscal funds. (1) The municipal finance authority was mainly responsible for making coordinated and balanced plans for the use of poverty-alleviation funds and assigning tasks, while the county finance authority was responsible for making good use of the funds. (2) The administration and disbursement of the poverty-alleviation funds was prioritized by strengthening the awareness of accountability and urgency. (3) The fund disbursement was sped up by clarifying requirements, implementing the advance allocation system and pooling of earmarked funds, and simplifying the reimbursement procedures. (4) Special efforts were made at counties, including targeted adjustment to speed up slower-than-expected projects. (5) The fund performance was enhanced by ensuring implementation of plans, strictly controlling the scope of fund using, standardizing subsides, strengthening financial management, and enhancing information disclosure. (6) Asset revenue was emphasized as a new approach for poverty alleviation.■

Hefei City, Anhui Province took four combined measures to accelerate the government procurement of services

According to the news released by the Finance Department of Anhui Province on October 24, since 2016, Hefei City has been aligning its policies to the overall plan of the central government and of Anhui Province on comprehensively deepening reform with a view to pushing forward the government procurement of services. (1) Combine the expansion of the procurement scope with the modernization of the procurement catalogue, and fully implement the requirements of MOF and the Finance Department of Anhui on the catalogue's compilation. (2) Combine the open and transparent operation with the enhanced accountability, and introduce documents to regulate the operation of procurement procedures. (3) Combine the development of credit system with the cultivation of social organizations, accelerate the development of a credit system for service procurement, and draft and enforce the Measures for Administering the Register of the Discredited Service Procurement Firms. (4) Combine the reform of public institutions with the transformation of government procurement of services, and undertake systemic review of the function, staffing and financing of those public institutions.■

Guangxi Zhuang Autonomous Region took four measures to increase the transparency of treasury operation so as to lay the foundation for transparent public finances

According to the news released by the Finance Department of Guangxi Zhuang Autonomous Region on October 25, in recent years, the Treasury Division of the Finance Department of Guangxi Zhuang Autonomous Region has taken four measures to increase the transparency of treasury operation. (1) It made government affairs and treasury operation open, transparent, and consistent with laws, and used the portal website and office automation system to effectively enhance the transparency of government affairs. (2) It conducted the preparation of fiscal final accounts in Guangxi and accomplished the work as scheduled and as required by the Budget Law during the 12th Five-Year Plan period. (3) It undertook the preparation, review, approval and disclosure of the departmental final accounts in Guangxi and helped lay solid foundation for the transparent government. (4) It took the initiative to publish all the information related to fiscal revenue and expenditure to allow the general public to better understand the fiscal performance in Guangxi.■

Jincheng City of Shanxi Province adopted eight measures to improve the management of earmarked funds

According to the news released on October 31 by the Finance Department of Shanxi Province, Jincheng City adopted eight measures to improve the management of earmarked funds. (1) The establishment of earmarked funds should comply with relevant laws and regulations. (2) The application for establishing new funds should be submitted by the municipal project supervisor to the municipal government. The municipal government should relay the application to the municipal Finance Bureau for reviewing, and based on the review results, decide on the approval of the application. (3) The budget preparation of the earmarked funds should specify the targeted region and project. (4) Municipal matching funds should be arranged. (5) A clear implementation schedule should be established for the funds. (6) After the approval of the establishment of special funds, the municipal Finance Bureau should work with the project supervisor to develop specific management rules, so as to have a set of specific rules to follow. (7) Establish regular assessment and exit mechanism for the funds, and regulate and consolidate the existing funds. (8) Enhance efficiency of the budget implementation of the funds.■

Chongqing Municipality based budget allocation on performance evaluation

According to the news released on November 3 by the Finance Bureau of Chongqing Municipality, performance evaluation was conducted on 45 key projects under 6 agencies receiving budget financing. (1) The evaluation was carried out by diversified panel members, including representatives from the municipal People's Congress for the first time. The review panel included experts randomly selected from the expert bank, relevant professional officials, and members from the municipal People's Congress. (2) The projects were subject to both group review and individual review. (3) The whole process of performance management was established, covering the budget preparation, traceable budget execution, performance evaluation, and performance result-based budget allocation in the future.■

The finance authorities of Hubei Province yielded effective outcomes in the implementation of social security policies

According to the news released by the Finance Department of Hubei Province on November 7, the finance authorities of Hubei has been making their best efforts to support the development of social security. (1) From May 1, 2016, the proportion of pension contribution by employers is cut from 20% to 19%; the aggregate unemployment insurance premium rate is cut from 2% to 1%, and will be implemented on an interim basis for 2 years. The subsidies for unemployment insurance will be scaled up. (2) A total of 2.7 billion RMB has been disbursed as employment subsidies, which ensured the province-wide implementation of policies related to employment and starting-up business. (3) Make the funds available and use the funds as subsidies to ensure the smooth implementation of the pension reform in the provincial-level public institutions. Work in conjunction with other government agencies to formulate the policies aimed at the transition of the pension scheme of the township staff. (4) Implement the health reform policies, move forward the reforms of the pharmaceutical, health insurance and health care systems, and work with competent authorities in integrating the basic health insurance schemes for urban and rural citizens. (5) Disburse 2.2 billion RMB of general transfer payment for minimum living allowances and targeted poverty reduction in rural areas, and support the poverty reduction efforts of counties and cities.■

The comprehensive reform in the rural areas of Yunnan Province helped Mouding County to boost collective economy, promote development and eradicate poverty

According to the news released by the Finance Department of Yunnan Province on November 9, it has guided and helped 43 poor villages in Mouding county to boost the local economy, raise the village income, and ensure that Mouding can deliver poverty eradication targets as scheduled. (1) Provide guidance on the formulation of village economic development plan consistent with the geographical environment and development conditions in rural Mouding. (2) Channel funds to the 10 village committees in 5 townships which have high growth potentials and prospects of income increase, prioritize the development of industries with local advantages, and foster strong local brands. (3) Develop 3 leading village committees, establish 10 village committees with special highlights, select 11 demonstration village committees, and spur the collective economy of 43 weak villages. (4) Explore the tripartite cooperation involving village collective, farmers' cooperative and rural households and improve the models of "village collective + farmers' cooperative", "village collective + rural households", and "farmers' cooperative + rural households" to broaden the opportunities for rural economic development. ■

Shanxi Province promoted targeted poverty alleviation efforts by using equity incomes

According to the news released on November 15 by the Finance Department of Shanxi Province, the provincial authority issued the *Guiding Opinions on the Pilot Project of Poverty Alleviation through Equity Incomes*. (1) Rural collective economic organizations are encouraged to convert natural resource assets into equity, and share it among the members of local organization. (2) When allocating rental and equity incomes, the required contribution to public welfare funds can be allocated to poor households at certain proportion. (3) When building hydropower, wind power and other natural resource development projects in poverty-stricken areas, project equity can be shared with members of the local economic organization or relocated households in the occupied land. (4) The assets of profitable projects supported by fiscal funds or other agricultural funds can be converted into equity to poor households at a certain proportion as appropriate. (5) Poor households are encouraged to take equity in joint-stock land cooperatives, farmers' cooperatives or grass-roots marketing cooperatives, which are established by rural collective economic organizations. (6) When promoting poverty alleviation through financial measures, credit rating should conducted for poor households to make it easier for them to get loans. ■

The Finance Bureau of Zhenjiang City, Jiangsu Province adopted four measures to promote agricultural modernization

According to the news released on November 16 by the Finance Department of Jiangsu Province, the Finance Bureau of Zhenjiang City adopted four measures to speed up agricultural modernization. (1) 49.02 million RMB of fiscal funds was allocated to the construction of major water conservancy projects. (2) The development of high-standard farmlands was supported, in an effort to improve agricultural production conditions, enhance comprehensive production capacity, and strengthen food security. (3) Policy incentives were given to facilitate modern agricultural development for higher quality and efficiency. (4) In order to promote sustainable agricultural development, 4.25 million RMB was arranged to support the comprehensive utilization of straw, agricultural source pollution control, green pest control technology, agricultural products of higher quality and safety. 5.85 million RMB from the Green Fund of Zhenjiang was used to promote green landscaping in high-speed roads and urban areas.∎

92 Jiangxi Province regulated the procedures for the declaration of "three public expenses" and made the government spending traceable

According to the news released by the Finance Department of Jiangxi Province on November 21, it has recently issued regulations on the declaration of "three public expenses", which provides the following. (1) When making the declaration of expenses, the "three public expenses" of the units that are placed under the departmental budget management and are funded by public finance shall present the tax invoice issued by the merchants, the POS receipt for government spending, and the list of expense details input, uploaded and printed on the Jiangxi Government Spending Supervision Platform. (2) Merchants can register at the Supervision Platform, and simply provide the required basic information online, which, once validated, will enable them to become qualified supplier for government spending. (3) The supervision over the "three public expenses" of the budgetary units is conducted online so that the entire process is traceable and transparent.∎

93 Henan Province achieved preliminary outcomes in the operation of the online mall for government procurement

According to the news released by the Finance Department of Henan Province on November 23, the trial operation of the online mall for government procurement in Henan has achieved preliminary outcomes. (1) Through the comparison of online merchants' prices, the disclosure of the quotation information and the minimum price procurement, the prices of the products on the online mall are closer to the market. (2) The effective connection between the online mall and the government procurement management system helps do away with such things as the approval number and the contract record filling, and thus enhances the work efficiency. (3) The procurement on the online mall is traceable throughout the process, and the finance authorities can exercise effective supervision through the IT system. (4) The online mall forces some contracted suppliers to change their operation model, and as a result, some contracted suppliers are creating or using e-commerce platforms to make deal both online and offline. (5) The procurement planning, online price comparison, order placing, contract record filing, and payment upon acceptance are all well recorded throughout the process and can be operated online in a paperless manner to ensure high transparency.∎

Shandong Province accelerated reform in government procurement of services

According to the news released on December 1 by the Finance Department of Shandong Province, the *Opinions on Further Promoting Reforms in Government Procurement of Services* was issued recently, which provided the following. (1) The reform in government procurement of services is to be further deepened, through expanding the reform scope, supporting reform in public institutions and the development of social organizations, and establishing incentive and disincentive mechanisms for better regulation. (2) Innovations should be made to the implementation of government procurement, including improving the centralized procurement catalog, raising the procurement quota and public bidding thresholds, enhancing the flexibility of procurement models and organization, and giving universities and research institutes more purchasing autonomy, so as to give full play to the policy function of government procurement. (3) Efforts are to be made to improve the efficiency of government procurement and its management functions, including allowing the procurement agency to play a more dominant role, promoting standardized development of proxy procurement agencies, establishing a dynamic management mechanism for the evaluation expert pool, and optimizing oversight mechanisms. (4) Guarantee mechanisms for work are to be further improved.■

Huai'an City of Jiangsu Province made effective efforts in reducing burdens for the real economy

According to the news released recently by the Finance Department of Jiangsu Province, Huai'an City achieved remarkable results this year in deepening the pricing reform and removing administrative fees. (1) Removal of certain fees led to lighter burden for the economy and unleashed policy dividends. In implementing the supply-side structural reform in pricing, the city lowered the electricity prices for general industrial and commercial as well as other enterprises by 0.0312RMB/kWh, which is expected to reduce nearly 90 million RMB costs for enterprises each year. (2) Efforts were made to clean up administrative fees. The city has established a series of mechanisms to cover the annual report, oversight tour, collection notification and policy evaluation of administrative fees, so as to strengthen supervision. (3) Special inspection was conducted for reducing costs and burdens. (4) Special supervision was conducted for pricing reform and administrative fees.■

Yulin City, Shaanxi Province has introduced 7 measures to support the promotion of PPP

According to the news released by the Finance Department of Shaanxi Province on December 5, the government of Yulin City has introduced measures to support the promotion of PPP pilot projects. First, for each city-level demonstration PPP project, the finance authorities of Yulin will provide 0.3 to 1 million RMB of subsidies and 3 to 5 million RMB of rewards. Second, a fund dedicated to the financing of PPP projects in Yulin will be set up. Third, if the pilot PPP projects involve government spending obligations, the finance authorities at the city and county level shall incorporate them into their annual fiscal expenditure budget and medium and long term fiscal plan. Fourth, financial institutions or quasi ones are encouraged to explore credit products and financing services that suit the features of PPP projects. Fifth, supportive land policies are introduced. Sixth, city and county-level government are required to improve the mechanism for the adjustment of public service prices. Seventh, a public service platform for PPP projects is required to be quickly established.■

The Finance Bureau of Wuhan City, Hubei Province has fully advanced the development of the internal control system featuring "1+6+N"

According to the news released by the Finance Department of Hubei Province on December 8, the Finance Bureau of Wuhan City has fully advanced the development of the internal control system with "1+6+N"at its center. First, a committee on the internal control work was set up in the Finance Bureau to oversee the internal control work. Second, a dedicated working group was created to thoroughly study the relevant documents. Third, study sessions were conducted to collect and study information from various channels. Fourth, *Notice on Soliciting Comments* was issued to seek the opinions of relevant divisions and revise the documents on the basis of those comments. Fifth, a bureau-wide meeting was organized to review the basic control system and the 6 risk management measures with a view to refining and finalizing the comments. Sixth, in accordance with the comments from the review, a DG-level official was designated to lead a team to revise and refine the basic control system and the 6 risk management measures in detail.■

Yunnan Province introduced the *Management Measures for the Earmarked Transfer Payment for Village Public Welfare Projects on a Case-by-Case Basis*

According to the news released on December 12 by the Finance Department of Yunnan Province, the Office of Rural Comprehensive Reform Leading Group of Yunnan issued the *Management Measures for the Earmarked Transfer Payment for Village Public Welfare Projects on a Case-by-Case Basis*, which provided the following. (1) The transfer payment is disbursed based on the factor approach. The approval procedure is decentralized and streamlined, and various funds are to be consolidated to support poverty alleviation. (2) Advance planning and guidance is to be given to projects preparation, and a supervision mechanism is to be established to cover the whole process of the projects. Authorities at various levels should take corresponding responsibilities. Performance evaluation is to be carried out and the results are to be applied for future funding allocations. (3) The distribution arrangement, process and results of the transfer payment should be made public. Project organizers should disclose the use of the village-raised funding and transfer payment. (4) An interconnected oversight mechanism should be established to include auditing and supervision of the funds.■

Bozhou City of Anhui Province improved five mechanisms to enhance the safety and efficiency of fiscal funds

According to the news released on December 13 by the Finance Department of Anhui Province, Bozhou City has recently introduced the *Management Measures for the Fiscal Funds in Bozhou*, which provided the following. (1) The finance authority is responsible for the development of the management, budget approval, funding disbursement, supervision and performance evaluation of the fiscal funds. (2) Special funds should be properly established, with corresponding management measures and an execution term of 3-5 years. Funding allocation should follow the factors method, projects method, or a combination of both. (3) For all the funds allocated to villages, relevant information relating to the arrangement and disbursement of the funds should be made public at the county, township and village levels. (4) The whole-process budget performance management mechanism should be established. Projects without required performance targets cannot receive budget funding, while those which fail to meet the target or miss the deadline should have their budget reduced. (5) Financial disciplines should be strengthened by establishing a"zero tolerance"mechanism for violation.■

Finance authorities of Hubei Province took four measures to promote PPP

According to the news released by the Finance Department of Hubei Province on December 19, it has solidly promoted PPP to inject new vitality to the supply-side structural reforms of Hubei. (1) The division of responsibility and the policy support for advancing PPP are clearly specified. PPP experts are openly solicited and a PPP expert pool is created to make the management of PPP projects more science-based and well-regulated. (2) Radio, television, press, internet and other media are fully used to raise the publicity of PPP. MOF officials and relevant experts are invited to training sessions targeting local government leaders as well as officials from finance and competent authorities in Yichang, Xianning and Ezhou. (3) Innovative modalities for PPP are actively explored and the cooperation with international financial institutions is strengthened. (4) The finance authorities in all cities, prefectures and counties as well as relevant provincial government departments are required to conduct self-inspection and oversight to ensure clear accountability and accurate data collection.■

The Finance Bureau of Chongqing Municipality took five steps to evaluate the performance of budget management in municipal government departments

According to the news released by the Finance Bureau of Chongqing Municipality on December 20, it has required accountability throughout the process of budget management in municipal government departments. (1) All aspects of budget compilation, approval, execution, final accounts and disclosure are subject to better regulated management. (2) 18 indicators are developed for the compilation of revenue and expenditure budget, the execution of departmental budget, and the budget oversight. (3) All departments are required to make self-assessment of their budget management of the last year and report the results of their assessment. The Finance Bureau will verify and aggregate their reports on the basis of the data from their departmental budgets and final accounts. The budget performance management will be exercised in a steady manner, and a performance target system be established so as to promote budget performance management at both the municipal and the district (or county) levels and cover all the project expenditure in municipal government departments.∎

Yunnan Province made innovative use of agriculture funds to facilitate pro-poor reforms through capital gains

According to the news released on December 26 by the Finance Department of Yunnan Province, the People's Government of Yunnan recently issued a *Circular on the Quantitative Reform of Converting Agricultural Funds to Equity Assets*, which provides the following. (1) By converting assets into equity, farmers are allowed to take equities and share in benefits, so as to make active use of rural assets. (2) Equities can be formed by assets invested by fiscal resources, including in agricultural facilities, aquaculture, photovoltaic projects, hydropower and tourism. (3) For assets of direct investments in farmers' cooperatives and rural collective economic organizations, the assets can be directly quantified. (4) Policy guidance should be improved, with standardized operational procedures for assets return and steady implementation. (5) Organization of the reform should be strengthened with specified roles and responsibilities for various authorities.∎

Shandong Province actively improved fiscal supports for industrial policies, which boosted structural upgrading and enhanced economic efficiency

According to the news released on December 29 by the Finance Department of Shandong Province, finance authorities in Shandong have improved fiscal supports for industrial policies, which boosted structural upgrading and enhanced economic efficiency. (1) Comprehensive efforts were made to cut overcapacity, reduce costs, and shore up weak links of the national economy, with cutting costs as the main objective. (2) Policy supports were given to guide enterprises to make innovations and strengthen new driving forces for the economy. (3) A series of policy measures were launched to help enterprises enhance their competitiveness. (4) Various funds were consolidated to explore market-based operations. Diversified supporting mechanisms are to be established, combining paid support, leading investment and result-based incentive subsidies.∎

REMARKS & OPINIONS

REMARKS & OPINIONS

President Xi Jinping: the AIIB is to effectively increase infrastructure investment in Asia and promote regional connectivity and economic integration

On January 16, Chinese President Xi Jinping attended the opening ceremony of the Asian Infrastructure Investment Bank in the Diaoyutai State Guesthouse in Beijing, and delivered a speech. President Xi pointed out that the AIIB will effectively increase investment in infrastructure, and enhance connectivity and economic integration in the Asian region. By improving the investment environment for developing countries in Asia, the Bank will create jobs, improve long-term development potential, and give a boost for economic growth in Asia and the world. The launch of the AIIB is of significant importance to the reform and improvement of the global economic system and governance. This initiative conforms to the trend of global economic architecture evolution, and nudges the global economic governance towards a fairer, more equitable and effective direction. We hoped member states could uphold the spirit of unity and cooperation, and actively increase input to the Bank, so the Bank can start operation as soon as possible. As the Bank grows bigger and stronger, it will add to the overall strength of multilateral development banks, and make greater contribution to international development. The AIIB should pursue open regionalism, complement the existing multilateral development banks by adding new vitality with its advantages and features, and strive to build a professional and efficient financing platform for infrastructure investment. Given the huge infrastructure financing gap in Asia, the new and old organizations can cooperate and compete with each other to jointly promote infrastructure connectivity and sustainable economic development in Asia. The Bank should take into account the new trends in international development and the diverse needs of developing member countries, adopt innovative business models and financing instruments to assist member states in developing high-quality, low-cost infrastructure projects, thus becoming a bridge for South-South and North-South cooperation. The Bank should follow the models and principles of existing multilateral development banks, fully draw on their good experiences and practices, shy from pitfalls, and achieve high-quality operation from the beginning. ∎

Lou Jiwei: the greatest potential of China's economy lies in reform

In his recent article, Finance Minister Lou Jiwei said that in the current and future stage, it is important to comprehensively implement the requirements of the Fifth Plenary of the CPC, shift the engine of growth from input of factors towards innovation, and provide institutional backing for enhancing productivity, maintaining medium-to-high growth rate and moving up the value chain. The specific tasks include: (1) deepen price reform and reduce government's interference in price formation to provide true and reliable price signals to market and investors and to give the basic guarantee for structural optimization and indigenous innovation. (2) Accelerate the market-based reform of factors of production, improve the modern system of property rights, and refine the bankruptcy and exit mechanism of enterprises. (3) Expedite the SOEs reform, build a modern enterprise system, strip SOEs of public administration functions, focus on the management of capital, and enhance the dynamism, competitiveness and influence of SOEs. (4) Move forward fiscai and tax reform, build a comprehensive, well-regulated, open, transparent and modern budget system, put in place a tax system with scientific design of tax types, optimal structure, sound legal framework, and fair and efficient administration, improve the match between government duties and spending obligations, and properly increase central government duties and spending obligations; deepen interest rate and foreign exchange rate reform. (5) Deepen social security system reform, advance the pension system reform, focus on improving the individual account and maintaining the actuarial balance, build an incentive and disincentive mechanism where the more you contribute, the more benefits you get, create a more transparent and easily understood collection and payment system, realize the national pooling of basic pension for employees, transfer state capital to the social security fund, develop the complementary pension, and foster a system that enables reasonable increase of basic pension and link it to the contribution of premiums. (6) Reform the health insurance system, build a sustainable funding mechanism with reasonable sharing of costs, study the policy of letting retired employees pay to the health insurance, establish a benefit adjustment mechanism that fits the level of funding, comprehensively enforce the critical illness insurance system for urban and rural residents, reform the health insurance payment method, consolidate the basic health insurance system, and build an orderly and tiered treatment system. (7) Speed up the household registration reform and enable agricultural population to work in non-farming sectors to raise labor productivity. (8) Advance the scientific and technological system reform, revamp the central government funding for scientific and technological schemes, build an open and unified national platform for science and technology, and let government agencies stay out of directly managing specific projects. (9) Move forward land system reform, amend the regulations regarding the expropriation and compensation of houses built on state and collective owned land, and encourage the sale, lease and equity investment of rural collective construction land. (10) Accelerate the new-type of urbanization and agricultural modernization, develop compact cities in metropolitan areas, increase the intensity of cities, and promote the intensive use and conservation of land; create a system where fiscal transfer payment is linked to the urbanization of rural migrant population, and gradually turn the eligible rural migrant population into urban residents; push forward the agricultural modernization in parallel, reform and upgrade the agricultural subsidy policies, cut the excessive use of pesticides and chemical fertilizers, and reduce the distortion of the agricultural product market. ∎

Lou Jiwei: improving fiscal policy and promoting institutional innovation to boost the new-energy vehicle sector

In his recent address, Finance Minister Lou Jiwei said that boosting the development of new energy vehicles is an important move to upgrade the automotive industry and part of the efforts of promoting green and innovation-driven growth. On one hand, subsidy policies need to be adjusted, and the mechanism for selecting the eligible subsidy recipients and for knocking out the unqualified recipients shall be created. The eligibility threshold for subsidies shall be raised to highlight the support to superior enterprises; and the subsidy standard also needs to be gradually lowered to force enterprises themselves to grow effectively in market competition. On the other hand, it is important to adhere to the market-oriented principle and establish a long-term mechanism for the development of new-energy vehicle industry. Over the past few years, MOF has been pushing forward the credit-trading mechanism for new-energy vehicles, a system that is technically neutral, sustainable and combines incentives with disincentives. The major auto-producing countries have stepped up their R&D in new-energy vehicle technologies which encompass extensive areas such as material science, IT, control technology, manufacturing technique, equipment manufacturing and etc. In these areas, there is still large gap between domestic and foreign producers. As the technological weakness is increasingly evident, more resources shall be focused on scientific and technological research to

REMARKS & OPINIONS

strive for decisive progress in core technologies. To this end, supportive fiscal policies will be scaled up: resources will be directed to the areas that matter most; approaches of fiscal support provision will be innovated to maximize the leverage effect. Currently, the market environment of new-energy vehicles remains imperfect, constraining the development of this industry, and thus needs to be improved promptly. The central public finance authorities will study more targeted supportive policies to improve the soft environment pertaining to relevant systems and standards and shore up the hard infrastructure facilities for power charging, battery replacement and etc.■

Jia Kang: why China needs supply-side reform today?

Recently, Dr. Jia Kang, the head of the Huaxia Research Institute of New Supply-side Economics, pointed out in an article that the underlying factors for economic growth, especially from the long-term perspective, lie in five main areas: labor, land and natural resources, capital, technology innovation and institutional arrangement. International experience shows that before an economy enters the middle-income stage, the contribution of the first three factors to the economy is more apparent. As a result, when an economy is in an early phase and the "take-off" phase of development, the so-called "factor inputs driven" growth model is usually emphasized, which is reflected as extensive development. After an economy enters the middle-income stage, the latter two factors, i.e. technology and management innovation, are crucial and may deliver greater contribution. The "total factor productivity" is a catch phrase nowadays, and mainly refers to the contribution by the latter two factors. Therefore, the driving forces for China's economic growth in the new era, in fact, are the processes of industrialization, urbanization, marketization and internationalization, informatization, and democracy and the rule of law, which compose of the five factors of the supply-side. It is a hybrid driving system which requires improvement. There are obvious supply constraints and suppression for those factors in current China. Therefore, comprehensive reform is needed to resolve the constraints, especially for the latter two elements to play a bigger role and substitute for the contribution of the first three factors. Such reform should give more play to market players, so as to enhance economic vitality. The so-called "supply-side structural reforms" and "total factor productivity enhancement" lie in the improvement of quality and efficiency of the supply system. China used to have "advantages" of a later comer, but now it needs to take proactive initiative to cultivate supply-side strength. While fully respecting the market as the decisive force in allocating resources, the government must combine the management of aggregate demand and structural supply. In particular, rational supply management is a crucial component and inherent requirement for the structural upgrading and sustainable development of China's economy during the 13th Five-Year Plan Period and beyond, and should be tightly integrated with the reform to ensure effective and systematic supply.■

Liu Kun: strengthening management to ensure the healthy operation of the National SME Development Fund

In one of his recent speeches, Vice Finance Minister Liu Kun pointed out that in order to ensure efficient operation of the National SME Development Fund and achieve both policy goals and economic returns, the Fund should follow the general rules of fund management and establish a structure with binding interests. The organizational structure of the Fund should adhere to market rules, implement the basic system of equity investment, and give play to endogenous strength of fund governance. The management should adhere to market operation to avoid administrative intervention. Meanwhile, it should adhere to scientific supervision to prevent regulatory loopholes. On one hand, we should provide safeguarding mechanism for the market-based management and structure of the Fund. At present, government agencies often make administrative intervention in fund management, which may substitute management decisions and interfere with investment choice, or even constitute multiple layers of review and examination. The management of the National SME Development Fund should be rationalized and avoid such pitfalls. Therefore, efforts should made in, first, ensuring the decision-making authority of the management team; second, establishing the pluralistic ownership structure; and third, strictly implementing the partnership agreement. On the other hand, the government should perform regulatory authority properly. Currently, there are still many blind spots in the regulation of local funds. Relevant agencies may not know how to regulate, or how to fulfill their regulatory duties according to market rules. The regulation of the first national fund should focus on the following areas: first, the government is to participate in the internal governance of the Fund as investor. Second, external oversight is to be strengthened. Upon the consent by its partners, the Council of the Fund is to conduct, or delegate a third party to conduct, regular checking on the investment operations, revenue and expenditure of the Fund. Third, the Shenzhen Municipal Government should strengthen its regulatory responsibilities. As the Shenzhen Venture Fund is a state-owned entity of the municipality, the Shenzhen government should give play to its regulatory advantages and strengthen local management.∎

Zhu Guangyao: the economic fundamentals of BRICS countries remain unchanged

In his recent published article, Vice Finance Minister Zhu Guangyao said that the international economic and financial situation is confronted with daunting challenges and the downward pressure on the world economy is growing. Some BRICS countries are confronted with temporary difficulties in economic growth, yet their economic fundamentals remain unchanged. Facing both challenges and opportunities, more coordination and cooperation among BRICS countries are needed. On one hand, BRICS countries account for over 20% of the world economy and are home to 40% of the world's population. Meanwhile, BRICS countries are major markets for consumer goods and important suppliers of resources. Their economic strength and level of human resources are on the rise, which will keep lifting up the economic growth of BRICS countries and contribute to world economic growth. On the other hand, cooperation among BRICS countries is deepening and widening, particularly, with the visionary leadership and efforts of BRICS leaders, seven leaders' summits have been successfully held, and the all-round cooperation covering economic, financial, cultural, political and diplomatic areas also keep moving forward. In addition, there is solid foundation for economic cooperation among BRICS countries, and notably, substantial progress has been achieved in the financial infrastructure cooperation. Thanks to the efforts of BRICS leaders, the NDB is now up and running and the Contingency Reserve Arrangement has been established, which marks an epoch-making milestone for financial cooperation among BRICS countries. As the economic strength of BRICS countries keeps rising, they also involve more actively in global economic governance, and support and collaborate with each other to speak up for the demands of developing countries. Despite the temporary economic setbacks and financial market volatilities in some BRICS countries, BRICS countries have huge resource endowments, strong human resources, powerful foundation and potential for economic growth, and sound policy space, which will help BRICS countries tackle the current challenges. We have every reason to believe that the deepening economic reform and opening-up of China will ensure the Chinese economy will remain on the track of sustainable and healthy growth and meet the development targets identified in the 13th Five-Year Plan. China, along with other BRICS countries, will push forward economic structural reform to improve economic structure, unleash growth potential, bring benefits to the peoples of BRICS countries, and contribute to world economic growth.■

Liu Kun: strengthening the coordination of fiscal and financial policies to move forward structural reform

In his recent address, Vice Finance Minister Liu Kun said that 2016 is the beginning of the decisive phase of building a moderately prosperous society, and also marks a critical year of China's efforts to advance structural reform. This year's four priorities in fiscal and financial areas are: (1) keeping the economic performance within a reasonable range, intensifying the proactive fiscal policies and adopting a flexible approach to prudent monetary policies. In 2016, macroeconomic environment is complicated and the pressure of maintaining stable growth is rising, which requires the government to have relatively high expenditure and to cut the investment and operating costs of market entities. Therefore, it is necessary to implement both tax cut and deficit in the fiscal policies. (2) Enhancing the quality and efficiency of the supply system and the effectiveness of investment. While new driving forces of growth are nurtured, traditional comparative advantages will also be reinvented to foster the momentum for sustained growth. Targeted industrial policies, solid reform measures and sound social policies will be adopted, and fiscal and financial policies will be more integrated with market mechanisms. (3) Strengthening the awareness and capacity to prevent risks, and controlling and resolving risks in a scientific way. Currently, the economic risks of China are centered on local government debt and the financial sector. To control the former, local government debt management shall be further strengthened, the stock of debt be properly handled, the debt service and payment obligations be honored, and the early warning of risks be enhanced; to contain the financial risks, greater supervision is required and all sorts of financing activities be regulated. (4) Deepening engagement in international economic and financial cooperation and involvement in global economic and financial governance. On the basis of implementing the Belt and Road Initiative, MOF will deepen international economic and financial cooperation to help promote domestic innovation, reform and development.■

Lou Jiwei: build consensus on structural reform and promote global economic growth

During his speech on February 26 in the G20 High-level Seminar on Structural Reform, Finance Minister Lou Jiwei noted that the global economy is still facing serious challenges. IMF has lowered its forecast for global economic growth from 3.6% to 3.4%, and other important international organizations have also lowered their forecasts for 2016. Under this background, it is still a daunting task for G20 to promote strong, sustainable and balanced growth. It is apparent that global economy is in a low growth territory, as reflected by weak aggregate demand, prominent unemployment, heavy debt, and sluggish trade and investment. Such difficulties are closely related to cyclical factors and short-term downside risks, but the deeper causes are rooted in the long-term structural problems of the global economy. Especially after the financial crisis, the major economies are witnessing slower TFP growth and lower potential output, which constitute fundamental constraints on stronger growth of the world economy. The solution for strong, sustainable and balanced growth is to deepen structural reforms. The correlation between structural reforms and macroeconomic performance has been confirmed by many theoretical studies and country-specific empirical analysis, and by international experience as well. Early stage of economic development of a country mainly depends on factor inputs, while in the later stages of development the contribution of TFP would gradually increase. In general, structural reforms have attracted growing attention by G20 in recent years, and many policy efforts were made in this regard. In 2015, G20 countries have updated their growth strategies based on new developments, and made new policy commitments. However, on the whole, the reform progress still lags behind expectations. We still need to further strengthen the structural reform agenda. First and foremost, G20 needs to strengthen top-level design of reform initiatives. While considering the differences in national conditions and stage of development of each country, G20 can seek "common ground" on some basic principles and areas of reform, and set priorities and guiding principles for structural reforms. This will help G20 members to jointly promote and implement the reforms and maximize the positive spillover effects.

In light of major global structural challenges and existing focus of reform commitments of G20, the following areas deserve further exploration. First, to promote trade and investment. In the last two years, international trade and foreign direct investment growth was significantly lower than pre-crisis levels, thus their contribution to the global economy declined significantly. G20 should strive to reduce market access barriers, eliminate tax barriers to cross-border trade and investment, and improve labor market flexibility, all in a bid to increase private investment, foster trade growth, so as to restore the traditional growth engine of the global economy. Second, to promote labor market reforms. Affected by aging and other factors, the structure of the global supply of labor is changing, and the labor participation rate is on a declining path. G20 should strive to break the fragmentation of the labor market, reduce barriers to employment, and encourage labor mobility. Some countries should make necessary reforms to their social security system, encourage employment through competition, and prevent labor costs from rising too fast. At the same time, we should increase investment in education, improve the quality of education and make education better match the demands of labor markets. Third, to encourage innovation. On one hand, we should continue to give greater support to technological progress, including policy incentives as well as institutional and non-institutional protection for improvement of technical innovations, so as to foster early advent of new technological and industrial revolutions. On the other hand, we should make necessary institutional innovations. These include institutional reforms and innovations in taxation, industry regulation, social security, protection of property rights, intellectual property rights at the country level, and further multilateral reforms in monetary, trade and investment, finance, taxation at the international level, so as to improve global economic governance. Fourth, to improve fiscal sustainability. After the financial crisis, the size and duration of heavy government debt across the world is unprecedented, causing serious impacts on financial stability and market confidence. To some extent, it has become a structural problem in the global economy. In the medium to long-term, G20 needs to ensure debt sustainability, and gradually restore fiscal space, in order to lay the foundation for sustained economic growth. In addition, countries are generally faced with medium to long-term challenges in infrastructure, competition, financial reform, environmental sustainability, etc., which should become priority areas for structural reforms in the future.

REMARKS & OPINIONS

While enhancing the top-level design, G20 should strengthen monitoring and analysis of the progress and effectiveness of the reforms, to better implement reform commitments. Currently, progress on structural reforms was mainly measured through qualitative analysis, while quantitative evaluation is lacking, so the evaluation findings are not clear and intuitive. To this end, G20 may consider building quantitative analysis framework through a set of structured indicators. Such framework could, on one hand, objectively measure the overall effectiveness of reforms in the economic, social and environmental aspects; and on the other hand, summarize progress and deficiencies of structural reforms in various areas of a country in an intuitive way, and to provide reference and guidance for the next stages of reforms.■

Zhu Guangyao: with downside risks to the global economy, G20 needs to strengthen policy coordination

In his remarks on February 25, Vice Finance Minister Zhu Guangyao noted that with downside risks to the global economy, G20 members needed to strengthen policy coordination to address the challenges and boost confidence in the global market. The G20 Finance Ministers and Central Bank Governors Meeting is mainly tasked to analyze the current global economic situation and discuss coping strategies. This year's meeting has attracted special attention, because firstly, the host is China, and secondly, the world economy is experiencing "cold snaps". In January, IMF lowered its global economic growth forecast for 2016 to 3.4%, slightly higher than last year's 3.1%; the World Bank lowered its 2016 forecast to 2.9%, lower than the estimate in mid last year; the latest report by OECD also lowered its 2016 global growth forecast from 3.3% in November last year to 3%. The above data more or less reflect the fact that the global economy is facing downside risks. The G20 finance ministers and central bank governors will discuss at the meeting how member states are to strengthen policies coordination and cooperation and solidarity, so as to bring the global economic growth back on track, and strive to achieve balance between immediate, medium and long-term economic growth. As the second largest economy, China's policies will have impacts on other countries, so will the Fed's policy. Countries should strengthen policy coordination, which makes the G20 meeting all the more important. Furthermore, we can not rely solely on monetary policy, fiscal policy should also play a role, so as to achieve better policy portfolio. At the same time, we need to have good communication with the market to clarify policy intentions.■

Lou Jiwei: strengthening international cooperation and coordination to jointly counter global economic challenges

In his recent address, Finance Minister Lou Jiwei said that with the hard efforts, coordination and communication of all parties, G20 Finance Ministers and Central Bank Governors Meeting reached consensus on key issues, basically met the expectation of China, helped secure the major deliverables of this year's G20 finance track, and defined the timetable and roadmap for the work of the next phase. The meeting has the following highlights. (1) It reached agreement on the assessment of the state of macroeconomy, sent a positive signal to the outside world, and boosted market confidence. The price volatility of stock, bond, commodity and gold during the Lunar Chinese New Year showed the bearish sentiment of global investors on economic outlook, but the overall view at the meeting was that the magnitude of the recent market volatility did not reflect the underlying fundamentals of the world economy. We expected activity to continue to expand at a moderate pace in most advanced economies and growth in key emerging market economies to remain strong. The representatives at the meeting also agreed to confront the problems and risks squarely and avoid exaggerating the problems. (2) We agreed on policy responses and committed to use all policy tools—monetary, fiscal and structural—individually and collectively to foster confidence and preserve and strengthen the recovery. Given the variations of growth trend, economic situation, monetary policy space, policy urgency and political environment among countries, there were diverging views among G20 members in this regard, hence the different priorities underscored by different countries. (3) We agreed on the importance of structural reform, and secured two outcomes proposed by China, i.e. developing a set of priorities and guiding principles for structural reform and creating an indicator system to measure the progress of structural reforms. G20 started to notice structural reform in 2009 and intensified its focus since then, but this is the first time that structural reform has been elevated to the current level. (4) We reached agreement on the reform of the global economic governance system, and would continue to push forward the international financial architecture reform and enhance the coordination of international tax, green financing, climate finance and counter-terrorist financing. With coordination among G20 parties, we added new elements to this year's G20, for example, we, for the first time, made green financing and counter-terrorist financing the formal agenda items of the G20 finance track. We hoped to consolidate the previous reform outcomes, continue to advance the reform agenda and improve the global economic governance framework. As the constructor and participant of the global economic governance system, China does not want to unravel the existing system and create a new one to replace it. However, as the existing system fails to reflect the changes in the world economic governance landscape and some aspects are ill-suited for the new developments, it is important to reform and improve it in a constructive way.■

Li Keqiang: accelerating shifts in driving forces for development to promote steady, effective and high performance of China's economy

In his remarks on March 6, Premier Li Keqiang pointed out that faced with complex domestic and international situation and various challenges, China has the capacity and condition to maintain sustained and stable economic and social development. There was considerable leeway for macro-control policies, and room for innovative regulatory tools. Measures adopted last year were still effective in maintaining growth, promoting reform, adjusting economic structure, and delivering benefits to people's livelihood. All those would contribute to maintaining a medium-high rate of growth and promoting the development of industries towards medium-high end. The key, as emphasized by the Premier, lies in fostering new driving forces for growth and the new economy. We should support innovative, coordinated, green, open and shared development, push forward structural reforms, especially on the supply-side. Following the global trend of a new round of scientific revolution and industrial evolution, we should implement the strategy of innovation-driven development, encourage the public to start businesses and make innovations to tap into their potential of creativity, and promote integrated progress of Made in China 2025 and Internet +. With revolutionary new technologies as well as emerging industries and business models, we could upgrade traditional growth engines, resolve excessive capacity in an orderly manner, and make advanced manufacturing and modern services pillars for the national economy. When the economic

REMARKS & OPINIONS

engines shifted smoothly from traditional ones towards new ones, the double engines would take the Chinese economy to steer on a more solid, more sophisticated and steadier track. The key for the shift was to deepen reforms by building scientific and institutional platforms and engaging various market players. When various sizes of enterprises, higher learning institutions and entrepreneurs were well connected through the platform of synergy, new business model would emerge and the sharing economy would grow. With active participation of private investors and firms, the gene of innovation would grow across the board, helping to improve the performance and upgrade China's economy. The shift of driving forces required accelerated transformation of government functions to streamline administration, delegate more power, improve regulation and provide better services, all in a bid to encourage entrepreneurship and innovation and foster a market environment with fair competition and facilitated access. We would take measures to reduce tax and fees to ease the burden for businesses, so as to make them more competitive. In the work of the government, we would prioritize weak links most concerned by the people such as education, medical service, housing, social security and food security, ensure people's basic livelihood, speed up efforts in tackling poverty, so as to enhance people's sense of benefit in society when building a moderately prosperous society in all respects.■

Lou Jiwei: higher deficit won't trigger government debt risks

In his remarks at the press conference during the fourth session of the 12th NPC on March 7, Finance Minister Lou Jiwei said that there was room for China to increase its deficit. According to the budget report, the fiscal deficit for 2016 was projected to be 2.18 trillion RMB, an increase of 560 billion RMB over last year, raising the deficit-to-GDP ratio to 3%, 0.6 percentage point higher than in 2015, making it the highest deficit since we launched the reform and opening-up. It was difficult to gauge the appropriate size of deficit. China has certain room, but there was a limit. The fiscal revenue of China accounted for around 30% of GDP, below the average in the international community, and far below that of the developed economies. Therefore, we could afford a higher deficit. A properly increased deficit could help to sustain medium to high rate of growth and support structural reform. The fiscal priorities in 2016 were to ensure input in key areas, optimize investment structure, and support people's livelihood. We would strictly control the growth of "*three offcial expenses*", and cuts would be made to those costs if necessary, so as to ensure spending on basic public services and key welfare programs. Minister Lou noted that during the process of optimizing the expenditure structure, timely measures were to be adopted to, based on rational evaluation, reduce policy related expenditures or unsustainable investment over-committed during the high revenue period. Meanwhile, re-balancing transfer payment should be increased to empower local and provincial government with greater discretionary financial resources. With government debt hovering around 40% of GDP, it was well within the safe zone compared with other countries. The central government debt, in particular, totaling 11 trillion RMB, was considerably low in relation to the GDP. There was room for the central government to issue debt. The key is to make the debt properly regulated. To ward off government debt risks, it was crucial that local governments should not incur additional debts beyond stipulation of the *Budget Law*. Two issues deserved special attention. First, we should keep a lid on the debt for which the local government is liable. Such debt might rise when the economy slowed down. Second, local government should be forbidden to take on more debt through various circumvention and disguise, and regulations have to step up in this regard. In this year's report on the work of the government, there was a specific timetable for the piloting reform of replacing business tax with VAT to be rolled out to all sectors starting from May 1. It was on the must-do list of the year. Currently the piloting measures were still to cover construction, real estate, financial and consumer services industries, which were the toughest areas for the reform. Due to the complex situation of the reform and challenges on fiscal revenue, the reform was not extended across the board in 2015.■

Shi Yaobin: continuing the efforts to innovate and advance the international economic and financial cooperation

In his recent address, Vice Finance Minister Shi Yaobin said that China has become the world's second largest economy, the biggest exporter and a major country with huge foreign exchange reserve, commanding increasing influence on the world stage. Particularly since the outbreak of the global financial crisis, China has been moving faster to the center stage of global affairs. Recognizing China's strength, some developed countries are asking China to take on more international responsibilities and obligations, and some developing countries are also expecting more from China. Against this backdrop, the leadership at MOF proposed the concept of "public finance for China as a major country". Guided by this concept, MOF has been actively engaging in international economic and financial cooperation and achieved fruitful outcomes. (1) It actively involves in bilateral and multilateral economic and financial dialogues which have seen increasingly higher level and greater influence. (2) It engages in cooperation with the World Bank, the ADB, foreign government lenders as well as other bilateral and multilateral lending institutions; it also created new MDBs such as the AIIB and the NDB. The establishment of the AIIB and the NDB is unprecedented and calls for extremely arduous efforts. To evolve from vision to reality, the AIIB went through 8 rounds of negotiations, numerous discussions and consultations; the NDB underwent 7 rounds of negotiations and several multilateral and bilateral dialogues. The creation of these two MDBs is of great significance at both national and international level. This is a "win-win" move as it not only supports global recovery, promotes regional infrastructure and economic development, and demonstrates the efforts of China to take on more international responsibilities to complement and improve the existing global economic system, but also aligns to China's general diplomatic strategy of "focusing on the Asia Pacific and projecting into the surrounding areas" and facilitates Chinese capital, industries and talents to "go global". "Public finance for China as a major country" means that we cannot afford to be inward-looking, instead, we need to take into account and use the markets, resources and rules at both domestic and international level, put the formulation of economic and financial policies under the context of global governance, actively involve in the reform and rule-setting of the global economic governance system and maintain the global economic order to foster an enabling external environment for China's development. Going forward, we need to earnestly implement this concept, and play a more active role in international economic and financial cooperation with a view of preserving and enhancing the national interests; make good use of bilateral and multilateral dialogue mechanisms and China's cooperation with bilateral and multilateral lending institutions to promote the institutional innovation at home and expand external space for China's development; and leverage the resources from bilateral and multilateral channels to advance fiscal and tax reform and build up the capacity of officials in the public finance system.■

REMARKS & OPINIONS

Zhou Xiaochuan: reducing leverage through the development of capital markets

In his recent marks during the China Development Forum, the Chinese central bank governor Zhou Xiaochuan gave three observations on the cause of high leverage in China. First, China has a high national savings rate. The usual ratio of national savings to GDP is about 20%-30%, while the aggregated savings ratio in China was over 46% last year, among which 35% was contributed by the household sector. There are multiple reasons for the high savings rate, but with such huge savings, it is just normal for business to have high level of debt financing through banks and bonds. If China's corporate debt is higher than that of other countries, it would not be surprising. Second, China is a late starter in equity market. There was no stock market until early 1990s. With such a short history, the proportion of financing from capital markets is small. Private equity financing is also relatively weak. Third, the Chinese are getting rich fast since the reform and opening-up, but the accumulation of private wealth is relatively small, so the amount of private-money-turned equity is also small. As a result, the businesses are having a high level of borrowing. Heavy debt across the board may lead to macro risks. There are a variety of approaches to resolve such risks, one of which is to accelerate the development of capital markets. Such development can channel more private savings to equity financing, so as to help to reduce the debt-GDP ratio and debt-equity ratio.■

Zhu Guangyao: global economic uncertainties have increased

In his recent address, Vice Finance Minister Zhu Guangyao identified 8 headwinds faced by the world economy. (1) Global economic recovery remains sluggish and uneven, and downside pressure keeps mounting. In early 2016, IMF lowered its forecast for global growth in 2016 from 3.6% to 3.4%, which implies that the global economic situation is grimmer in 2016 than in 2015. (2) Global trade growth continues to lag behind global economic growth. The average growth of global trade has been faster than that of global economy in the past 20 years, but in recent years, the annual growth of global trade has fallen below that of global economy. (3) Global employment rate has yet to bounce back to the pre-crisis level. In the longer run, high unemployment rate will have adverse effect on state, and also jeopardize social stability by providing the breeding ground of terrorism. (4) Global interest rate is at the lowest level since the Second World War, and poses more complex, grave and challenging problems when global economy situation, political ecology and social ecology are at play. (5) There is severe divergence of monetary policy among major advanced economies. The Federal Reserve of the U.S. embarked on the normalization of interest rate policy in December 2015, while ECB decided to further expand QE on March 10, 2016 and BOJ adopted negative interest rate and pressed ahead with QE. (6) Commodity prices continue to drop. The decline will persist in 2016 and is expected to be less sharp and intense than in 2015. (7) Emerging market economies are facing increasing pressure. For example, except for China and India which still maintain robust growth, both Brazil and Russia have slipped into recession in 2015, and South Africa posted subdued growth. (8) Geopolitical risks are escalating and the world has entered the most challenging period since the end of the cold war.■

Li Keqiang: lay a solid foundation for the full implementation of VAT reform, and deepen reform to promote steady growth, structural adjustment and new growth engines

Recently, Premier Li Keqiang paid study tours to MOF and State Administration of Taxation (SAT) and chaired meetings on the full implementation of VAT reform. Premier Li pointed out that the full implementation of VAT reform was a significant step for structural reform as well as for fiscal and tax reforms, which would generate multiple policy impacts. First, it helps to evidently relief enterprises of tax burdens. With weak economic recovery globally and downside pressure domestically, the proactive fiscal policy is to play a stronger role. The expansion of fiscal deficit this year is mainly attributable to reduced tax revenues from businesses as the result of VAT reform, which cuts tax burden for businesses by over 500 billion RMB, the largest cut in recent years. Now that the real estate sector is also covered, it helps to increase effective investment by businesses. As fish grows bigger in a deeper pond, the reform will make the growth be stronger and last longer. Second, the reform is a major booster for structural upgrading of the economy. The VAT reform is conducive to the development of service sector, especially output related services. It promotes optimized division of industries, extends the industrial chain, and fosters manufacturing upgrading. Third, it helps to create a fair competitive market environment. Through unified tax code, the VAT is applied to all sectors and the deductible chain is integrated among various service industries and between the secondary and tertiary industries, thus eliminating double taxation from the tax regime, which is of long-term significance to the improvement of the tax regime. At present, the development of new economy, emergence of new growth engines and upgrading of traditional industries have spawned a large number of new technologies, industries, and business models. The full implementation of VAT reform helps the enterprises get lower cost of innovation and faster upgrading of equipment. It fosters crowd-innovation, crowd-sourcing, crowd-supporting and crowd-funding platforms for the implementation of innovation-driven development strategy, and encourages start-ups and innovation by the general public. Private companies and small and micro-enterprises may enjoy better market environment as a result, leading to stronger job creation, especially for the over 10 million graduates from universities and vocational schools. The reform will accelerate the shift of growth engines while maintaining medium to high rate of growth and advancing the economic structure towards higher levels. The fiscal and taxation system is in the front-line of VAT reform, and the last stop of policy implementation. Relevant government agencies should spare no effort in the preparation and implementation. Line-agencies should strengthen coordination to form synergy, push ahead with reform while giving detailed policy interpretation to address concerns of the public in time and stabilize market expectations. Efforts should be made to strengthen training and services for taxpayers, help enterprises to improve financial management, and guide taxpayers to correctly understand and make good use of the policy. Relevant agencies should step up research, follow and analyze the operation of pilot programs, conduct in-depth analysis on typical problems and come up with timely countermeasures. Transitional measures should be adopted to ensure the tax burden for industries to be put on a declining path. Meanwhile, we should enhance institutional building and policy guidance to prevent local protectionism and market segmentation. Tax evasion and fraud will be cracked down according to the laws.∎

REMARKS & OPINIONS

Li Keqiang: accelerating the transition from old engines of growth to new ones and promoting steady, efficient and high-level development of the Chinese economy

In his published speech on March 6, Premier Li Keqiang said that despite the complex domestic and external situation and various daunting challenges, China has the capability and condition to maintain sustained and stable social and economic growth. The leeway for macro regulation remains ample, the space for developing innovative management tools is still large, and the measures unveiled last year to maintain steady growth, promote reform, adjust structure and improve people's livelihood will continue to take effect. All these factors will sustain the momentum of medium-to-high growth and underpin the transition to medium-to-high level of development. To this end, it is important to actively foster new engines of growth and develop the new economy. Specifically, we need to pursue innovative, coordinated, green, open and shared economic development, deepen structural reform, particularly the supply-side structural reform, adapt to the new round of global technological revolution and industrial changes, adopt an innovation-driven growth strategy, promote the public to start businesses and make innovations, unleash the creativity of people, accelerate the fusion of "Made in China 2025" and "Internet+", incubate disruptive technologies, facilitate the emergence of new industries and new business models, reinvent and enhance traditional engines of growth, reduce excess capacity in an orderly way, make advanced manufacturing and modern service industry the key pillars of the Chinese economy, engineer the stable transition from old engines of growth to new ones, and harness the "twin engines" to put the Chinese economy on a higher and more steady and sound path of development. The key to the transition lies in deepening reform and creating technological and institutional platforms for market players. We need to create such platforms for businesses, universities, research institutes and makers, develop innovative operation models, advance the shared economy, mobilize private businesses and catalyze private capital, make innovation part of the DNA of all the industries and sectors, and upgrade the quality and level of the Chinese economy through vibrant innovation and creative activities. The transition towards new growth engines also requires the government to move faster to change its functions. We need to press ahead with deregulation, improve regulation, deliver better government services to lessen the burden of businesses when they engage in innovation or create start-ups, and foster a fair, convenient and enabling market environment. We will cut taxes and fees to reduce the costs of businesses as they move forward. We will focus on addressing the areas of people's concern, such as education, health, housing, social security and food safety, strengthen the social safety net, accelerate the pace of poverty reduction, and ensure people can gain greater benefits in the course of building a moderately prosperous society in all aspects. ∎

Lou Jiwei: relevant players should make joint efforts to tackle poverty and unemployment

In his recent remarks on the 93rd Session of the Ministerial Conference of the Development Committee, Finance Minister Lou Jiwei said that despite continuous moderate recovery, the global economy is still beset by many uncertainties and unstable factors. There is a serious shortage of resources for development. In particular, displaced population is surging lately, causing drastic pressure on economic development and social stability in some countries, and further exacerbated the fragility and complexity of the international environment for development. The main cause of displacement is protracted poverty, unemployment and long-term war and conflict, which calls for joint efforts by the UN, influential nations and the international community. The fundamental resolution towards this problem is to end regional conflicts, maintain peace and foster development. Taking promoting poverty reduction and development as its principle mandates, the World Bank should abide by its Charters, uphold its mission and utilize its comparative strength, and based on that, play its due role in addressing poverty caused by the displacement. During this process, the Bank should properly handle its relationship with UN agencies and multilateral development banks to give play to their complementary advantages; and strike a balance among maintenance of peace, humanitarian assistance and long-term development, while focusing on supporting long-term economic development of recipient countries. At the same time, the Bank should develop uniform principles and standards internally to ensure equal treatment of recipient countries and see to that funding commitment to poverty reduction and to other borrowing countries is unaffected. The Bank may consider capital replenishment as the main channel to enhance its capital strength, in order to improve the lending capacity and financial sustainability. The Bank should keep the equity review process on schedule, so as to objectively reflect the evolvement of global economic landscape, and to give more voice and representation to developing countries. Meanwhile, the Bank should strengthen all-round cooperation with developing countries, better cater to the needs of developing countries, and provide customized solutions, so as to maximize development efforts. ∎

Lou Jiwei: "replacing business tax with VAT" reform is an important step forward in China's structural reform

In his recent speech, Finance Minister Lou Jiwei said that the comprehensive implementation of the "replacing business tax with VAT" reform is an important move for promoting the supply-side structural reform, and is expected to deliver multiple benefits and exert far-reaching impact since it will not only underpin current growth but also sustain future growth. The tax reform in 1994 gave rise to a tax system featuring the co-existence of VAT and business tax. Under this tax regime, VAT was levied on goods and the processing and repair services, and business tax was levied on other services, real estate and intangible assets. This arrangement played an important role in economic development, however, the co-existence of VAT and business tax also resulted in the increasingly acute problem of double taxation, making it imperative to reform the system to subject goods and services in all industries to VAT. As many industries and firms are facing difficulties in their operation, the comprehensive VAT reform will invigorate the businesses and boost the economy. Meanwhile, this VAT reform is leaning towards R&D and other producer service industries, which will help optimize division of labor, lengthen the production chain and upgrade the manufacturing industry. One of the objectives of the VAT reform is to ensure the tax burdens of all industries will decrease rather than increase, which is also an important political task. When designing the pilot program, MOF and SAT placed equal emphasis on reform and growth, properly handled the pace and intensity of reform, and determined the appropriate VAT rate for each pilot industry. Meanwhile, the previous tax incentives for the four new pilot industries are retained. With respect to policy implementation, MOF and SAT require all levels of finance and tax authorities to fully implement the policies. To ensure reform dividends are truly delivered to businesses, training programs are also organized to help fiscal and tax officials as well as financial staff in businesses to better understand the policies and avoid the case where tax burden of businesses is increased due to misunderstanding and incorrect enforcement of policies. Monitoring over the pilot program is also enhanced to timely

REMARKS & OPINIONS

and properly address the emerging problems. After the roll-out of the VAT reform, the central and local share of the VAT revenue needs to be adjusted. While maintaining the general stability of the central and local income level, interim measures for the sharing of VAT revenue between central and local governments will be drawn up, and localities will be guided to develop industries that suit local circumstances to enhance the local income-generating capacity. As the tax reform is yet to be fully in place and it still takes time to complete the division of government duties and expenditure obligations between central and local governments, an interim plan is needed for the sharing of the VAT revenue between the central and local governments to rationalize the intergovernmental income distribution. VAT reform will cut tax revenue for both central and local governments, and after the adjustment of VAT income distribution, the central government will take more loss of revenue. In addition, the central government will give tax rebates to local governments to ensure the existing interests of central and local governments remain basically unchanged.■

Lou Jiwei: rating agencies are biased

In a response to recent downgrading of Chinese sovereign credit rating outlook to "negative" by two rating agencies, Finance Minister Lou Jiwei said in a speech that the downgrading has not reflected the actual situation of the Chinese economy. Moody's and Standard & Poor's have cited the rationale behind the negative rating as concerns over China's economic slowdown, higher government debt, increased capital outflows and doubts on the macro-management capabilities and reform determination of the Chinese government. But the outlook did not reflect the actual situation of China's economy. The recently published first-quarter GDP growth was 6.7%, a considerably high level. Though the figure was slightly lower than last year, it was within the expectation range. In terms of government debt, China has taken measures to curb the rising debt of local governments. The debt level of the central government is not very high, and it is to help the deleveraging process of the private sector that the central government is taking on more debt. Such reforms take time, but rating agencies may not know that China is considering those reforms. The international community has been questioning the credibility of these rating agencies for some time. Historically, the market performance of China's sovereign bond has been higher than the ratings for most of the time, which indicates that the rating agencies are "biased". Rating agencies should carry out in-depth communication with the rated countries before making more objective and fair assessment. On the Chinese economic policy, Lou Jiwei said that on one hand, we are managing the aggregate demand management to keep growth at a reasonable range; on the other hand, we are focusing structural reforms on the supply side. Structural reform has made significant progress, which will improve the allocation of resources and raise growth rate over the long-term. China's economy is also facing unfavorable factors such as aging population, so the policies and reforms must be "more forceful" to deal with downward pressure.■

Zhang Gaoli: strengthening international tax cooperation to promote world economic development

In his recently published speech, Vice Premier Zhang Gaoli said that China attaches great importance to international tax cooperation. Chinese President Xi Jinping stressed the need for enhanced international tax cooperation, the combat of tax evasion and assistance to help developing and low-income countries with capacity building in tax matters. Premier Li Keqiang also made specific requirements in this regard. Tax is the pivotal foundation for state governance system and capacity as well as key means for global economic governance. Strengthened international tax cooperation will be critical for better protecting the tax interest and tax base safety of nations, promoting economic growth and raising people's wellbeing. 2016 is an important year for comprehensively implementing the outcomes of G20 tax reform. Zhang Gaoli raised three suggestions: (1) deepen international tax cooperation, build a mutually beneficial international tax relationship, earnestly strengthen international tax policy coordination and tax administration cooperation, and jointly promote the development of international tax administration capacity. (2) Combat international tax avoidance and evasion, move faster to build a new order of international taxation featuring fairness, justice and openness, safeguard the tax interests of nations, protect the legitimate rights and interests of cross-border taxpayers, and regulate the conduct of cross-border taxpayers. (3) Promote inclusive development, scale up technical assistance and support in tax matters to developing countries, and help developing countries enhance their tax administration capacity. China is in the decisive stage of building a moderately prosperous society in all aspects. The Chinese economy has entered the New Normal and is faced with downside pressure, but it still has high resilience, great potential and ample room for maneuver, and the positive trend of its growth remains unchanged. We will stick to and pursue the development philosophy of innovative, coordinated, green, open and shared growth, adhere to the overall principle of progressing while maintaining stability, continue to carry out proactive fiscal policy and prudent monetary policy, make great efforts to promote supply-side structural reform and keep developing innovative means of macro management. We have introduced a series of significant measures, including tax reform measures. Since this year, the Chinese economy has been basically stable and moving forward in a steady way, and it has got off to a good start featuring economic growth, optimal economic structure and improved living standard of the people.■

Wang Yang: promote integration of agriculture-related fiscal funds to improve the effectiveness of poverty reduction

Chinese Vice Premier Wang Yang said in a recent speech that promote integration of agriculture-related fiscal funds is the key to improve the effectiveness of poverty reduction and ensure financial resources for tackling poverty. Following the instruction of the CPC Central Committee and the State Council, and based on poverty reduction plans for poverty-stricken counties, we should focus on major poverty reduction projects by making coordinated use of agricultural related fiscal funds, so as to improve the effectiveness of poverty reduction efforts and achieve poverty alleviation. Integration of funds is a necessity for poverty reduction efforts, and also an integral part of deregulation and improvement of government services. The central, provincial (autonomous regions and municipalities), and city (prefecture) authorities should allow the funding for agricultural production and rural infrastructure construction to be pooled into poverty reduction funds in pilot counties. We should enhance fiscal resources for and policy support to poverty-stricken counties, while strengthening financial regulatory and policy related services. Piloting counties should design proper development plans, identify key projects and development agenda, improve fund management and decision-making process, adopt innovative funding mechanism, and emphasize supervision of funds management, all in an effort to improve the effectiveness of poverty reduction.■

REMARKS & OPINIONS

Hu Jinglin: focusing on five priorities to advance the agricultural modernization

In his recent speech, Vice Finance Minister Hu Jinglin said that the agricultural modernization requires the comprehensive development of agriculture to focus on the following priorities. (1) Spend funds mainly on the program of developing high-standard farmland and make great efforts to enhance the comprehensive production capacity of agriculture; catalyze financial and private capital alongside fiscal input for this program; develop a high-standard and substantive program; and improve the supporting facilities and supervision mechanisms to sustain the program's long-term benefits. (2) Ensure the high output of farm produce and, more importantly, shore up the weak links in the production chain, optimize the production structure and raise the quality and efficiency of product; support the formation of agricultural industrial chain and value chain and develop a modern agricultural production system; and study targeted supportive policies and specific measures. (3) Further optimize the overall development arrangement, apply differentiated policies to areas where development is encouraged, restricted and due consideration for conservation is required, and improve the dynamic management of county-level projects; make efficient water use an important criteria for the high-standard farmland, support the low-carbon agricultural technological equipment and facilities, support project areas where resources are over developed and the ecological environment is fragile to treat pollution, restore vegetation, and conserve ecological system; and promote the spread of improved grain variety and farming technology and methodology. (4) With national food security, higher agricultural efficiency and increased farmer income as targets, advance the development of high-standard farmland, agricultural industry and agriculture-related services, promote the orderly transfer of land operating rights, cultivate a new-type of agribusiness system, and develop diversified and properly scaled-up operation of agriculture. (5) Further tilt project funding to poverty-stricken areas and earmark a certain proportion of funding to poor villages; while promoting the development of high-standard farmland and strengthening the foundation for agricultural and rural development, make greater efforts to support poor areas to take advantage of local resources to develop agricultural industries with local specialty to eradicate poverty.■

Zhu Guangyao: expand mutual benefit to serve Chinese and the U.S citizens

In his recent remarks, Vice Finance Minister Zhu Guangyao said that the 8th China-U.S. Strategic and Economic Dialogue was to be held on June 6-7 in Beijing. As special representatives of President Xi Jinping and President Obama, Vice Premier Wang Yang and Treasury Secretary Jacob Lew were to co-host the economic track meeting. During the dialogue, the two sides were to hold discussions under the theme of "strengthening China-U.S. communication and cooperation, enhancing bilateral economic relations". The meeting included three sessions: first, on the macro-economic situation and policies; second, on open trade and investment; and third, on financial stability and regulation cooperation. There were also two strategic sessions, on G20 economic agenda and the global economic situation and risks, respectively. This round of dialogue was of significant importance. Both sides attached great attention and strived for positive deliverables. The meeting was to focus on priority issues, present highlights, and solve difficult problems, so as to make policy preparation for the G20 Hangzhou Summit in the economic area, showcase the will and action by the both sides in strengthening economic cooperation and jointly promoting strong, sustainable and balanced growth of the global economy, and further enhance the strategic and over-arching status of the dialogue mechanism. The two sides had sent senior delegates of major economic and financial agencies to the dialogue. 14 U.S. agencies and 15 Chinese agencies attended the meeting. Under the direct leadership of Vice Premier Wang Yang and Secretary Jacob Lew, the two sides were engaged in intensified consultation of outcomes. This year is the tenth anniversary of the dialogue mechanism. Over the past decade, the S&ED has played a positive role in enhancing mutual trust, avoiding miscalculation and expanding cooperation between the two sides. The economic relationship is the blaster and propeller of the overall China-U.S. relations. The Chinese side stands ready to work with the U.S. in fulfilling the important consensus reached by the two heads of states, meeting each other half-way, and seeking positive outcomes in the dialogue. ∎

Lou Jiwei: sluggish recovery of the global economy is caused by deep-seated structural factors

In his recent address at the 8th U.S.-China Strategic and Economic Dialogue, Finance Minister Lou Jiwei said that eight years after the outbreak of the global financial crisis, the global average GDP growth rate is just 3.5%, 1.6 percentage points lower than the average level of the five-year period preceding the crisis. The sluggish recovery is caused as much by cyclical factors as by structural factors such as declining potential output, lack of effective demand and slow progress of structural reform. In the U.S., bolstered by the QE policy, economic recovery is strengthening and most of the economic indicators are turning for better; however, structural reform in the U.S. is not yet completed, investment gap remains huge, trade and fiscal deficit is high, and the long-term growth prospects are still faced with challenges. In China, since this year, economic performance has been on a stable path, indicators of growth, price and employment are within policy expectation, bright spots are emerging in service sector, consumption, high-value added manufacturing and business startups; nevertheless, the inherent problems in the economy are still not thoroughly resolved. China and the U.S. reaffirmed their commitments made at the G20 Finance Ministers and Central Bank Governors' Meeting in Shanghai, including to use all policy tools to support growth and counter potential risks and to intensify structural reform so as to boost potential growth rate and promote long-term and stable growth of the world economy. At the Dialogue, China made it clear that to adapt to and steer the new normal, China, while properly expanding aggregate demand, would focus on strengthening supply-side structural reforms, press ahead with the five priority tasks of reducing excess capacity, destocking, deleveraging, cutting costs and shoring up weak links, continue with proactive fiscal policy and prudent monetary policy, and seek to create a stable macroeconomic environment for structural reforms. The U.S. stated that it would closely monitor the impact of the adjustment of its monetary policy on world economy, particularly on the emerging economies and global financial market, make its policies more forward-looking and transparent, and reduce the negative spillovers; it would also continue to advance the adjustment of economic structure, take measures to increase investment and savings rate, raise labor participation and productivity, and realize medium-term fiscal sustainability. China and the U.S. positively acknowledged the important exemplary role of the two countries working together to address global economic challenges, and were committed to working alongside the international community to further enhance the coordination and cooperation of macroeconomic policies, raise medium and long-term growth potential through structural reform and innovation, improve global economic and financial reform, promote international trade and investment, build an open world economy, implement the 2030 Agenda for Sustainable Development,

REMARKS & OPINIONS

and contribute to inclusive and sustainable development of the world. ■

Liu Kun: accelerate the implementation of PPP projects and further reduce tax and fees

In his recent remarks, Vice Finance Minister Liu Kun said that PPP promotion in recent years achieved positive results, but some problems have surfaced through the inspection, one of which is the absence of PPP legislation. As a result, policies and measures introduced by various government agencies may not be consistent, and it led to difficulties in PPP implementation. In addition to the legislation gap, there are three problems: first, there are many potential PPP projects, but it is difficult to launch them. It is a prevalent problem. PPP project has high requirements for the participating parties, including government participants. The difficulty in launching the projects is, to a certain degree, related to the government's governance capacity. Second, entrepreneurs are under the impression that good PPP projects are mostly dominated by SOEs, while the threshold for private investment in PPP is high, especially for the good projects. Third, some local governments may have relatively poor credit, so investors are concerned that the government may randomly change contract terms. The central government has taken several measures to reduce the burden of tax and fees. First, promote VAT reform pilot. The reform has led to a total of 641.2 billion RMB of tax reductions as of the end of last year. With the full roll-out starting from May 1, the tax cuts are expected to reach 500 billion RMB by the end of this year. Second, support the development of small and micro enterprises, through tax breaks, exemption of administrative fees and etc. Fourth, encourage investment in technological innovation through the introduction of R&D expense deduction, accelerated depreciation of fixed assets and other preferential policies. Fifth, clean up and standardize fees and government funds. Feedback from the inspection showed that some companies didn't feel evident relief of tax and fees, while other companies still complain heavy burdens. Given the challenging business environment at present, business profit is falling. Therefore, even there are tax cuts, the businesses may still be under pressure. In addition, the tax cuts are uneven across sectors. While some sectors enjoyed more generous tax relief, others may still struggle. There are several reasons: the current tax regime is complex, and administrative fees are to be further cleaned up; tax policy is being implemented gradually; the effects of some preferential policies are still to be materialized; some companies did not keep up with the VAT reform, so the chain of deductions is not complete. Next, we must continue to follow the deployment and request of the CPC Central Committee and the State Council, further reduce taxes and fees to lighten the burden on enterprises and reduce market operating costs. We should also pay close attention to the implementation of policies to strengthen the policy awareness, so as to deliver tangible benefits to private enterprises. ■

Hu Jinglin: working in a pragmatic and innovative way to bring the comprehensive development of agriculture to a new level

In his recent address, Vice Finance Minister Hu Jinglin said that the comprehensive development of agriculture is of great significance to the national food security and agricultural modernization. At present and in the future, the comprehensive development of agriculture shall focus on the following priorities. (1) Give full play to the decisive role of the market in resource allocation, incentivize all players to engage in comprehensive agricultural development, and enable fiscal funds to leverage financial and private capital for the pilot program of developing high-standard farmland. (2) Implement "innovative, coordinated, green, open, and shared" development concept in comprehensive agricultural development, take the opportunities offered by the amendment of departmental directives to explore innovative policy system for the new era, and develop innovative project management model to allow leading agribusinesses, farmers' cooperatives and other market entities to play a major role in project management. (3) Enhance the whole-life management of funds and projects, improve systems related to legal person, tendering, supervision and public disclosure of project and county-level financial reporting, further simplify and optimize process and procedures to raise efficiency, advance budget transparency and accelerate budget implementation, and gradually create a modern management system that is adapted to the comprehensive agricultural development in the new era. (4) Engage with the grass-root community to better understand people's needs, which is the basis for the reform of the system and improvement of management. Establish a science-based, complete, streamlined, efficient and coordinated management system, and create internal control and risk prevention mechanisms for the management of funds and projects so as to better monitor key links and high-risk areas. (5) Foster the culture of learning in government agencies, improve the learning platforms, encourage regular learning and constantly enhance the competence of cadres.∎

Lou Jiwei: attach great importance to infrastructure investment and cooperation, give full play to multilateral development banks

In a recent speech at the Infrastructure and Global Economic Growth Seminar held during the first annual meeting of the AIIB, Finance Minister Lou Jiwei made the following remarks. The world economic recovery is slow and uneven, downward pressure still exists, and there is a long way to go to realize the goal of strong, sustainable and balanced growth. The global economy continues to face multiple risks and challenges, including rising external uncertainties and slumping commodity prices. The recent Brexit from Europe further exacerbated the international financial markets uncertainties. The international community highly anticipated G20 to play an important role in promoting world economic growth and improving global economic governance, and had high expectation for the Hangzhou Summit. Under the authorization of the summit, the G20 Finance Ministers and Central Bank Governors Meeting played an important role in strengthening macroeconomic policy coordination, promoting economic growth and fostering financial market stability. The international community recognized that sustainable economic growth should rely more on structural reforms. G20 is identifying the priority areas and guidelines for structural reforms, and developing a measurement system for reform progress. In the current challenging circumstances with short-term risk of weak recovery and long-term risk of stagnant growth, the infrastructure investment can be used as an effective tool in adjusting aggregate demand to foster short-term economic recovery, and as a measure to promote supply-side structural reforms, raise potential growth, and support long-term economic growth. G20 attaches great importance to infrastructure investment and cooperation, stresses the need to give full play to MDBs to enhance the size and quality of infrastructure investment, and develop quantitative targets in supporting high-quality projects. The Chengdu meeting in July is expected to accomplish all economic and financial outcomes of G20. Multilateral development banks play a leveraging role in infrastructure investment, and have unique advantages in capital, experience, knowledge and institutional capacity in promoting infrastructure development. As important development partners, the AIIB and NDB carried out

REMARKS & OPINIONS

pragmatic cooperation with existing multilateral development institutions such as the World Bank and the ADB, and issued joint statements supporting infrastructure through G20 and the Global Infrastructure Forum. Such action sent a consistent message from the multilateral development bank community, which will effectively boost the confidence of global investors, and leverage more capital into long-term infrastructure investment. As the international debut of the AIIB, such action testifies to the positive role of the AIIB as an international development institution in supporting high quality infrastructure investment. ∎

Li Keqiang: economic transformation is required for stronger world economic growth

Premier Li Keqiang recently delivered an address at the Opening Ceremony of the 10th Annual Meeting of the Summer Davos Forum. According to Premier Li, since the international financial crisis broke out eight years ago, countries have resorted to various policy tools to grapple with the crisis and stimulate growth. Eight years on, recovery of the world economy has fallen far short of expectations: global trade and investment are lackluster; commodities and financial markets have experienced volatility from time to time; growth prospects of developed and emerging market economies are diverging; and geopolitical risks and destabilizing factors are both on the rise. Just a few days ago, the UK voted to leave the EU in a referendum. This made an impact on the international financial markets and added to the uncertainties in the world economy. Against such a backdrop, to promote world economic recovery and the growth of all economies, we need to make joint efforts to tackle challenges, strengthen confidence, foster a stable international environment and find solutions to address root causes of the problems we face. European countries are important partners for China. Under the new circumstances, China will continue to maintain and develop its relations with the EU and the UK. The theme of the forum, "the Fourth Industrial Revolution and Its Transformational Impact", offers people a new perspective and is thus forward-looking and relevant. First, to promote steady recovery of the world economy, we must actively carry out structural reforms. To address the deep-seated problems in the world economy, we need to both strengthen demand management and advance structural reforms to eliminate the root causes that trigger problems. Countries may face different situations, yet they should all move toward addressing economic imbalance by way of promoting fiscal and financial reforms, easing regulation, facilitating competition, supporting innovation and expanding opening-up, and should all work together to ensure strong, sustainable and balanced growth of the world economy. Second, to promote steady recovery of the world economy, we must speed up economic transformation and upgrading. For the world economy to walk out of the woods, the ultimate solution lies in shifting the growth model and replacing old growth engines with new ones at a faster pace. The advent of a new round of technological and industrial revolution has provided a historical opportunity for this. The emergence of new technologies, new tools and new materials, which are of pace-setting and transformational significance, has given a strong boost to the growth of the new economy and the upgrading of traditional industries. Countries should follow this prevailing trend by focusing their policies on supporting economic transformation and upgrading, and strengthen the new drivers of economic growth. Third, to promote steady recovery of the world economy, we will need efficient and orderly global governance. In the face of common challenges, we need to uphold the spirit of solidarity and work for common progress. This is a sure way for us to move forward. Countries need to adopt more growth-friendly policies, strengthen macro policy coordination, steadfastly advance trade and investment liberalization and facilitation, firmly oppose protectionism and build a fairer, more just and open international economic system. The world's major economies, while making macro-economic policies, should consider not only their own growth needs but also the spillover effects of their policies.■

Sheng Laiyun: Chinese economy in the first half of the year is stable and progressive, with new growth engines and positive developments, but challenges remain

Recently, the NBS spokesman Sheng Laiyun captured China's economic performance in the first half of the year with five words, i.e., stable, progressive, new, positive, and hard. "Stable" refers to the steady and sound economic operation. First, economic growth is relatively stable. The rate of growth in both the first quarter and the second quarter was 6.7%, showing a trend of stabilization. Growth in the first half of the year was 6.7%, which dropped by 0.3 percentage point over the same period of last year, but calculated at constant prices of 2010, the GDP grew by an additional 23 billion RMB compared with the same period of last year. Second, employment was stable. In the first half of this year, 717 million new urban jobs were created, completing 71.7% of the annual targets. Third, the prices were stable. The CPI rose by 2.1%, remaining with the first quarter. CPI in June rose by 1.9%. Fourth, growth in income and consumption was stable. Real income for households rose by 6.5% in the first half of the year, which remained the same as in the first quarter. Total retail sales of consumer goods grew by 10.3%, on par with the first quarter. "Progressive" refers to steady progress of the supply-side structural reforms and transformation and upgrading of the growth model. First, the service sector continued to expand rapidly. Services accounted for 54.1% of GDP in the first half of the year, up by 1.8 percentage points over the same period last year. Second, the structure of demand was improving. Among the three major demands, the final consumption contributed to 73.4% of the economic growth, a 13.2-percentage-point increase over last year. Capital formation contributed 37%, and the contribution by net exports of goods and services was -10.4%. Third, the catch-up advantage of the Midwest regions was still playing out. Value-added by Midwest industries generally grew faster than in the eastern regions and above the national average. In addition, the three strategic initiatives-- the Belt and Road Initiative, the Beijing-Tianjin-Hebei Economic Zone, and the Yangtze River Economic Belt-- are steadily advancing. Fourth, the supply-side structural reforms are implementing effectively. The efforts in accomplishing the "five tasks" 1 have achieved initial results. "New" refers to the development of the new economy with new growth engines. According to the State Administration for Industry and Commerce(SAIC), the first half of the year saw an average of 14 000 newly registered companies daily, up from the 12 000 daily figure of last year. Strategic emerging industries grew by 11.8% in the second quarter, 1.8 percentage points higher than in the first quarter. New industries and new business model maintained a high growth rate. "Positive" refers to improvement in the quality of economic operation. The positive factors are in accumulation. In the first half of the year, energy consumption per unit GDP fell by 5.2%. The decline of PPI narrowed for six consecutive months. From January to May, the profits of industrial enterprises above designated size grew by 6.4%, an improvement over last year. "Hard" refers to two aspects: first, the international environment remains complex and challenging. The world economic

---

1 Reducing excess capacity, de-stocking, de-leveraging, cutting costs and shoring up weak areas of the economy.

recovery is slower than expected, trade remains weak, and economic uncertainties have increased, including the recent Brexit referendum. Second, domestically, China's economy is in a crucial stage of restructuring, transformation and upgrading, the growing pains of adjustment continue, and the real economy is under stress.■

Lou Jiwei: the NDB should foster the sound image as a new MDB in the 21st century

In his recent address at the first Meeting of the Board of Governors of the NDB in Shanghai, Finance Minister Lou Jiwei said that the NDB should prioritize knowledge service, expand financing channel, streamline operational procedures, and foster the image of a new MDB in the 21st century. The NDB should look ahead from strategic and long-term perspectives. On one hand, it needs to draw upon the mature experiences and good practices of the existing MDBs, uphold international norms and high standards, and constantly enhance its operational transparency; on the other hand, it should improve and innovate the existing policies and system, and develop tailored and diversified products and services. It is important for the NDB to prioritize service. In addition to financial support, the NDB should also commit itself to providing high-quality services for developing countries. On the basis of project implementation, it should support the efforts of member countries in making institutional innovation and exploring the development paths and models that suit their national circumstances. Meanwhile, it should deepen south-south cooperation and promote the sharing of development experiences among developing countries. Second, the NDB should expand its financing channel. The recent volatility of the international capital market has posed considerable challenges to developing countries' access to foreign capital. Against this backdrop, the NDB should actively develop local currency financing, and provide stable and inexpensive capital for member countries. Furthermore, it needs to mobilize resources from policy financial institutions, commercial banks, insurance funds and private sector for infrastructure investment, properly adopt the PPP model and assist the member countries with economic and social development. Last but not least, the NDB should streamline its operational procedures. It should be lean and efficient, reduce operational costs, cut hidden costs, and maximize development impact. As it strives to be more efficient in decision-making and management, it should also put in place complete policies and procedures, ensure the high quality of projects and foster the sound image as a new MDB in the 21st century.■

Lou Jiwei: build a new international tax regime to promote strong, sustainable and balanced global growth

Recently, Finance Minister Lou Jiwei delivered a speech at the G20 High-level Tax Symposium. He pointed out that as an important and integral component of global governance system, tax policy plays a significant role in the coordination of global economic rules, and can be used as an effective tool to promote global economy recovery. Against the backdrop of economic globalization, the mode of production, the organizational form of enterprises and the international trade structure have all changed dramatically, imposing severe challenges to the existing international tax system. Therefore, the G20 countries should explore a more equal and rational international tax regime, which will promote international coordination and cooperation in taxation, and make greater contribution to achieving strong, sustainable and balanced global economic growth. At present, G20 countries still have ample opportunities to further strengthen international tax cooperation and coordination. As the major global governance platform, G20 should play a leading role in improving the international tax governance, continuously expand and deepen international tax coordination and cooperation, and support the development of a fair, equal, inclusive and organized international tax system. First, we should closely monitor the development trends of global taxation. The G20 countries should take a global perspective and strengthen studies on the strategic, macroscopic and institutional issues in tax areas, while ensuring fiscal safety and sustainable development objectives of member countries. Second, we should deepen the international tax cooperation. Building on the existing tax cooperation mechanisms, the G20 countries should consider carrying out global, regional, multilateral and bilateral tax cooperation in larger scopes, at higher levels and in more sophisticated areas. Third, we should strengthen tax capacity building. With economic globalization and the development of digital economy, now we are facing a big challenge of capacity building for tax administration, which is especially acute for developing countries. It is very important for developing countries to enhance their tax capacity, and it is a matter of significance for the balanced growth of global economy. Fourth, we should apply tax tools rationally. Improving international tax governance and building a fair and efficient international tax system will provide policy opportunities for the strong, sustainable and balanced economic growth. ■

Shi Yaobin: MOF should play a leading role in advancing the work of PPP in the public service area

Recently, Vice Finance Minister Shi Yaobin made a study tour to Chengdu City, Sichuan Province to inspect the work of PPP in Sichuan. He said that PPP is not only a major innovation for the provision of public services, but also one of the key measures at present to catalyze private investment and boost economic growth. PPP is also an important part of the 13th Five-Year Plan and Government Work Report. PPP requires the public sector and private sector to participate, as equals, in the supply of public services, and is conducive to the improvement of government management system. To ensure the success of PPP, three pillars are required: (1) laws. The Executive Meeting of the State Council has explicitly asked the Legal Affairs Office of the State Council to work with MOF and the National Development and Reform Commission (NDRC) in drafting the PPP laws so as to address the most salient problems, remove the concerns of private sector and encourage the investment by private sector. (2) Regulation. PPP is not merely a financing tool, and shall not be regarded as only a method of investment and financing. Government shall participate in the whole-life management of projects, determine the payment by government on the basis of project performance, avoid any preset and fixed return on investment, and eliminate the fake PPP projects. As Sichuan is taking the lead in doing PPP projects and has many projects in the pipeline, it is thus required to make greater efforts to ensure its projects are well-regulated and well-implemented. (3) Guidance. MOF will study the way of giving more fiscal support to PPP projects in the public service area to further catalyze private capital and amplify the leverage effect of fiscal funds. Finance authorities at all levels of government shall work with other competent authorities to explore the possibility of changing the method of fiscal support and allocating a certain proportion of funds for PPP projects with a view to mobilizing more resources while ensuring stable resources for public service projects. Meanwhile, MOF will coordinate the efforts of the World Bank and other international organizations to increase their

REMARKS & OPINIONS

support to PPP projects, and capitalize on the advantages of their loans, including long maturity, low interest and strong credit enhancement, which will meet the project financing needs while helping lower the financing costs. ■

Ouyang Huang: five policies to support economic development

In one of his recent articles, Mr. Ouyang Huang, Deputy Director General of the Finance Department of Hunan Province pointed out that the provincial government should maintain stability while making progress, and promote sustained and sound economic and social progress through coordinated application of the macro, industrial, micro, reform and social policies. The macro policy should be steady in three aspects. First, the policy should be well-timed to deliver stabilizing effect. Second, remain focused on priority areas. Third, stabilize investment and consumption confidence through strengthened public education of relevant policies. The industrial policy should be precise in three aspects. First, well-calibrated to support a number of flagship industries with potential, features and competitive advantages. Second, well-positioned as complementary to market force. Third, it should be targeted and effective. The micro policies should underpin dynamics in three aspects. First, support market competition, so as to promote substantial transformation of government functions. Second, support entrepreneurship and innovation, while further streamlining administrative approval, breaking up monopolies, and lowering market entry threshold. Third, expand corporate financing. Efforts should be made in developing the local financial industry in the medium-to-long term, and improving the credit guarantee system. The reform policy should be substantive in three aspects. First, the reforms should be real and focused on key areas of taxation, finance, agriculture, education, social security, etc., to speed up the introduction of a number of substantial, influential and workable reform initiatives. Second, the reforms should be effectively implemented. Third, real benefits from the reforms are expected. The social security policies should ensure stress safeguard in three aspects. First, guarantee people's livelihood, continue to increase fiscal support to education, health care, health, social security and other key areas of people's livelihood. Second, protect the poor population. Third, remain vigilant against risks, by following closely the potential government debt and risks relating to Internet banking and illegal fund-raising, and develop plans in advance to eliminate potential risks. ■

Zhou Xiaochuan: continuing to improve the RMB exchange rate formation mechanism

In his recent remarks at the G20 Finance Ministers and Central Bank Governors Meeting in Chengdu, Zhou Xiaochuan, the Governor of PBoC, said that China's economy was running smoothly in the first half of 2016 as it was progressing in a stable way, growth was within a reasonable range, and price and employment remained stable. After the UK referendum to leave the EU, the external environment facing China's economy became more complicated. The Chinese government would maintain the stability and continuity of its macroeconomic policies while making efforts to move forward supply-side structural reform, which was the surest path to resolve structural problems such as excess capacity. After a period of adaption, market participants have had better understanding of the RMB exchange rate formation mechanism. Since the resumption of the International Financial

Architecture Working Group, all work has achieved notable progress. G20 should continue to move forward the 15th general review of IMF quotas to further increase the shares of emerging market economies and developing countries; continue to incorporate the enhanced contractual clause into sovereign bonds and welcome the Paris Club to broaden its membership to more emerging creditors; call for greater cooperation between regional financial arrangements and IMF as well as further work to refine IMF lending toolkit. Meanwhile, it is also important to increase the use of SDR. PBoC has published the SDR-denominated foreign reserve data and BOP and IIP data and is studying the potential issuance of SDR-denominated bonds. Recent years have seen remarkable progress in financial sector reform and the resilience of the international financial system has been effectively enhanced. G20 should remain committed to a more open, strong and resilient financial system, including continuing to advance the reform of international financial sector, summing up the experiences regarding the macro-prudential framework and tools, and strengthening the supervision of the financial market infrastructure. He pointed out that G20 made positive progress in promoting digital financial inclusion and in developing indicators and data for financial inclusion, and going forward, more efforts would be made to further advance the financial inclusion so as to enable all groups of people to share the benefits of economic growth.■

Gao Peiyong: the key for tax reform is the reform on direct taxes

In one of his recent remarks, Mr. Gao Peiyong, the head of the Institute of Strategic Research on Finance and Economics of Chinese Academy of Social Science, pointed out that 70% of China's current tax was derived from the consumption tax, business tax and other indirect taxes, so the basic approach of this round of tax reform was to increase the individual income tax and other direct taxes, lower the contributing proportion of indirect taxes, so as to optimize the tax regime by making the tax structure fairer and more equitable. The government tried to adjust the household income through means of taxation, but could only do so through the individual income tax at present. After over 30 years of reform and opening-up, some residents had accumulated considerable wealth, but currently there was no property tax, which limited the government's tool in regulating income distribution. The Gini coefficient gap in the initial distribution was not significant between China and Western countries; some years even saw lower Gini coefficient in China. However, after the secondary distribution of incomes through taxation and fiscal arrangement, China's Gini coefficient become evidently higher than that in Western countries. That was due to insufficient adjustment by tax tools, or the tools were not as effective as we hoped for. Therefore, China's tax regime needed an overhaul, which was consistent with our objective of modernizing the national governance capability. This round of tax reform involved a total of six taxes, including VAT, consumption tax, environmental tax, resource tax, individual income tax and real estate tax. Among those, the individual income tax and real estate tax were direct tax, while the consumption tax, VAT and others were indirect taxes. As the reform on the two major direct taxes led to real challenges for the existing taxation collection mechanism, The *Tax Administration Law* was adopted as a supplement measure. Therefore, the whole package of the tax reform included six taxes and one law. In the context of supply-side structural reforms, the major macro-adjustment tool was tax policy, or tax reforms to be more accurate. In 2015, the fiscal revenue of China totaled over 15 trillion RMB, meaning a per capita tax burden of over 10,000 RMB. Such tax burden would have varied effects in different regions. It was fair to say that each individual and household had a stake in China's tax system reform. While keeping the overall tax burden stable, we should gradually increase the proportion of direct taxes and

REMARKS & OPINIONS

reduce the indirect taxes, so as to improve the tax structure and make the tax burden fairer and more equitable.∎

Lou Jiwei: major outcomes of this year's G20 Finance Track have basically been achieved

In his recent speech, Finance Minister Lou Jiwei said that the world economy and the international economic cooperation are at an important inflection point, and the role of G20 is also undergoing an adjustment. As the presidency of G20, China is prioritizing the innovation of G20 mechanism by promoting the shift of G20's role from being a crisis response mechanism to one of global economic governance and by switching G20's focus from short-term policies to structural reforms. For example, China's efforts to promote the G20 Blueprint on Innovative Growth and growth pattern featuring new industrial revolution and digital economy, along with structural reforms, will give impetus to the sustainable development of the world economy in the medium-to-long term. For instance, China is making great efforts to advance the enhanced structural reform agenda. All the three G20 Finance Ministers and Central Bank Governors Meetings reached the consensus that monetary policy will continue to support economic activity and ensure price stability, consistent with central banks' mandates, but monetary policy alone cannot lead to balanced growth. structural reforms should thus play a key role. With great push from China, G20 achieved landmark outcomes in the top-level design of the enhanced structural reform agenda by identifying 9 priority areas and 48 guiding principles of structural reforms and developing a set of indicators to measure the progress and effectiveness of structural reforms. The 9 priority areas include the slowdown of labor productivity and other issues that face all the countries and are intended to boost labor market productivity, promote investment and trade openness, improve business environment and enhance infrastructure development. According to Minister Lou, it is the first time in G20 history that the initiative of tackling both the symptoms and root causes of economic problems to boost growth is championed.∎

Lou Jiwei: inclusive growth and structural reforms

Recently, Finance Minister Lou Jiwei attended the High-level International Symposium on New Approaches to Address Economic Challenges, which was jointly organized by MOF and the OECD, and delivered a speech. Minister Lou pointed out that the world economy was still in deep adjustment, the growth momentum was sluggish, and the impacts of non-economic factors such as terrorism and refugees became more evident. The development of major economies and their macro-policy orientation became more differentiated, international financial market was unstable, commodity prices were hovering at low levels, and emerging economies were faced with increased risks and difficulties. In particular, the recent Brexit caused short-term shocks to the global finance, trade and capital flows. In the long term, EU breakup might become a new source of risks. The deeper roots of the growth challenge of the global economy lay in structural contradictions and problems. While countries differed in national conditions and stages of development, and their structural problems were different, but the international community have common consensus on recognizing the importance of promoting structural reforms and enhancing potential growth. Inclusive growth was related to equitable access, optimal efficiency, reasonable sharing and sustainable growth, and the key was to reduce or eliminate the unfairness in development opportunities. Inclusive growth required inclusive supporting mechanisms and structural reforms. We should use reform to break down the institutional obstacles, foster enabling and inclusive institutions for factor accumulation and technological innovation, which would facilitate free movement of labor, fair competition and the play of market forces. The key of structural reforms was to balance the relationship between government and market, give full play to the decisive role of market in resource allocation, and give better play to the role of government. Structural reforms were difficult processes as they involved complex interests and various risks, which required overall planning and rational prioritization of the timing and pace of structural reforms. Meanwhile, the relationship between macroeconomic policies and structural reforms also deserved attention. Some structural reforms might have tightening effects in the short term, which should be accompanied by expansionary fiscal and monetary policy. The focus of structural reforms was on the supply side, while the demand side mainly relied on policy support. The supply-side structural reforms and demand-side policy should be effectively coordinated, which may pose problems, and countries may have various room to cop.■

Shi Yaobin: expanding investment in African agriculture and promoting its sustainable development

At the Opening Ceremony of the 8th China-Africa High-level Experiences Sharing Program, or the China-IFAD Workshop on South-South Cooperation, Vice Finance Minister Shi Yaobin said that the economic cooperation between China and Africa has reached an unprecedented level. Agriculture and rural development have always been the key area of economic cooperation between China and Africa and received high attention from both sides. Enhanced investment cooperation is an important driver of agricultural development and serves the common interests of both sides. Shi offered 5 suggestions for stronger investment cooperation between China and Africa: (1) stay open and inclusive, pursue mutual benefits and win-win outcomes, uphold the spirit of openness and cooperation, respect and accommodate the reasonable concerns of all parties, leverage comparative advantages, and realize common development. (2) Allow businesses to play a major role with guidance from the government, strengthen coordination between Chinese and African countries' governments, and foster a sound investment environment. (3) Enhance exchanges and interaction, and effectively connect investors with investment needs. (4) Promote synergies among international financial institutions such as the World Bank and IFAD to strengthen the "tripartite cooperation" in the area of investment and financing for African agriculture, explore models that promote partnership between private capital and government investment and boost agricultural and rural development in Africa. (5) Guard against potential risks when seizing investment opportunities, and expand agricultural investment cooperation between China and Africa while raising risk awareness to ensure the safety and efficiency of investment.■

Liu Shangxi: PPP is a major initiative no less important than the market reform

In his recently published article, Liu Shangxi, Director General of the CAFS, said that PPP is another

REMARKS & OPINIONS

momentous reform no less important than the market reform. PPP will change the interest and risk structure of the entire society. The old approach means that government must tax more if it wants to build infrastructure and provide public services. But if public services can be jointly provided through the partnership between the public and private sectors rather than by the public sector alone, a new interest structure will emerge, so will the risk structure. By virtue of PPP, government will be able to supply more high-quality public services in a more efficient way, and the general public will access better public services, which will lead to more public consumption, better household consumption, and less risks from the lack of public services, facilities and consumption for the individuals. As a result, the risk structure of society is also changed. In this sense, PPP is significantly impactful and is a major initiative no less important than the market reform. ∎

Zhao Mingji: strengthen accounting-related work and promote accounting reform

Assistant Finance Minister Zhao Mingji pointed out in his recent remarks at the National Accounting Working Conference that, at present, China's accounting profession is facing historical opportunities and challenges. We should take full account of new requirements, new situation and new challenges, understand future development trends of this profession, recognize existing shortcomings, and push for reform in the job function, services, customers, working techniques and management. Accounting has an enormous role to play. Regulatory authorities and accounting professionals should follow strategic policy guidance, take the lead in accounting development and reform, and make efforts in institutional building and innovation. Grassroots professionals should enhance capacity in learning and research. The whole profession should push for effective progress in 15 priority reform areas, endeavor to realize the grand vision of making China a strong accounting power by 2020. ∎

Lou Jiwei: G20 should earnestly implement the consensus of Hangzhou Summit

According to the recent speech of Finance Minister Lou Jiwei at the G20 Finance Ministers and Central Bank Governors Meeting in Washington D.C., the recovery of the world economy is slow, growth is moderate in advanced economies, and emerging market economies are turning around, which supports global growth. Meanwhile, the uncertainties and risks facing the world economy are rising, as some major economies are entering the general election season, the fallout of Brexit is uncertain, vulnerabilities of the financial system are rising, expectation of Fed interest rate hike is increasing, geopolitics are tense and terrorist attacks are frequent, all of which may have significant impact on the global economy and international financial market. Against this backdrop, G20 should closely watch the development of the situation, continue to strengthen the coordination and cooperation of macroeconomic policies, and earnestly implement the consensus of Hangzhou Summit, including using all policy tools to support growth, pressing ahead with structural reform, expanding infrastructure investment, strengthening financial regulation, improving international financial architecture and promoting trade liberalization, so as to achieve strong, sustainable, balanced and inclusive growth of the world economy. In response to the requirements of the Communiqué of the April meeting, the Financial Action Task Force (FATF) and the Global Forum on Transparency and Exchange of Information for Tax Purposes made initial proposals on ways to improve the implementation of the international standards on transparency, including on the availability of beneficial ownership information, and its international exchange. The meeting discussed the initial proposals and agreed that enhanced transparency of beneficial ownership is vital for protecting the integrity of the international financial system and preventing the misuse of all sorts of entities for corruption, terrorist financing, money laundering and tax evasion. G20 countries should lead by example in actively implementing the standards on the transparency of beneficial ownership.∎

Lou Jiwei: a bigger and better World Bank Group is of great significance

According to the recent speech of Finance Minister Lou Jiwei at the 94th Development Committee Ministerial Meeting, the world economic recovery continues, but remains moderate and trade and investment are still sluggish. The problems confronting the world economy are not cyclical in the short term, but structural in the long term, which will lead the world economy to a low-growth path. In the next 15 years, building a better and bigger World Bank Group will be vital for achieving the twin goals of "ending extreme poverty and promoting shared prosperity" and for advancing the 2030 Agenda for Sustainable Development. The WBG needs to enhance its institutional capacity, explore innovative ways to foster stronger cooperation with developing countries, and strengthen its financing capacity through capital increase; champion south-south cooperation, tripartite cooperation and regional economic cooperation to mobilize resources, including from the private sector, to support the economic growth of developing countries. The WBG should also be more responsive to the needs of their clients and help its member countries address the impediments of their economic development, advance their structural reforms, promote economic diversification and accelerate the upgrading of industries. The allocation of the shares of IBRD should reflect the Istanbul Principle and Lima Principle and proceed according to the requirements of the 2030 Agenda for Sustainable Development so as to raise the overall shares and voting power of developing countries, enhance the voice and representation of developing countries, objectively reflect the changes of the world economic landscape, and increase the legitimacy and effectiveness of the WBG's governance structure.∎

Lou Jiwei: improve accounting-related work and promote accounting reforms

In his recent remarks during the National Conference on Accounting Management, Finance Minister Lou Jiwei pointed out that it was important to improve accounting-related work and promote accounting reforms, as it helped the market play a decisive role in the resources allocation, and gave better play to the government. In recent years, all regions, departments and agencies followed guidance of the CPC Central Committee and the State Council, and made solid progress in improving the basic functions of accounting, enhancing auditing and accounting supervision, and strengthening management, which safeguarded the interests of the government and the public, and facilitated sound and sustained economic and social development. At present, the Chinese economy

REMARKS & OPINIONS

has entered a stage of New Normal, which required further progress in supply-side structural reforms, especially in the five priority tasks, and deeper fiscal reforms to establish a modern fiscal system. The accounting profession is faced with daunting tasks of reform and upgrading. The accounting-related work should be more comprehensive, targeted and proactive. ∎

Liu Kun: follow the guidance of the five development concepts and comprehensively move forward the treasury work during the 13th Five-Year Plan period

According to the recent speech of Vice Finance Minister Liu Kun, the concept of "innovative, coordinated, green, open and shared development" proposed at the 5th Plenum of the 18th Central Committee of CPC should guide the reform and development of treasury work during the 13th Five-Year Plan period and be implemented in every aspect of the treasury operation in public finance. (1) To implement the concept of innovative development, it is critical to focus on major issues related to the overall development of treasury. Those issues include: first, compile the accrual-based government financial statement and develop innovative fiscal reporting system; second, establish a robust debt financing mechanism and develop innovative debt issuance system; third, create a result-oriented government procurement system and develop innovative procurement system. (2) To implement the concept of coordinated development, it is critical to fully enhance the synergy of the treasury system. A modern treasury system that is efficient and transparent should be established, more efforts need to be made to promote coordinated and synergistic development of the treasury system, and a balance should be struck among efficiency, effectiveness and benefits. (3) To implement the concept of green development, it is critical to keep strengthening the policies that are conducive to energy conservation. Green development reflects people's aspiration for a better life and is the prerequisite for the harmonious co-existence between human and nature. (4) To implement the concept of open development, it is critical to take the initiative to adapt to economic globalization. The Chinese economy has been integrated into the economic globalization. In this context, it is important to take into account and deploy both the domestic and foreign markets, resources and rules while following the requirements proposed by Finance Minister Lou Jiwei on building a public finance system that fits China's status as a major power. (5) To implement the concept of shared development, it is critical to demonstrate the outcomes of treasury reform through improved service. General Secretary Xi Jinping pointed out that shared development is the development being comprehensively and gradually created and shared by all. This should also be purpose of treasury reform. Public finance is the foundation and pillar for state governance, and treasury is the cornerstone of that foundation. It is critical to give full play to the fundamental role of treasury, so as to ensure the outcomes of treasury reform are shared by all. ∎

Zhu Guangyao: rapid corporate debt growth warranted attention

In one of his recent speeches, Vice Finance Minister Zhu Guangyao said that China's debt level was open and transparent, the overall risk was under control but challenges remained, and rapid corporate debt growth warranted attention. According to the IMF, China's non-financial sector debt in 2015 amounted to 153.4 trillion RMB, accounting for 220.40% of GDP; while according to the

China National Finance and Development Laboratory (NFID), the figure was 154.3 trillion RMB, accounting for 227.92% of GDP. The two figures were basically consistent, with the discrepancy mainly resulting from different statistical approaches. The data from the IMF and NFID were also in line with each other in view of the central government debt, household debt and corporate debt. Regarding the local debt, the data from the two sources for the combined debts of local governments and local financing platforms were also very close, with the IMF figure at 28.2 trillion RMB, and the NFID figure at 27.8 trillion RMB, only slightly different in structural terms. The generally quoted IMF debt ratio of 220.40% included the debts of the central government, local governments, financing platforms, households and the corporate sector. In terms of government debt alone, both the IMF and NFID data showed that the debt ratio of the central and local governments, including debts from local financing platforms, did not exceed 40%. So the overall debt ratio was reasonable. Those data affirmed that the debt risk in China was completely under control. Nonetheless, challenges also remained, such as the recently fast expansion of corporate debt, which called for serious attention. The Chinese government has taken multiple measures to address corporate debt risks, especially the debt of SOEs. Policy measures relating to debt-to-equity swap were released, using market function to address the rapid growth of debt. Furthermore, the NDRC has established an inter-ministerial joint meeting mechanism to address corporate deleveraging. The current steps and processes were very clear. Cutting excess capacity should follow market principles to promote M&A, and allow bankruptcy and liquidation through legal process. At the same time, zombie enterprises should be eliminated. Those measures were of great significance for the sound and sustainable development of the Chinese economy.■

Liu Kun: deploy fiscal and tax policies to promote venture capital and spur innovation

In his recently published speech, Vice Finance Minister Liu Kun said that the *Several Opinions on Promoting the Sustainable Development of Venture Capital* by the State Council made systemic plan on the development of venture capital and the promotion of innovation and set the direction for the sustainable and healthy development of the venture capital industry. MOF will earnestly implement the Opinions through enhanced fiscal and tax policies and better deployment of government investment funds to provide policy support and guidance. First, MOF will improve fiscal and tax policies and foster an institutional environment conducive to the growth of venture capital. In accordance with the principles of tax neutrality and fairness and with the requirements of tax reform, MOF will work with relevant ministries to study the tax policies aiming at innovation activities during the seed stage and the early stage. The preliminary plan will extend the income tax credits from small and medium-sized high-tech firms to tech firms in the seed stage and early stage, ease the criteria for preferential tax treatment, make it easier for the eligible start-up firms to be identified as high-tech firms, and scale up the supportive tax policies for innovative tech firms. Meanwhile, the venture capitalists are also likely to get income tax credits so as to encourage them to invest more into tech firms in the seed stage and the early stage. Second, government will provide better guidance and improve the management funds aimed at promoting venture capitals. At present, all sorts of government investment funds including the guiding fund for venture capital are operating at a large scale. To regulate the management of government investment funds, MOF published in 2015 the *Interim Measures for Administering Government Investment Fund and the Guiding Opinions on Injecting Fiscal Resources into Government Investment Fund to Support the Development of Industries*.

REMARKS & OPINIONS

In accordance with the No. 53 document of the State Council, MOF will work with relevant ministries to strengthen the management of those funds. The national funds such as the National SME Development Fund and the National Guiding Fund for Venture Capital in Emerging Industries shall play a leading demonstration role, and the fiscal resources shall be used to catalyze private capital and to guide the development of entrepreneurship and innovation.■

Hu Jinglin: support poverty-stricken counties to make integrated use of agriculture-related funds, and adopt targeted efforts for poverty alleviation

In his recent remarks, Vice Finance Minister Hu Jinglin pointed out that while finance authorities at various levels are increasing poverty alleviation inputs, poverty-stricken areas are faced with difficulties in making integrated use of poverty alleviation funds. For example, due to the mismatch between the fiscal powers and responsibilities, poverty-stricken counties do not have the authority to arrange fiscal funds for projects. The provision of earmarked funds has caused fragmentation of projects and funds, which hindered the effectiveness of poverty alleviation. The pilot of making consolidated use of fiscal funds in poverty-stricken counties is a key measure to improve the efficiency of poverty alleviation funds, and helps to ensure the success of poverty alleviation. It is also an important manifestation of the central government's efforts of delegating powers to lower levels and streamlining administrative procedures, and promoting the transformation of government functions. The pilot reform is unprecedented in the history of agricultural funding reform. The basic thinking of the pilot is to fully delegate the rights of using agriculture-related fiscal funds from the central, provincial and municipal authorities to the poverty-stricken counties. The poverty-stricken counties will, according to local poverty alleviation plans, prioritize poverty alleviation projects and construction tasks, and make good use of agriculture-related funds. This will help to optimize the allocation of agriculture-related funds, stimulate local growth engines, reduce financial capital precipitation, and address fragmentation and mismatches in agriculture-related funds, which reflects the requirements of the supply-side structural reforms. In poverty-stricken counties, the consolidation of agriculture-related funds should aim at improving the effectiveness of poverty alleviation. To ensure target measures and address funding fragmentation, the project and finance-related powers should be truly delegated to break various constraints. In addition, scientific planning should be made and projects should be launched through effective platforms, so as to ensure the most efficient and targeted use of fiscal funds. The pilot requires the central government not only to delegate funding and project-approval powers to pilot counties, but also to improve management and services. It is in essence an inward, self-motivated revolution, which reflects the requirements of government reforms in facilitating poverty alleviation efforts.■

Hu Jinglin: step up efforts to support infrastructure development along international transport corridors

Vice Finance Minister Hu Jinglin said in a recent speech that in the face of complicated international and domestic situation, MOF of China, while pressing ahead with supply-side structural reforms and cultivating new drivers of growth, will actively implement the national strategy of opening-up and promote a new opening-up system aligned to international investment and trade rules. (1) Foster a freer and more conducive trade and investment environment and facilitate the creation of a new system for market-based allocation of resources. MOF will actively take steps to advance the liberalization and facilitation of trade and investment, facilitate the internal and global flow of production factors in an orderly and free way, and promote effective allocation of resources in the world. (2) Build an all-round international economic and financial coordination mechanism and establish a new model for economic management. China will participate in the global coordination of macroeconomic policies, conduct all-round international economic and financial exchanges and cooperation, and establish a management approach in accordance with the high-standard global investment and trade rules. (3) Implement regional development strategy and usher in an all-round opening-up. Under the "Belt and Road" Initiative, China will step up efforts to support infrastructure development along international transport corridors, promote cross-border infrastructure connectivity, and expand space for the development of an open economy. Meanwhile, it will also develop innovative approaches to support the establishment and operation of multilateral development banks. (4) Promote the transformation and upgrading of domestic and global industries, and foster new competitive edge in global cooperation and competition. China will comprehensively move up along the global value chain, promote the transformation and upgrading of domestic and global industries, support the development of trade in services and technologies, and cultivate new competitive edge in foreign trade. The industrial capacity cooperation between China and the global market will not only further China's opening-up, but also help developing countries to accelerate industrialization and urbanization, and promote common development among all countries. The new round of opening-up in China is high-level and two-way as it encourages both exports and imports, and facilitates both outbound investment and inbound investment. Hu Jinglin also promised that China will create a more open, convenient and transparent environment to provide better conditions for the investment and operation of foreign enterprises in China. ■

Lou Jiwei: the development of modern fiscal system has made substantial progress

During the recently held Seminar on the 60 Years of Public Finance and National Governance and Financial Think-tanks, the then Finance Minister Lou Jiwei pointed out that centering on improving budget management, tax regime and the alignment of administrative power and spending responsibility, the fiscal and tax reform introduced a number of substantive efforts, and achieved remarkable progress in developing the modern fiscal system. (1) The reform on the budget management system has made decisive progress. With the publication of new *Budget Law* and the *State Council's Decision on Deepening the Budget Management Reform*, the basic framework for the modern budget management system has been established. (2) Tax reform has made solid achievements. The VAT pilot was fully rolled out, covering all goods and services. Policy measures were carefully designed to ensure that tax burdens were reduced for all sectors. At the same time, the sharing of VAT revenue between the central and local governments was adjusted. Consumption tax was improved to better guide production and consumption. Resource tax was re-structured to base on prices. Relevant fee-related funds were cleaned up. (3) Fiscal reform was making steady progress. The State Council has issued the *Guiding Opinions on Promoting the Re-alignment of the Fiscal Administrative Powers and Spending Responsibilities between the Central and Local Governments*, clarifying the relevant requirements on how to draw the line between the central government and local governments, and designed a timetable and roadmap for the reform. This reform is extremely complex and difficult, but there is no return, and relevant efforts need to be continued. While building the modern fiscal system, we should also keep an eye on global macro risk prevention and build a fiscal system matching China's status as a major power and push for global governance reform. We have successfully launched the AIIB and NDB, and pushed for the development of those new MDBs. We hosted the finance track meetings of the 2016 G20 Summit, which facilitated macroeconomic policy coordination, structural reforms and infrastructure investment among G20 members. We also improved bilateral and multilateral dialogue mechanisms to safeguard and enhance national interests. ∎

Xiao Jie: corporate tax cuts topped 500 billion RMB in 2016

During his recent speech at the National Finance Work Conference, Finance Minister Xiao Jie pointed out that fiscal reform has made remarkable headways in 2016. First, effective proactive fiscal policy was implemented. The VAT reform was rolled out nationally, and the overall tax burden for newly covered sectors has been reduced. Corporate tax cuts topped 500 billion RMB in 2016. A number of government funds have been cancelled, stopped or combined. The exemption scope of relevant government funds and 18 types of administrative fees has been expanded. Second, efforts were made to cut overcapacity, reduce inventory, deleverage, reduce cost and shore up weak links of the economy. Special funds were established and allocated for the resettlement of workers in steel and coal industries in the process of cutting overcapacity. Support was given to the renovation of shantytowns and resettlement of residents. Reforms for the procurement and storage of important agricultural products were deepened. PPP was expanded in public service sectors. Third, fiscal and tax reforms were enhanced. VAT covered both goods and services. Resource tax was advanced and to be levied based on prices of resources. Water resources tax reform was piloted, and the tax legislation on environmental protection was promoted. Fourth, efforts were made to improve people's livelihood. A more active employment policy was introduced. The public expense standard for per student was unified for urban and rural areas to promote balanced development of education. Financially difficult students were exempt from tuition and fees. Reform was promoted for secondary vocational education to gradually remove tuition and fees. Pension reforms were carried out in public institutions and ministries. Basic pension standards for retirees were further increased. Fifth, fiscal management and supervision was strengthened. Efforts were made to promote the introduction of the *Asset Evaluation Law*, to develop the implementation rules for law-based finance system, and clean up departmental rules and regulatory documents, to give play to the local advantages of the Inspector's office, and strengthen the supervision over local use of the central budget funds and transfer payments. Sixth, international financial cooperation was strengthened. MOF successfully held a series of meetings under the finance track of the G20 Summit, and achieved important outcomes in pushing relevant parties to advance structural reforms and promote infrastructure construction. The AIIB was officially launched. Support was given to the NDB to achieve its annual operational objectives. Bilateral and multilateral financial cooperation was strengthened. ∎

Zhu Guangyao: the concept of inclusive development of the world economy will have far-reaching impact on the course of G20's development

Vice Finance Minister Zhu Guangyao said in his recent speech that the concept of inclusive development of the world economy has become the consensus of G20 countries and will have far-reaching impact on the course of G20's development. G20 Hangzhou Summit placed particular emphasis on inclusive development, which directly responses to world's demands for shared development and addresses some issues related to the anti-globalization trend. Building on the success of the Hangzhou Summit, Germany will set the tone of its G20 presidency in 2017 to maintain the continuity with the development initiatives of the Hangzhou Summit, especially the inclusive development and the reform of the world economic governance. In the meantime, to implement these important consensus, Germany also identified three major tasks for its 2017 summit. First, strengthen economic resilience; second, increase investment in Africa; and third, develop digital economy. Investing in Africa also expands and reflects the inclusive development concept proposed by China, and needs to be prioritized as an important strategic task under Germany's G20 presidency in 2017. President Xi Jinping attaches great importance to Africa's development. China's initiatives and the consensus of the Hangzhou Summit will continue to move forward and become more specific under Germany's G20 presidency. ■

Shi Yaobin: PPP reform is faced with bottlenecks and challenges which requires urgent attention

During his recent speech at the PPP Promotion and Showcase Project Guidance Meeting of the National Fiscal System, Vice Finance Minister Shi Yaobin pointed out that there were still challenges to be addressed in PPP reforms, including mindset change and imbalanced development. First, some local authorities still need to change their mindset. Correct theoretical understanding is the foundation for pushing ahead reforms, without which low efficiency or mistakes may occur. Typical mistakes would be over-emphasis on investment and GDP growth, over expansion of PPP model, using PPP only as a financing tool, and setting high thresholds of guarantee funds, registration capital, or bank deposits. Second, the reform progress is uneven. The development of various industries is unbalanced, leading to varied degree of enthusiasm among relevant authorities and diversified challenges. Furthermore, regional development is uneven. Judging from the project pool, central and western regions are making rapid headway. As of the end of October this year, the top five provinces, excluding Shandong, are all central and western provinces. Third, participation of private capital is not enough. As a matter of fact, private capital is not so enthusiastic about participating in PPP. Some local governments have not ensured protection for private capital, while private capital has yet to enhance their own capacity. Fourth, some project procedures are not standardized. At present, some irregularities of project implementation require close attention, including PPP disguised financing, deliberate circumvention of management requirements, over-emphasis on quantity and under-emphasis on quality, shaky project preparation and so on. Fifth, legal protection and policy framework need to be improved. At present, the basic institutional framework of PPP has been established, but legal framework needs to be enhanced. There are many issues to be address, such as legal protection and supporting policy measures. ■

Zhu Guangyao: cooperation between China and the U.S. will make positive contribution to the world, whereas trade war between them will lead to lose-lose situation

In his recently published speech, Vice Finance Minister Zhu Guangyao said that cooperation between China and the U.S. will make positive contribution to the world, whereas trade war between them will lead to lose-lose situation. The combined size of Chinese and the U.S. economy accounts for nearly 40% of the world economy, and their combined trade is around 23.5% of the world trade. Given the impact of China and the U.S. in the world, their bilateral cooperation will generate positive spillovers and foster a positive momentum. China-U.S. cooperation also matters a lot for global governance, in particular, both countries maintain close policy coordination on G20, the most important platform for global economic governance. The good cooperative relationship between China and the U.S. is based on the principle of non-conflict, non-confrontation, mutual respect and win-win cooperation. Nevertheless, on issues related to China's core interests, such as territorial integrity, sovereignty and political system security, there is absolutely no room for negotiation. Tension and frictions are unavoidable in the course of the development of China-U.S. cooperation. In addressing the problems and tension, it is crucial that both sides must abandon the zero-sum mentality and avoid lose-lose results in the event of trade war. A report by the Peterson Institute for International Economics suggested that Trump's trade protectionism measures against Mexico and China will have significantly negative impact on the U.S. If an asymmetrical trade war broke out between China and the U.S., China would take some counter measures, including banning the Chinese state-owned enterprises from purchasing the services offered by U.S. companies, which would cost 85,000 jobs in the U.S. In addition, the ban on the import of American soy beans would cost 10% jobs in 21 farming counties in the U.S.. Vice Minister Zhu also hoped that more Americans will visit China and more Chinese go to the U.S., and the cultural exchanges between the two countries will help boost their economic relationship. ∎